Library of
Davidson College

Teaching Reading For Human Values In High School

The Charles E. Merrill
COMPREHENSIVE READING PROGRAM

Arthur Heilman
Consulting Editor

Teaching Reading For Human Values In High School

Compiled by
James Duggins
San Francisco State College

CHARLES E. MERRILL PUBLISHING COMPANY

A Bell & Howell Company   Columbus, Ohio

Copyright © 1972 by Charles E. Merrill Publishing Company, Columbus, Ohio. All rights reserved. No part of this book may be reproduced in any form, electronic or mechanical, including photocopy, recording, or any information storage and retrieval system, without permission in writing from the publisher.

International Standard Book Number: 0-675-09133-0

Library of Congress Catalog Card Number: 75-184568

2 3 4 5 6 7 8 9 10—76 75 74 73

PRINTED IN THE UNITED STATES OF AMERICA

For Frona Caroline Grimes

who knows about human values

Foreword

In a world where cliches such as "alienation," "plastic society" and "urban sprawl" gloss over the basic conditions of human deprivation, the examination of human values becomes urgently relevant to man's hunger for dignity and beauty. In spite of all that is known about human beings, the meaning of Erich Fromm's phrase "man for himself" is more than ever an imperative for survival in the struggle of man against himself.

American education has an historic commitment to perpetuating values which achieve delicate balance between individual freedom and social obligation. Yet social change occurs so rapidly today that imbalances are constantly presented to us in the forms of brutality and violence, slums and suburbs, world disunity, and economic poverty. Irrationality outweighs rationality and American youth, along with the adults who teach them, are confused about where to find the value fulcrum which will restore society to more humanistic behavior.

We believe the record of human behavior documents man's search for personal and social values which has brought civilization to its present state. These ideas are similar to the values man affirms as cornerstones of contemporary society. One reads these records as he examines the humanistic tradition that is part of our cultural heritage. Reading for human values, therefore, is an active reaffirmation of one's own culture. This book is concerned with how such a reading experience occurs, why it is important to the enhancement of human values, and what the reader gains from a deepening understanding of his own humanity.

If one accepts the premise that the reading experience is an affirmation of values, one can then examine values more closely as they relate to the reading experience. Four statements, or propositions, which demonstrate the validity of teaching reading for human values seem relevant to this concept: 1) the reader accepts or rejects what he reads in terms of his expressed beliefs or values; 2) these values are revealed and are consciously expressed in reading by a person's cultural identity; 3) some central beliefs are organized into institutionalized value systems that are examined and evaluated in the reading experience; 4) values that remain vital and operative must be reconstructed through the reading experience by each generation of readers.

Four Propositions about Human Values as They Affect the Reading Experience

Proposition I: *Values express the priorities we assign to the beliefs of our society. Effective reading experiences affirm and extend these values.*

Our interpretation of the beliefs of our society are what most people call values. The one thing we know is that everyone has them. These expressions of belief, or values, are what we consciously use to describe our behavior. We act upon what we believe. When someone acts differently and we do not approve, our disapproval is called a value conflict.

If values prompt behavior, then, this behavior is ultimately rooted in the culture which is the source of these values. Culture represents the sum total of a society's beliefs. Beliefs common to all of us are called the "core values" of a society. That core values differ from one society to another explains one reason why peoples of the world do not always act in the same way. In the United States, for example, elders encourage youth and do not stand in their way. In China it is the elders for whom youth makes way. Our society emphasizes priorities put upon youthfulness; in China, the value priority is put upon the wisdom and experience of the elders. This is not to say that Americans disrespect their elders or that Chinese are uninterested in their children. It is a question of degree, a difference in the value priorities of the two cultures.

Reading as all other experience is interpreted through the values we hold. An American may read a comparative essay on youth culture in the United States and China, for instance, and find himself defending the child-rearing practices of this country even though, on occasion, he might grumble about them. If the reader sees himself in the humanistic tradition that allows for differences he will not reject the values emphasized among the Chinese, but at the same time he might not feel that he need change parental roles with his counterpart in China. The interpretation of what we read becomes an affirmation of our personal and cultural identity.

We usually reflect our own values in the reading experience in many subtle ways. The columnists we choose to read are most often those who appear in newspapers whose editorial policies agree with our own ideas. The magazines we subscribe to reflect value choices. Or if we are not interested in reading books of poetry, for instance, it is because we do not place a very high value on poetry even though we may not object to people who do. In those books we do choose to read, there is much evidence to suggest that we distort the author's message to suit our own values. People are often quite unconscious of value choices in selecting their reading fare. The average American might express his choice by saying, "I read what I like to read. Something I'm interested in." He is unaware that he has made value choices. He is not conscious of his cultural identity.

Still other people quite consciously make reading choices that are exclusive in nature. Such persons eliminate everything that disagrees, questions, or offends their own views. They read only the "right" books. If far right politically, they eliminate anything that smacks of a moderate position. If politically far left, they read only attacks on the far right. Still other orthodoxies extend to such questions as morality, religion, health or economic systems. They read by a process of culling out any literature that would threaten their own dogmatism.

Schools usually deal with youngsters who come from homes where value choices in reading matter are made unconsciously rather than from homes of extremism. Unfortunately these families who are indifferent to choices of reading matter also negatively affect the child's reading culture before he reaches school. The school, if it is to accept a humanistic role in which differences are examined rather than judged, must deal with reading in a way that moves the student toward a conscious attempt to examine values in what he reads. Only by such conscious examination can students become aware of the implications of what they read upon their cultural identity.

Proposition II: *Values express our "cultural identity." Effective reading experiences lead us to become conscious of our identity.*

When an individual makes a decision that results in his taking some action or supporting an idea, he reveals his value priorities in ways that describe his cultural identity. Cultural identity is the way a person sees himself in his cultural role. Such identity is usually explained in terms of personal feelings and desires. Thus one's identity is both cultural and individual in character.

Much of our identity is unconscious; we find it difficult or even impossible to explain why we do certain things. To the extent that we become more conscious of our identity in our thoughts and actions, we become more aware of our values and the choices we make that are dependent upon them. Consciousness of identity is reached through a process of inquiry into our motives, our feelings, outside influences, response to group pressures and many other factors that operate in making decisions.

This process of inquiry occurs only when a person can make choices freely and when he examines these choices in terms of his own personal and cultural motivations. We believe today that such process operates better under inductive than deductive conditions of thinking. Historically, however, much of the instruction in American schools has been geared to deductive thinking in which the student must adapt his thought processes to a prescribed formula and to the value premises of a definitive authority. The implications of instructional patterns based on one or the other of these thought processes are central to an understanding of the concepts of the teaching of reading as they are being developed in this book.

Perhaps one of the most important educational developments of the 1960s was the attention given to the effects of inductive-deductive thinking as it relates to learning. This development came about through curriculum experimentation that lent itself more to inductive learning. In deductive thinking the student infers concepts from information prescribed for him. He is required to study through methods organized by the teacher and materials furnished by the school. The teacher and the materials are the authorities from which inferences must be made. Lesson plans, assignments, and formal testing reinforce the authority roles of teacher and text. The student arrives at a point where he achieves competency on a measure external to himself.

Inductive thinking places emphasis on the student's discovering for himself what he needs to know through a process of inquiry. Instruction based on inductive learning does not challenge the authoritativeness of teachers or materials in the various subject fields nor does it deny the usefulness of practice and skills development. Perhaps most educators today believe both inductive and deductive thinking are used by students in the learning process. The question is one of balance in methodologies based on one kind of learning process to the exclusion of the other.

Proposition III: *Values become organized into systems that support the institutions of society. Effective reading experiences examine the institutionalized value system.*

Reading has too long been considered a separate and private act. This does not deny the ultimate privacy of some aspects of reading such as that moment when the reader internalizes what he has read and establishes its meaning for him. The reader, however, also lives in a highly charged and complex communication environment of which reading is only a single part.

Furthermore, the reader reads for many different purposes in many different places. He reads in different moods at different times. The notion that there should be a set time and place or a set pattern for reading completely denies these factors. Librarians, for example should be reminded that libraries started in coffee houses where laughter and argument, food and drink were part of the convivial warmth for the eighteenth century Britisher who dropped by to read the latest edition of *The Spectator.* One need only watch a youngster happily reading a book with stereo accompaniment or with the television set flickering in the corner to see a more contemporary illustration that denies the idea of all reading as a private and separate experience.

The importance of the reading experience lies in the nature of the reader's involvement, his directions of inquiry, the meanings of the experience to him as these elements of the experience emerge at a given time. The reading experience, if it is a meaningful one, should mirror the public or private, noisy or silent atmosphere of its purpose. Enter a house where reading is thought a separate or special kind of experience and one finds the books neatly shelved, magazines prettily arranged on the coffee table, and probably not a comfortable reading chair in the room. In a household of readers one finds some of the books in the library, others scattered from the bathroom to the garage, with a magazine or two chucked under the bed. Walk into a classroom where reading occurs as a separate and formalized experience. Like the nonreading household, the books are in the back of the room, shelved class sets in categorical precision. Enter the classroom where reading occurs as a natural part of learning, and there will be great gaps in the library shelves at the back of the room. Books are being read. Books casually lay about in handy spots where students find them convenient to use.

Reading as a human experience creates its own richly eccentric environment. Reading in an academic setting often is strangely quiet, somehow divorced from living. School reading sometimes makes the shelving of the book and the conditions under which it can be read more important than the person. Instruction in reading that honors this compulsive use of books is sure to fail to create a reading population.

Most complex societies have developed four basic social institutions around which they organize the activities of their culture: the family, the church, the state, and the school. These institutions have systematized the functions of family life, religion, citizenship, and education. The customs of each institution are passed on to the younger generations through the rules and regulations which each of them has established.

The systematization of core values through social institutions is illustrated by the teaching of reading. A basic belief in American society has always been that its citizens should be literate. Public schools were established very early in our history to assure us of that accomplishment. Since one of the school's chief functions was to help children become literate, the values surrounding a belief in literacy soon became systematized by the school and transmitted to the child.

From the beginning the teaching of reading has reflected several of these cultural values. For example, reading was viewed in a moral as well as a utilitarian context in colonial schools, culminating in such tract-like textbooks as the *McGuffey Readers*. Here, the child was taught not only reading skills but moral dicta as well. The necessity for certain moralisms which we associate with the puritan ethic in American education remains with us today in most primary readers. The "good life" that we extol through the adventures of all the Dicks, Janes, Sams, and Suzies in these books has only recently been questioned by teachers as representing an unrealistic version of our culture. Realism in these books is sacrificed to moralism. At the secondary school level, the moral content of reading materials is assured by a censorship system in which the school authorities who select materials consider only those that are conducive to their own moral codes.

While it is certainly true that through textual materials positive models for behavior may be presented, it is also true that today's well-educated youth will not tolerate one-sided or biased reporting. Much contemporary value conflict stems from the selection of literature that reflects only the social mores approved by school administrations. Thus, literature dealing with sexuality, economic systems other than "free enterprise" or the role of the United States as a world power is still banned from many school libraries. A librarian in a West-Coast city dramatically demonstrated this point by purchasing from drugstores and supermarkets within a three block radius of the high school twenty-five paperbacks not allowed in her library. In a follow-up study she found that over eighty-five percent of her readers purchased and read these titles on their own. Often the censorship imposed reflects values of two or three generations past. The case of ethnic minorities is an area of literary censorship recently highlighted by civil rights movements. It is perhaps significant that only at the insistence of civil rights workers were materials positively depicting minority groups developed. The tragedy for youth, in a personal sense, is that schools often do not offer literature that would be enlightening and helpful to them in their own lives. Problems of sexuality and sex role, problems of divorce, alcoholism, and drug addiction, religion and the draft are censored. Often the literature which does exist in these areas is so banal that students turn from it with mistrust and cynicism.

Proposition IV: *Values that remain operative and vital must be reconstructed by each generation. Effective reading experience is one of the chief ways by which such reconstruction occurs.*

Other than the family, the school is the chief conservator of the cultural heritage in a society. There are other agencies, libraries and museums, for example, but the school remains the most active culture transmitter in an organized form.

There is one great difference between the ways by which the family and the school pass on the cultural heritage. In the home, cultural traditions are transmitted by members of the child's family. The child is taught to use a knife, fork and spoon because his family does not eat with their hands. He learns to keep parts of his body covered because complete nudity is associated with sexual promiscuity. There is little concern for the historical roots of these folkways and mores in teaching them to the child; he is simply told how to behave because it is the "correct" or "decent" way.

When the child enters school, however, he is exposed to a process of culture transmission that quickly goes beyond the direct experiences reinforced by members of his family. He begins to assimilate symbolic behavior that reflects cultural expectations far abstracted from direct experience. Each time a child stands to salute the flag, for instance, he is engaging in symbolic behavior. The school assumes a greater and greater share in developing symbolic behavior as the child matures. By the time he reaches high school the expectations of the culture through direct and symbolic experiences extend to nearly every avenue of his behavior.

Perhaps the most significant analysis of the relationship between direct and symbolic behavior was made by John Dewey in *Experience as Education*. Fundamentally, Dewey derived a formula by which direct and symbolic experience are reconstructed into new forms that in turn provide the individual with bases for future behavior. One begins by analyzing what he experiences directly. If students are asked to examine their concepts of democracy, for example, they begin by analyzing the current beliefs that motivate their behavior as democratic persons. Following this analysis, the student tries to trace, consciously and unconsciously, the experiences in society that contribute to his behavior. It is at this point that the student establishes the link between his behavior and the cultural expectations of his society. In pushing his analysis into his own past he must necessarily include older generations who have influenced his behavior: his parents and other adults who overlap his generation but who also precede his own lifetime. He eventually extends these links beyond his own time in the history of events into such ancient roots of his culture as the Greek States or Roman Law. As this examination of the past continues the student gradually reconstructs his current experiences by acquiring greater awareness and new alternatives to behavior.

Though the question of the role of experience in learning was first raised by Dewey in 1938, its resolution has been delayed the past two decades by several factors in American education. The translation of his idea into curriculum practice was damaged almost beyond repair by literal interpretation. The construction of experience was centered on direct experience or if this were impossible a kind of acting out or pseudo-reconstruction of events and ideas. In elementary schools it was often characterized by a ludicrous literality such as the not-too-far-fetched satire in *Auntie Mame* where youngsters leap nakedly over each other as sperm and eggs, fertilizing each other into tadpoles and little froglets. In secondary schools Dewey's idea was often given a utilitarian interpretation that limited study of subject matter to its usefulness or at best to some current application of experience no matter how superficial. Some curriculum experts of this period claimed, for example, that students could study the whole field of literature by pursuing their interest in automobiles or baseball as it related to literary heritage.

During this same period, however, there was a much more serious effort towards the genesis of general education in the subject fields. The development of the language arts programs by the Progressive Education Association or the introduction of an integrated social studies curriculum by the National Council of Social Studies are illustrative of two outstanding contributions that singularly changed many of the programs in these fields over the past half century.

It has taken certain events in current education to reexamine Dewey's concept and place it in its proper perspective as an important part of learning theory. The reevaluation of learning that has contributed most to forwarding Dewey's idea was best stated by Jerome Bruner and others who worked with him in the construction of new science curricula through the National Science Foundation. When the goals of education as they viewed them are concerned with a "process" rather than "product" (the traditional view), then Dewey's theory becomes central to the implementation of the educational process.

Reading for human values only occurs when the reading program in schools is humanistic and when the teaching of reading gives priority to value orientations of the individual. In materialistic societies such as ours human values are seemingly buried under a culture that dehumanizes the individual by his acceptance of technological and economic motives as prime motives for existence. But an awareness of human values lurks within the quiet desperation that, as among the Hippies and social activists, often explodes into open protest against the unnaturalness and indignities of a materialistic establishment.

Unfortunately, reading programs unwittingly support a culture where materialism outweighs humanism in the social balance. These programs violate humanistic goals in three ways: 1) they are skills-oriented to the exclusion of human factors in the reading act; 2) they support mass education rather than individualized instruction; 3) they ignore or suppress the value predilections of the reader instead of using his value orientations productively in the reading experience. When students are exposed to these reading programs, it is small wonder that they reflect upon their school experience with two common reactions: 1) "teachers are not interested in us as human beings but as educational products, stamped in approved moulds and certified to uniform standards," and 2) "books are really not very helpful or interesting when our life-needs are to make money, establish security for ourselves and our families, and enjoy the pleasures of life." This latter hedonistic conclusion, it is true, reflects the culture of the middle class in America, but it is significant that these materialistic values are not challenged by the school sufficiently to change them. If the school graduate is haunted occasionally by the thought that life holds something other than a completely materialistic existence, he ignores the idea by turning up the volume or taking the pill that will take him on a trip away from it all.

We begin a decade with uncertainty and protest toward a society which dehumanizes or destroys the individual. There is a growing cry against a materialism that shuts out the inner light of human values. This cry comes from many thoughtful people who are widely read in a literary construct that affirms their own life values and goals. It is significant, too, that many of those protesting form their questions *outside* the classroom. But, since many of the questioners are to be found in the present generation it is inevitable that they present their case to schools.

Reforms in reading programs have high priority among the demands of youth in the campus protest movements. "Teach us to read," they say, "so that we can have educational equality." "Give us material that relates," they ask, "or allow us to find it for ourselves. Don't push us out of school if a method fails, but find one that succeeds." Finally these students demand their share of decision-making in the learning experience. They feel that the only educational process which is valid for them is one in which they participate. Even the uncompromising militancy of a few may represent one of those rare opportunities when sizable numbers of students ask for guidance and help in determining their educational destiny. To teach reading isolated from the needs of these students denies them those life values which will affirm their humanity in a world becoming increasingly inhumane.

Jerome G. Disque
San Francisco State College

Contents

Part One: Reading for Social Values   **1**

Chapter One: The Role of Reading in an Open Society   **3**
The Thesis, *Wilbur Schramm,* 5
Influences Shaping American Reading Instruction, *Nila Banton Smith,* 11

Chapter Two: The Role of Reading in Attitude Change   **25**
Mass Communication, Popular Taste and Organized Social Action, *Paul F. Lazarsfeld and Robert K. Merton,* 27
The Influence of Reading on Concepts, Attitudes, and Behavior, *Fehl L. Shirley,* 46

Chapter Three: The Role of Reading in Youth Revolt   **57**
The Student Movement and School Reform, *Mario D. Fantini,* 59
Hermann Hesse's Curious Appeal, *Bruce Cook,* 78

Chapter Four: The Impact of Institutionalized Education upon Reading   **89**
Reading: A Search for Seeing Things Differently, *Frank G. Jennings,* 91

The Informational Needs and Reading Interests of Children in Grades IV Through VIII, *Herbert C. Rudman,* 102

Part Two: Reading for Personal Needs 113

Chapter Five: In Search of Self 115

Towards a Transactional Theory of Reading, *Louise M. Rosenblatt,* 117
Contributions of Reading to Personal Development, *David H. Russell,* 132
Goose Flesh and Glimpses of Glory, *Richard S. Alm,* 142

Chapter Six: In Search of Social Realities 151

How to Look at Television, *T. W. Adorno,* 153
The Adult Social Adjustment of Retarded and Non-Retarded Readers, *R. Phillip Carter, Jr.,* 170

Chapter Seven: In Search of Ethnic Identity 175

Distorted Accounts of Indians and Chinese, *Michael Harris,* 177
The Chicano in Fiction, *Nick C. Vaca,* 179
A TVA For Textbooks, *Meyer Weinberg,* 181

Chapter Eight: Reading for Utility 185

Illiteracy: The Key to Poverty, *Bernard Asbell,* 187
The Right To Read, *David Dempsey,* 196

Part Three: Promising Programs 201

Chapter Nine: Personalized Reading Programs for the Guidance of Emotional Growth 203

Contributions of Research in Bibliotherapy to the Language-Arts Program. I, *David H. Russell and Caroline Shrodes,* 205
Contributions of Research in Bibliotherapy to the Language-Arts Program. II, *David H. Russell and Caroline Shrodes,* 210
Bibliotherapy in the Development of Minority Group Self-Concept, *Eunice S. Newton,* 223

Chapter Ten: Individualized Reading Programs for Self-Selection of Materials 233

Well, What Did You Think of It? *Bruce C. Appleby and John W. Conner,* 235

Conducting an Individualized Reading Program in High School, *Jerry L. Walker,* 244

An Experiment in Improving Reading in the Junior High School, *Ruth E. Reeves,* 249

Chapter Eleven: Language-Experience Approaches for Student Initiated Materials 257

The Language-Experience Approach to the Teaching of Reading, *Lawrence W. Carrillo,* 259

Reading as Language, *Evelyn Jan-Tausch,* 266

Teaching Reading to the Culturally Different Child, *Josephine T. Benson,* 273

Chapter Twelve: Library Resources for Extending Reading Instruction 285

Reading Guidance in the Junior High School, *Anne E. McGuinness,* 286

The Reader with Mental and Emotional Problems, *Margaret C. Hannigan,* 293

The Librarian Goes to the Classroom, *Sarah Ryder,* 301

Textbook and Library Usage in Junior High Science, *Louis E. Barrilleaux,* 304

Teaching Reading For Human Values In High School

PART ONE

Reading for Social Values

CHAPTER ONE

The Role of Reading in an Open Society

Reading plays a very special role in an open society. Indeed, the right to read and its concomitant implication of ready accessibility of information carry a great deal of the burden for assuring the openness of our society. The early founders of the United States wanted to provide a system of public education that would spread literacy. They also wanted constitutionally to assure freedom of expression. In many ways they saw the right to read as an extension of the enlightenment of all men without regard for social class or ethnic origin. Reading programs in American schools, then, do more than just assist in vocational education or preparation for more schooling; they help defend a way of life that emphasizes the worth of the individual and human values.

Reading and a free press are not rights that come easily or without continual watchfulness, for human history reveals there are always the greedy who would rob us and the sincere, but overzealous, who would "protect" us from the freedom to choose. In this regard, it may be safe to speculate that the history of the dynamic struggle for both universal literacy and First Amendment freedoms reflects the stormy interaction of the democratic process itself. While the First Amendment was meant as a safeguard against political tyranny, even today a most frequent target of censors is deviant political opinion. Our ambivalence in this is both ironic and typically American: we continue to support the press, a power which we also fear.

The ability to read would disperse power. Influence is hoarded in the magic of sacred writings and the priests who guard and teach the marvels contained in them. Universal literacy mitigates such banks of power. In our complex times, the sheer volume of what is available to know prevents anyone from communicating with totality of knowledge about anything. Literacy makes vast stores of knowledge both available and avoidable among stored documents.

Under the conditions of our form of government, great responsibilities accompany the free press. Those who publish and those who read must exercise extraordinary discrimination. Although some claim us to be a nation of people more literate than most, self-government demands a high order of literacy. We may surely be more literate than most of our world neighbors of totalitarian states. But, when measured alongside the need imposed upon citizens to make choices about every aspect of life in the contemporary world community, our level of literacy may be found woefully lacking.

Wilbur Schramm

Now, well into the second half of the twentieth century, the very size of the mass media enterprise has seemed to call for new philosophical assumptions from publisher-producers. Wilbur Schramm examines some of the dimensions of these issues in this introductory section of his book, Responsibility in Mass Communication.

The Thesis

The present is a time of important changes in mass communication; a time of change is a time for redefining standards and responsibilities; and these new standards and responsibilities as they emerge are defining and delimiting a new philosophy of public communication for the United States.

The sense of new problems is everywhere around us. Within the last few years, codes of ethical conduct have been made in almost all the branches of mass communication. The industry has been looked at hard, from within and without. There has been an impressive amount of questioning and soul-searching by editors, publishers, broadcasters, and film-makers, and by associations and working groups made up of these men. There has been an increased governmental interest, indicated by Congressional committees, certain decisions of the Supreme Court, and the Federal Communications Commission—and in Great Britain by the Royal Commission. There has been also a considerable increase in public interest and concern regarding the social responsibility of the broadcasting industry, the film industry, and some branches of the printed media. This has been typified by printed and voiced criticism, by listeners' councils, by organizations to view and make recommendations on films, by the privately-supported Commission on Freedom of the Press, and by a series of well-publicized controversies, which in many cases took on the stature of debates.

Consider what has happened. Nineteenth-century mass communication was almost wholly by means of print. The newspapers were numerous and comparatively small, so that every group of the population could be

---

"The Thesis" from *Responsibility in Mass Communication* by Wilbur Schramm. Copyright © 1957 by The Federal Council of the Churches of Christ in America. Reprinted by permission of Harper & Row, Publishers, Inc.

fairly sure of having its shade of opinion represented. When Hartford, Connecticut, for example, had thirteen thousand people it had 13 newspapers. Today, we have in the United States one daily paper for approximately every ninety thousand people. Only 6 per cent of our cities with a local daily newspaper have competing ownership. Bigness and fewness have come to mass communication.

Furthermore, our century has seen the growth of the great media which we shall call machine-interposed—that is, films, radio, television. Drawing partly on the tradition of the theater, partly on the circus and vaudeville, partly on folk art, they have brought into existence a new form of entertainment which we call popular art, meaning a form of art intended for very large numbers of people, the success of which is to be judged primarily by the amount of money it makes.

The inexorable trend of economics and applied science which has brought bigness, fewness, centralization, and popular art to mass communication has brought with it striking new problems. Popular art, for instance, has raised questions which were never very important in the relatively restricted arts of theater, circus, and vaudeville, or the relatively indigenous folk art. What influence, for example, can a widespread popular art be permitted to exert on public mores, values, and tastes? Furthermore, such art is controlled by a relatively few people who are at a relatively great distance from the audiences they serve. The main sources of influence through popular art on public taste and mores are a few centers—New York and Hollywood, principally—and a few great production units—less than a dozen studios, a few great publishing houses, four radio networks, three television networks, all gigantic in size. In each of these a few people must prepare identical products for vast numbers of people. The old indigenous quality of folk art, as well as the ability of circus, vaudeville, and theater to adjust readily to the interests of small audiences, has been lost. This is a new problem, requiring as it does decisions on a gigantic scale that will balance the tastes, needs, and interests of smaller groups within the great audience against the common-denominator wishes of the great audience itself; and requiring also a set of basic decisions on what may acceptably be done with a medium that comes into the home and reaches as many as 50 million people with a single production.

In some ways the changes in the information media have been even more dramatic than the development of the popular arts. For, with the coming of bigness and fewness, the separate, clashing voices are no longer raised so readily in a "free market place of ideas." No longer is it easy for the self-righting process described by Milton and Mill, the very cornerstone of libertarianism, to operate. A new responsibility has come to rest on our news and opinion media. Whereas formerly they were responsible only for voicing clearly and vigorously the views each represented, in full confidence that the public would be able to read contrary views and decide between them, now it is coming to be obligatory for these media actively to seek out and represent *all* significant points of view.

Centralization of the information media has tended to change the old relationship of media, government, and people. The small, numerous media, as we knew them in the eighteenth and nineteenth centuries, were representative of the people in their checking on government; in fact *were* the people. But the larger and more centralized media have to some extent withdrawn from the people and become a separate set of institutions, parallel and comparable with other power centers such as business and government. And this in turn raises two other sets of problems.

For one thing, there is the problem how these larger and fewer and more centralized institutions of communication shall maintain their representative quality. In the second place, there is the problem how these institutions shall behave in their dual capacity as great business organizations and great communication organizations. For each of the great media organizations is really two enterprises, not completely compatible with each other. At the same time and under the same management, they are carrying out much the same responsibilities as a school system and a department store. They must maintain a certain level of economic strength and solidarity before they can properly carry out their communication responsibilities, but nevertheless their business responsibilities must not be allowed to interfere with their informational responsibilities. As business organizations they would readily be subject to the same close legal accountability as other business. Zechariah Chafee correctly observes that mass media are the only powerful business enterprises in the country which are subject to very little legal accountability. Our Bill of Rights begins with an explicit direction that mass communication shall not be restricted in any way that would affect freedom to say and comment. The result of all this is a delicate balancing of responsibilities and requirements, indeed a balancing act of the first order.

Freedom

Obviously, the basic responsibility of the mass media is to remain free. Their freedom must be defended against challenge from whatever source—whether from government, from opposing political philosophies, from business and class allegiances, from power and pressure groups, and from special-interest forces within the media themselves. What form does the threat of government control take in the mid-twentieth century? By many it is argued that the greatest threat to communication freedom is no longer the government, but rather forces from outside the government. For example, is communication "monopoly" a threat to freedom? What control over communications is exercised through financial support? To what extent do class or group allegiances, pressure-group activities, and favors threaten communication freedom? And how serious is the impact of expert manipulation of the media by public relations men and political leaders? These are all questions which must be faced up to in trying to assess responsibilities for maintaining a free communication system.

The Right to Know

The mass media must be free in order to represent the public's right to know. But what are the limits on that right? For example, what happens when the right to know conflicts with other old and honored rights: the right of an individual to privacy, the right of an individual to fair trial, the right of government to withhold information when it feels the public interest requires it, or the media's right to serve their own interest in withholding information? These are questions of conflicting responsibilities, which cannot be answered simply by saying that the public's right to know is overriding, and the right of free press is bounded only by law. In all these cases the boundaries of responsible performance need to be adjudicated and redrawn.

Truth and Fairness

If the preceding area was concerned with a *quantitative* ethic—*how much*, under given conditions, it is the responsibility of the media to tell the public—this area represents the *qualitative* responsibilities of a free and responsible communication system. Essentially, this is the problem of presenting a true and balanced picture of the world. What standards of accuracy shall be required? What are the obligations regarding objectivity as opposed to interpretation? What does it mean in practice to say that the media should be fair to minority viewpoints, to opposing political viewpoints, and to targets of attack? What is a "balanced picture"? These obligations are clearly not the same as they were one hundred years ago, when there were more newspapers per community, and when an editor or publisher could afford to operate his own political prism, confident in the knowledge that other political prisms were filtering the light in their own way, and the public could take its choice.

The Thesis 9

Popular Art

As the two preceding areas concerned chiefly the informing side of the media, so this one concerns the entertainment aspect. It is the problem of redefining standards in view of the new and unprecedentedly large audiences that have come with mass circulation and the electronic media. Within this area fall such questions as these: Should the public be given "what it wants" or "what it needs"? What is a "bad" picture, in the Platonic sense in which that question is usually asked? What constitutes indecency? When do the media threaten the social mores; when is the content "dangerous"? What are the assumptions regarding the nature of man and the world, and of media affect on man, which underlie the media codes and media practice, and are these adequate assumptions? Finally, what constitutes an adequate program service—in view, that is, of different tastes, minority interests, and the broadest concept of public good? These are not all new questions, but the mass media and the great audience require that they be asked again and reanswered in terms of the new conditions.

Our viewpoint is that the responsibility is shared by government, media, and public.

We could sum up by saying flippantly that the government's responsibility is to keep its hands off, the media's responsibility is to do for themselves what their critics want the government or some other policing body to do, and the public's responsibility is to be a responsive and critical audience. But this is too simple.

Therefore we shall have to ask, what are the limits on what government can and should do toward contributing to responsible communication? Of course, government should have as little as possible to do with the apparatus which exists to check on government, and indeed it may require a high order of responsibility for government to keep its hands off the communication system as much as it should. But, within allowable limits, what can government do? For example, what aspects of performance should it look at when it assigns broadcast channels? When and how, if at all, should it supplement the offerings of the privately owned mass media? If there must be some governmental check on motion pictures and textbooks, what are the responsible limits of that activity?

Communicators themselves can be expected to contribute to responsible mass communication. In general, the efforts of communicators have taken one of two forms: the adoption of self-regulating codes of ethical conduct, and the gradual professionalization of the industry. The first of these is swift and dramatic, but we are not persuaded that it can do what most needs doing. In any case, we must ask just what codes can do, and what they cannot; and what the present codes have accomplished. But we have more hope for the slower method, the gradual growth of the industry in responsibility and professional spirit. Under this heading, we must look at what has been accomplished and what might be accomplished by the increasing amount of professional education in the field, the activities of professional and trade associations in mass communication, the beginnings of self-criticism in the media, and the effects of awards and prizes for excellent performance in mass communication.

Finally, to what extent can the great audience be expected to take full partnership in the task of keeping mass communication responsible? Is the mass communication audience doomed to relative passivity or inarticulateness, to be represented only by a few organized minority groups and articulate critics? Is the stereotype of a "mass" audience, with tastes as simple as a baby's or as malleable as jelly, essentially correct? Or is it possible that an articulate, critical audience may develop to provide the check on mass communication which everyone feels is needed, but which nobody feels should be provided by government? Hardly anything would make as much difference in mass communication as an alert audience expressing to communicators its opinions and needs. And if indeed there are strong feelings within the public as to what kind of performance is wanted from mass communication, through what machinery can and should those feelings be expressed?

Nila Banton Smith

Just as communication, reading, and the arts mirror the history of a people, so does reading pedagogy. In this brief summation of one of her favorite topics, Dr. Nila Banton Smith demonstrates how reading instruction has followed the progress of the American pilgrim in the development of this country.

Influences Shaping American Reading Instruction

The story of American reading instruction from 1607 to 1965 is a fascinating one to pursue. Evolutionary progress in teaching this skill has been marked with a series of turning points. For a period of time methods and materials are quite similar. Then rather suddenly, both of these aspects of reading instruction change in design and in intent. What influences are responsible for bringing about these changes? What causes are sufficiently strong to wrest established procedures from the classroom and to initiate new ones?

More often than not these changes are brought about by the occurrence of a deep stress situation in American life. When an event occurs that threatens the national welfare and happiness of any people, reading instruction changes. Reading seems to be so intricately interwoven with the woof and warp of life that it becomes a part of the living fabric of the American people during crucial epochs in our history.

I shall attempt to sketch the influences that have been basically responsible for change and to indicate ways in which these influences have affected reading instruction.

The Period of Religious Emphasis (1607-1776)

The pioneers of America were, in general, deeply religious. Many of these early settlers came from among those people and from those lands which had embraced some form of the Protestant faith, and their purpose

---

Reprinted with permission of Nila Banton Smith and the International Reading Association.

in coming to America was to enjoy a religious freedom not possible in their own country. It was their religious convictions which caused these pioneers to face the dangers attendant upon the establishment of colonies in the wilderness of a new country, and it was these same religious convictions which caused them so courageously to endure the hardships with which they were confronted in the early years. Since the religious motive was the all-controlling force in their lives, it is quite natural that we should find it permeating and directing the instruction in their schools.

As a consequence, this concern was reflected in their teaching of reading both in the content of their readers and in their method. The materials for teaching reading consisted almost wholly of religious selections which it was deemed necessary for children to memorize in their "green and tender years." Oral reading played an important role in the lives of these people. There was a great dearth of reading materials during the colonial period. The Bible, generally speaking, was the only book the home libraries contained, and many families did not even have a Bible. Furthermore, illiteracy was highly prevalent at this time; so it was customary for the uneducated members of the family or the community to gather in little groups in the evenings and on Sabbaths to listen to the oral reading of the Scriptures by one who had mastered the art of reading, and many memorized long passages of scripture. Oral reading and memorization had strong functions to perform in the social and religious lives of these people. Consequently, reading was taught by oral and memorization methods and the content was entirely religious in nature. Thus reading instruction was shaped by the deep out-of-school concerns of early American settlers.

The Period of Patriotic Emphasis (1776-1840)

By the latter part of the eighteenth century the vividness of the early strife for religious freedom had been dimmed in the birth of new generations, who had learned of the ardent efforts and bitter struggles of their forebears only through hearsay, and whose own hearts and minds were completely occupied with the struggle for political freedom and the business of developing a young nation, strong, unified, and harmonious.

Reader content and method now departed from the religious objective and concerned itself with inculcation of loyalty for the new nation. Readers now contained selections which had to do with the traditions, occupations, and resources of America and with orations and poems written by American authors. Methods now came to lay great stress upon unification of the diversity of dialects; hence phonics was introduced by Noah Webster in his "Blue-Back" Speller to purify different brands of English in America.

Memorizing was now replaced with *eloquent* oral reading which might move its listeners to exalted heights of patriotism. So again we see how reading instruction was drastically changed by an out-of-school influence, emanating from a profound national concern.

Emphasis on Promoting Intelligent Citizenship (1840-1880)

We noted in the preceding period that the birth of our nation was followed by an emotional outburst of patriotism. As we neared the second half of the new century the effort to inculcate this intense type of patriotism began to subside and was replaced with a less emotional but still deeply felt national aim—that of preparing the great masses to discharge their duties of citizenship. Leaders now came to realize that the success of the new democracy depended not so much upon arousing patriotic sentiment as upon developing the intelligence of the people, whose ballots were to choose the leaders and determine its policies.

The aim of promoting good citizenry was two-fold: to provide information in all fields of learning, and to develop high morals.

The subject matter of readers now became broader. We find the intensive patriotic type of materials all but disappearing. There were some moralistic selections designed to develop noble and righteous citizens. With the new emphasis, however, upon reading as a means of obtaining information, we find the upper-grade readers filled with a wide range of informative selections in science, history, art, philosophy, economics and politics.

Our leaders in education eager to cooperate in the effort to provide a more effective education for the masses began to visit some of the experimental schools in Europe and came back with the ideas of organizing classrooms by grades and of teaching reading by the word method; hence McGuffey's readers, the first graded series to be published, and Webb's readers titled "The New Word Method" appeared. Methods and materials changed again, abruptly and rather completely.

Emphasis upon Reading as a Cultural Asset (1880-1910)

Sometime in the early 1880's a new movement began to shape itself in the field of reading instruction. At this time in history we have reached a status of tranquility and security. With the success of the American democracy assured, with threats of major wars no longer impending, with a population comfortable in a prosperous economy, a new trend emerged which affected the nature of reading instruction. The nation now had the leisure and peace of mind to turn to cultural pursuits in music, art, and literature. This concern for cultural development resulted in an emphasis upon the use of reading as a medium for awakening a permanent interest in literary material which would be a cultural asset to the individual in adult life.

Simultaneously with this settled state of affairs the Herbartian principles exerted a strong influence on reading instruction in America. Johann Herbart, who strongly advocated the teaching of literature, was responsible for a wave of educational enthusiasm known as the Herbartian movement in Europe and America. American educators went to Europe to study Herbart's theories, they returned and wrote books on these theories, and zeal for Herbart's ideas ran so high that the Herbartian Society was organized in 1892, and was very active for several years. It later became our present National Society for the Study of Education. Reading instruction was affected by the enthusiastic acceptance of Herbart's ideas.

Readers now became vehicles for acquainting children with folk tales in the primary grades and with the classics in the upper grades. Expressive oral reading for appreciation was the method adopted because it best served the purpose of these times.

The favorite procedure for introducing first-grade children to reading was to have them memorize, dramatize, and then finally read a folk story. "The Little Red Hen" was a story from literature which was especially appropriate for such treatment and this selection was used as the first story in practically all beginning readers. But finally "The Little Red Hen" was demised, and emphasis upon reading as a cultural asset passed away with her.

Initial Period of Emphasis upon Scientific Investigations in Reading (1910-1925)

The dramatic period beginning with the year of 1910 ushered in the first truly great breakthrough in American reading instruction. While there was no strong nationalistic aim for education or for reading at this time, a new development suddenly shaped up which had startling effects in changing reading methods and materials.

This era in the history of reading was marked by the birth of the scientific movement in education. In 1909 Thorndike made the initial presentation of his handwriting scale before a meeting of the American Association for the Advancement of Science, and in 1910 it was published. Generally speaking, the publication of the Thorndike scale has been recognized as the beginning of the contemporary movement for measuring educational products scientifically. In the immediately ensuing years scales and tests appeared rapidly: Courtis arithmetic tests, Hilligas' Composition Scale, Buckingham Spelling Scale, and then a reading test—The Gray Standardized Oral Reading Paragraphs. This test was published in 1915. Other reading tests, mostly silent reading tests, followed shortly.

With the advent of these instruments of measurement it was possible for the first time to obtain scientific information about the effectiveness of reading methods and materials and of administrative arrangements for teaching reading in the classroom. As a result, more innovations in reading instruction issued forth during this period than in all of the centuries of the past.

The initial period of emphasis upon scientific investigation in reading as described in this era extended from 1910 up to but not including 1925. This was, indeed, an eventful moment in the history of reading.

Up to the date of 1910 only 24 researches in reading had been reported in the English language and all of these had been of the laboratory type. From 1910 to 1924, a total of 436 accounts of reading studies had been published by investigators in the United States. This phenomenal spurt in scientific investigation in reading was due to the development of the basic tools of research—standardized tests. As would be expected, the majority of the first studies was concerned with tests and testing. As the period proceeded broader interests were reflected in the problems chosen for investigation. The great majority of these studies now had their settings in public schools, but some laboratory research continued.

The first doctoral dissertations in reading which came to my attention were conducted at the University of Chicago in 1917. Among these studies was a dissertation titled *Studies of Elementary-School Reading through Standardized Tests* by William S. Gray, who was our first great reading authority. Between 1917 and 1924 thirteen additional doctoral dissertations on reading were reported and among these there was a study bearing the title *The Psychology of Reading and Spelling With Special Reference to Disability.* And who was the young student who did this dissertation? None other than Arthur I. Gates, another "giant" in the field of reading. These two pioneers began their studies early in this initial period of scientific investigations and continued them throughout the years.

Now to note the effects of this influence: for one thing, research conducted during this period was largely responsible for causing the most drastic change in method that had ever taken place—the change-over from oral to silent reading. From the beginning of reading instruction, oral reading had maintained its supreme and undisputed claim over classroom methods. In marked contrast to this traditional practice, we find a period of years, let us say approximately between 1918 and 1925, marked with an exaggerated and, in some cases, almost exclusive emphasis upon silent reading procedures. Research had revealed that individuals could read silently with better understanding of meaning and with more speed. Thus two new techniques were ushered into the teaching of reading: those of silent reading and of speed.

The content of readers changed accordingly. Reading literary selections for appreciation was not consistent with procedures of detailed checking of comprehension or the development of speed, so readers now came to devote their pages to factual materials.

The use of standardized reading tests also ushered in an entire constellation of other new concepts and practices. Through their use it was found that wide individual differences in reading ability existed. As a result we first heard about "individual progression" in reading as developed by Washburne in Winnetka and Dalton in New York. Tests also revealed that large numbers of children were having difficulty in learning to read, and so the specialized branch of reading instruction known as remedial reading now became established in the public schools. And along with the remedial reading movement concerns began to take root in regard to reading specialization in teacher preparation.

It was a great day when the movement in scientific education began to operate in the field of reading. Even though investigators only scratched the surface during this initial period of research this was a momentous epoch in the history of reading, for it truly marked our first great breakthrough in improvement of reading instruction.

The First Period of Intensive Research and Wide Application (1925-1935)

While research got under way during the preceding period, during the next ten years it became intensive, extensive and widely applied. The years between 1925 and 1935 were remarkable in productivity of reading research. From July 1, 1924, to June 30, 1935, a total of 654 published studies were reported, dealing with problems related to an extraordinarily wide variety of topics. This wide and extensive research, together with its application, was the influence largely responsible for the innovations effected at this time.

One effect of this research was a broadening of the reading program in scope. In the new instruction, objectives were not strongly directed toward the development of any one or two skills or end points, but rather toward the development of several different abilities needed in the various purposes for which reading was used in well-rounded living. No one type of instruction was given an exaggerated emphasis overshadowing all others, as had been true in preceding periods.

Without a doubt the various investigations in regard to the reading interests, purposes, and habits of both children and adults were more influential than any other single factor in bringing about this emphasis upon a broader reading program. This decade was unusually fruitful in producing investigations of this type.

In addition to broadening reader content, skill programs, and methods, other notable developments were made—particularly, the initiation of the readiness concept for beginning reading and major advances in devising techniques for diagnosing reading deficiency.

The growing recognition of the complexity of the reading process and the multitude of problems associated with the teaching of reading carried in its wake increasing interest in supervision and in reading courses for teachers. The first supervisors of reading were appointed during this period, and colleges and universities began providing reading courses of varied types.

Period of International Conflict (1935-1950)

Once more an out-of-school stress situation began shaping reading instruction, even as it did in the Period of Religious Emphasis, even as it did in Revolutionary days. An event resulting from progress in science overshadowed all other indications of progress during the period of 1935 to 1950. The "birthday of the atomic age" is officially set as December 2, 1942, when Dr. Enrico Fermi turned on the first successful nuclear energy machine in Chicago. The first atomic bomb destroyed Hiroshima on August 6, 1945. The atomic age and reading immediately became interactive.

But we didn't realize this at the time. We were too close to this earth-shaking event to sense its import for reading instruction. The full impact did not become apparent until the period to be discussed in the next epoch. However, because of its grave significance in the future I am mentioning the initial release of nuclear energy at this point.

While the explosion of the atomic bomb had a delayed reaction on reading, international problems and World War II had some immediate effects, and I shall briefly review the events which brought about these changes.

During the years elapsing since World War I, the United States and other nations had lived through a period of peace. In the early 1930's, however, increasing dissatisfaction was heard concerning treaties and pacts, and in 1933 Hitler began to reveal his aggressive tendencies and continued to do so in the immediate years ahead. So the beginning years of the period covering 1935 to 1950 were marked with international strife and stress. This unrest continued and eventuated in the beginning of World War II in 1939. The United States soon became involved indirectly, but it did not declare war until after the Japanese attack on Pearl Harbor, December 7, 1941. Several trying war-torn years followed.

While the war ended in 1945, many problems still plagued the United States in the way of labor disputes; shortages in food, clothing and shelter; and Russian aggressiveness in building up communist governments in other countries and in extending its communistic party activities in our own country.

It is apparent then, that the entire period of 1935 to 1950 was marked with national and international unrest eventuating in another war.

With this brief consideration of national and international conflict in mind, I shall sketch its effects on reading instruction.

Probably the most obvious effect was a reduction in output of research and instructional materials. Research suffered a severe setback. While accounts of published research had previously numbered over one hundred per year, during the war year 1943–1944 only 54 appeared. Recovery in numbers was not achieved all through the 1940 decade. The number of doctoral dissertations completed was also drastically reduced.

The number of new series of basal readers published during this period decreased sharply. Sixteen basal series were listed as new in the preceding period. During this period, four series were published before the war, and two more got under way only in publishing their primary programs during the last two years of the period.

Another effect of world-wide tension was that it caused a few forethinkers to state a fresh viewpoint in regard to the contribution which reading might make to the American democracy. For half a century we had been concentrating in succession on literary appreciation, silent reading, and a broader program of skills with no mention of nationalism. During this new period the aim of living effectually in our democracy began to crop up. Social effects and uses of reading became a matter of concern. These indications of changing viewpoints concerning purposes of reading instruction were few in number, but even so they probably were the most significant effects of the new national tensions.

The content of basal reading series did not change drastically. The general acceptance of the readiness concept now caused authors for the first time to provide readiness books for the children and readiness instructions to the teacher. Preprimers were increased from one to two, three and four.

Advances in method included provisions for utilizing interrelationships of reading with the other language arts, addition of the use of context clues and structural analysis, and extensions in comprehension and work-study skills.

Interest in reading disability increased rapidly. The multiple-causation theory was developed, informal diagnosis was used for the first time, mechanical aids to reading appeared, and there was a beginning trend toward the development of clinics in public school systems.

Finally, a development in reading supervision should be mentioned. A number of school systems at this time had appointed a special person for supervisory service in reading, and the term "reading consultant" made its initial appearance in educational literature.

Expanding Knowledge and Technological Revolution (1950-1965)

In this long journey of reading instruction from 1607 to 1965 we have finally arrived at the epoch in which all of us are now living. Never since Revolutionary days has our national situation been so tense. Never since then have our democratic ideals been threatened. Once more, Americans are living in a critical period of national stress, perhaps the most critical one of our existence. What influences are causing strain in these troubled times? How are these influences affecting reading instruction?

Two of the influences which are fundamental in our current civilization and which are basically influential in shaping reading instruction are: expanding knowledge and technological revolution. Underscoring both of these and adding motive and impetus to them is deep concern for the survival of democracy. During this period United States citizens have become increasingly aware of the need for vigorous effort in maintaining our leadership as a nation and in preserving the way of life which we as a people cherish.

These combined influences have plunged us into the most serious problems in the history of mankind, and unexpectedly these problems are flinging out many new challenges to those engaged in the teaching of reading. In fact, because of these problems reading has suddenly leapt into a new magnitude.

The key solution and the one most frequently proposed for solving the problems that are currently plaguing humanity is *education* and *reading is basic to education.* Education cannot proceed without reading, hence there is a compelling new objective to increase literacy. This new objective is lifting the horizon of reading far above its established bounds, and revealing vast new frontiers—frontiers of creativity, of responsibility, of obligation and of privilege. The door to an exciting new epoch in the history of reading would seem to be not only ajar, but swinging wide open.

Now let us sketch broadly the more direct effects which these influences are having on the actual teaching of reading.

First, the accumulation of knowledge. We are living in the midst of an explosion of knowledge—social, scientific, ideological, economic, and political. This vast expansion of knowledge is changing continuously and will undoubtedly continue to change at ever-accelerating rates. We realize now that what a child is learning in school today or what an adult learned in school yesterday may be of little or no use to him tomorrow, metaphorically speaking. Therefore, if children in school and adults in present-day life are to keep in step with our ever-changing age they must be able to read well and with discriminating understanding in all fields of endeavor. So it is that these expanding and changing accumulations of knowledge are placing heavy new responsibilities on those who teach reading in all subjects and at all levels.

The technological revolution is also affecting reading instruction. Technology is rapidly replacing manpower with machines. Education will be necessary in holding the jobs of the future. Furthermore, the entire population will be consumers of products of this ever-advancing technology and as such they must read to make decisions as to whether or not to buy some of these technological products, how to use those that they do buy, how to live effectually with those not within their control. This situation in technological developments opens up an entirely new frontier in the field of reading.

Now to discuss the nationalistic concern. All through the late 1940's differences between the Western Powers and Russia continued to divide the world, and Russia's intention to expand communism was plainly evident in the fact that she had taken over seven small countries.

In 1950, shortly after communists had attacked the Republic of Korea, President Truman declared a national emergency as a means of strengthening the United States against communism. This meant enlarging our armed forces and producing large quantities of weapons. The feeling for nationalism now became strong, and its effect was immediately felt in education.

The concern for preservation of our democracy caused changes to be made in materials that children had to read in school, particularly in the fields of social studies and science, in trade books, and in weekly magazines taken for children in many school systems. Teaching reading in the content fields became more important. Interest in the whole subject of improving reading as a national asset picked up quickly.

It was not until 1957, however, that extraordinary concern about the teaching of reading began to manifest itself. This was undoubtedly due to an event of grave international significance—the release of the first Russian satellite, Sputnik. Up to this time the United States had possessed the most deadly weapon of warfare, and it had already sent a rocket 250 miles into space. These achievements assured its supremacy as a nation able to defend itself against aggression. But now the Russians were developing atom bombs, and, furthermore, on October 4, 1957, they startled the world by sending Sputnik 560 miles into space, where it began its orbit around the earth. The supremacy of the United States was now challenged by the technological achievements of another nation which avowedly was determined to establish world communism.

Education in all of its branches felt this challenge. As William Carr said in the January *N.E.A. Journal,* "The first Sputnik was followed by a thundering public demand for education." As part of this general demand reading instruction now became a subject charged with unprecedented activity.

Educators and laymen alike awakened to the sharp realization that we must put forth more vigorous effort if we were to preserve and improve the American way of life. In all aspects of national endeavor pressures were felt to produce more and more and to do it faster and faster. In reading, pressure to produce higher competency in a shorter time immediately became apparent. This trend reflected the larger motive and tempo which is now controlling increased production in all other aspects of American life. Investigators, authors, and publishers have been working feverishly in seeking new methods and in preparing new materials which they hope will produce faster and better results in learning to read. All this following the advent of Sputnik.

The culminating influence of this period and the one which more than any other gave a fresh and hitherto unrecognized status to competency in reading was governmental concern for and support of education for the masses. Former President John F. Kennedy took an unusual interest in education and asked Congress to aprove larger amounts to promote education than had previously been requested by other Presidents. In 1964 President Lyndon B. Johnson announced his intention to make war on joblessness, and on poverty, and to provide "Civil Rights" for all citizens. The basic medium advocated for furthering all three of these objectives was education, and, as previously stated, reading is commonly recognized as the foundation upon which education is built.

The strong new interest in teaching youth and adults who are not in attendance at school extends reading instruction far beyond its established bounds. First, in our history, we provided reading instruction to children in primary grades. It was then extended through the elementary school, then to high-school students, on to college students and in a limited way to adults outside of college. Now it suddenly has become mandatory that we teach millions of adults and millions of youths *out of school* to read better in order that they may hold jobs and lead productive lives.

Thus it is that the government's plans for improving the social and economic lives of our people involve education as a basic first step. The present administration fully recognizes the need for this basic step and is providing for it. In his message to Congress delivered on January 13, 1965, President Johnson proposed an expanded aid-to-education program and asked for new spending authority for the unprecedented sum of $1.3 billion for the coming fiscal year to finance the legislation he had proposed, and he received the amount that he requested.

So it is that the President of the United States and Congress in the interest of our national freedom and welfare, are advocating policies which require education for solution of our current problems, and are providing financial aid to implement their recommendations. Withal, it is gratifying to note that recognition is given to reading as the stepping stone to educational progress.

Never in the history of our country has reading been the subject of such high interest. Never have opportunities to learn to read been extended to so many individuals at all age levels, in school and out. Truly reading instruction has grown to entirely new dimensions in the enlarged and important role that it has to play in achieving national goals.

As a result of these stimulating influences authors of basal reading series are enlarging their programs with multiple texts and rapidly initiating methods reflecting the most recent research and trends. Many new approaches to beginning reading are being published. New reading materials are being prepared for teaching youth and adults who are illiterate or functionally illiterate. Interest in reading disability is expanding and increasingly making use of contributions from other disciplines. The demand for well-trained reading specialists is greater than the supply. Several states are now setting up special reading requirements in preservice and postservice preparation, and several require certification for reading specialists. Research, the common denominator in *all* aspects of reading, is now at an unprecedented high both in quantity and quality. And so this story of American reading instruction has a happy ending.

Change in the present century has been most exciting. In looking back in retrospect we might wonder whether ever another sixty-five years could be so productive as those which have elapsed since 1900. In consideration of the newly developed tools of investigation, evidence of our deep-seated motives to learn, the multitude of studies conducted, we might reason that practically all facets of reading instruction have been explored and thus another era could never be so great as this.

If we do reason to this conclusion, we probably are wrong. We pioneered during this period in unexplored territory. Metaphorically speaking, we chopped down and cleared away the large virgin trees, but perhaps some of the humble shrubs or creeping vines or fragile mosses may hold even more significance for us than the strikingly obvious, first-sight timbers. These more obscure constituents won't yield their significance with the use of heavy saws and axes. We shall need fresh, piercing insights in choosing which of these to select for dislodgment, and then we shall need unique, delicate tools to pry them loose from their tangled environment and to test the potency of their effect; and withal, great ingenuity will be required in shaping reading methods and materials in the image of our findings.

So to you who are involved in any aspect of reading instruction please be assured that there still are thrilling new worlds to conquer. With this expectation in mind, may progress in reading instruction march forward with ever-accelerating vigor and fertility, and may all of us join productively in the procession.

CHAPTER TWO

The Role of Reading in Attitude Change

Some of us expect that by their very nature books will be educational in the sense that we think reading will effect a change in readers. While we are rarely sure just what the nature of the effect may be upon any one individual, overall we expect literacy to contribute in humanizing, ennobling ways to the positive development of men. Through expanded contact with more and more articulate ideas, we assume that greater tolerance of a broader worldview becomes possible for the reader. Thomas Jefferson believed literacy, exposure to the world of ideas, would ward off the yoke of tyranny, and Emerson believed reading allowed men to discover the universality of the experiences they share with all men.

Arguments for censorship are based upon the same rationale. Some people regard books as a possible source of political and moral evil. Public libraries receive complaints nearly every day about the political ideas contained on their shelves. President Richard Nixon personally denied a contrary $2 million government study in his warning to Congress of the dangers of obscene materials.

One of the oldest fears we have of books takes the form of a kind of elitist snobbishness toward popular consumption of printed materials. The notion it supports is that literature itself is cheapened when it is made available to all. Figures from the literary world from Ben Johnson to Jacques Barzun have expressed such doubts culminating in contemporary self-recrimination about mass communication and pop culture. Americans, the largest producers as well as the largest consumers of "pop" art, music, and literature, reject their allegiance to it even as they demand more.

There is little "hard data" to support the idea that reading has any measurable effect at all. Researchers on this topic hesitate to predict specific *effects* from reading but confine themselves to descriptions of the *responses* of readers to certain materials under designated circumstances. Of course, we do indeed believe that reading affects people. We think, too, that we can influence people in predictable ways through exposure to quality literature of many kinds. But, we can seldom predict the precise effect of any one book upon a population or an individual.

It seems likely that differing social groups at different times interact with certain ideas presented by timely authors. Although President Abraham Lincoln may have noted that Harriet Beecher Stowe had written a book that started a war, it is more certain that a public appetite for it determined both the beginning of the war and the success of *Uncle Tom's Cabin*.

Paul F. Lazarsfeld
and Robert K. Merton

Obviously, there is much for the reading teacher to consider about the relationship of reading to social change. That, of course, is the external validation of the effectiveness of any reading program. In this selection, two of this country's most noted communications analysts examine possibilities of influence from the press.

Mass Communication, Popular Taste and Organized Social Action

Problems engaging the attention of men change, and they change not at random but largely in accord with the altering demands of society and economy. If a group such as those who have written the chapters of this book had been brought together a generation or so ago, the subject for discussion would in all probability have been altogether different. Child labor, woman suffrage or old-age pensions might have occupied the attention of a group such as this, but certainly not problems of the media of mass communication. As a host of recent conferences, books, and articles indicate, the role of radio, print, and film in society has become a problem of interest to many and a source of concern to some. This shift in public interest appears to be the product of several social trends.

Social Concern with the Mass Media

Many are alarmed by the ubiquity and potential power of the mass media. A participant in this symposium has written, for example, that "the power of radio can be compared only with the power of the atomic bomb." It is widely felt that the mass media comprise a powerful instrument which may be used for good or for ill and that, in the absence of adequate controls, the latter possibility is on the whole more likely. For these are the media of propaganda and Americans stand in peculiar dread of the power of

---

From *The Communication of Ideas* edited by Lyman Bryson. Copyright © 1948 by Institute for Religious and Social Studies. "Mass Communication, Popular Taste and Organized Social Action" by Paul F. Lazarsfeld and Robert K. Merton. Reprinted by permission of Harper & Row, Publishers, Inc.

propaganda. As the British observer, William Empson, remarked of us: "They believe in machinery more passionately than we do; and modern propaganda is a scientific machine; so it seems to them obvious that a mere reasoning man can't stand up against it. All this produces a curiously girlish attitude toward anyone who might be doing propaganda. 'Don't let that man come near. Don't let him tempt me, because if he does, I'm sure to fall.' "

The ubiquity of the mass media promptly leads many to an almost magical belief in their enormous power. But there is another and, probably a more realistic basis for widespread concern with the social role of the mass media; a basis which has to do with the changing types of social control exercised by powerful interest groups in society. Increasingly, the chief power groups, among which organized business occupies the most spectacular place, have come to adopt techniques for manipulating mass publics through propaganda in place of more direct means of control. Industrial organizations no longer compel eight-year-old children to attend the machine for fourteen hours a day; they engage in elaborate programs of "public relations." They place large and impressive advertisements in the newspapers of the nation; they sponsor numerous radio programs; on the advice of public relations counsellors they organize prize contests, establish welfare foundations, and support worthy causes. Economic power seems to have reduced direct exploitation and turned to a subtler type of psychological exploitation, achieved largely by disseminating propaganda through the mass media of communication.

This change in the structure of social control merits thorough examination. Complex societies are subject to many different forms of organized control. Hitler, for example, seized upon the most visible and direct of these: organized violence and mass coercion. In this country, direct coercion has become minimized. If people do not adopt the beliefs and attitudes advocated by some power group—say, the National Association of Manufacturers—they can neither be liquidated nor placed in concentration camps. Those who would control the opinions and beliefs of our society resort less to physical force and more to mass persuasion. The radio program and the institutional advertisement serve in place of intimidation and coercion. The manifest concern over the functions of the mass media is in part based upon the valid observation that these media have taken on the job of rendering mass publics conformative to the social and economic *status quo*.

A third source of widespread concern with the social role of mass media is found in their assumed effects upon popular culture and the esthetic tastes of their audiences. In the measure that the size of these audiences has increased, it is argued, the level of esthetic taste has deteriorated. And it is feared that the mass media deliberately cater to these vulgarized tastes, thus contributing to further deterioration.

It seems probable that these constitute the three organically related elements of our great concern with the mass media of communication. Many are, first of all, fearful of the ubiquity and potential power of these media. We have suggested that this is something of an indiscriminate fear of an abstract bogey stemming from insecurity of social position and tenuously held values. Propaganda seems threatening.

There is, secondly, concern with the present effects of the mass media upon their enormous audiences, particularly the possibility that the continuing assault of these media may lead to the unconditional surrender of critical faculties and an unthinking conformism.

Finally, there is the danger that these technically advanced instruments of mass communication constitute a major avenue for the deterioration of esthetic tastes and popular cultural standards. And we have suggested that there is substantial ground for concern over these immediate social effects of the mass media of communication.

A review of the current state of actual knowledge concerning the social role of the mass media of communication and their effects upon the contemporary American community is an ungrateful task, for certified knowledge of this kind is impressively slight. Little more can be done than to explore the nature of the problems by methods which, in the course of many decades, will ultimately provide the knowledge we seek. Although this is anything but an encouraging preamble, it provides a necessary context for assessing the research and tentative conclusions of those of us professionally concerned with the study of mass media. A reconnaissance will suggest what we know, what we need to know, and will locate the strategic points requiring further inquiry.

To search out "the effects" of mass media upon society is to set upon an ill-defined problem. It is helpful to distinguish three facets of the problem and to consider each in turn. Let us, then, first inquire into what we know about the effects of the existence of these media in our society. Secondly, we must look into the effects of the particular structure of ownership and operation of the mass media in this country, a structure which differs appreciably from that found elsewhere. And, finally, we must consider that aspect of the problem which bears most directly upon policies and tactics governing the use of these media for definite social ends: our knowledge concerning the effects of the particular contents disseminated through the mass media.

The Social Role of the Machinery of Mass Media

What role can be assigned to the mass media by virtue of the fact that they exist? What are the implications of a Hollywood, a Radio City, and a Time-Life-Fortune enterprise for our society? These questions can of course be discussed only in grossly speculative terms, since no experimentation or rigorous comparative study is possible. Comparisons with other societies lacking these mass media would be too crude to yield decisive results, and comparisons with an earlier day in American society would still involve gross assertions rather than precise demonstrations. In such an instance, brevity is clearly indicated. And opinions should be leavened with caution. It is our tentative judgment that the social role played by the very existence of the mass media has been commonly overestimated. What are the grounds for this judgment?

It is clear that the mass media reach enormous audiences. Approximately forty-five million Americans attend the movies every week; our daily newspaper circulation is about fifty-four million, and some forty-six million American homes are equipped with television, and in these homes the average American watches television for about three hours a day. These are formidable figures. But they are merely supply and consumption figures, not figures registering the effect of mass media. They bear only upon what people do, not upon the social and psychological impact of the media. To know the number of hours people keep the radio turned on gives no indication of the effect upon them of what they hear. Knowledge of consumption data in the field of mass media remains far from a demonstration of their net effect upon behavior and attitude and outlook.

As was indicated a moment ago, we cannot resort to experiment by comparing contemporary American society with and without mass media. But, however tentatively, we can compare their social effect with, say, that of the automobile. It is not unlikely that the invention of the automobile and its development into a mass-owned commodity has had a significantly greater effect upon society than the invention of the radio and its development into a medium of mass communication. Consider the social complexes into which the automobile has entered. Its sheer existence has exerted pressure for vastly improved roads and with these, mobility has increased enormously. The shape of metropolitan agglomerations has been significantly affected by the automobile. And, it may be submitted, the inventions which enlarge the radius of movement and action exert a greater influence upon social outlook and daily routines than inventions which provide avenues for ideas—ideas which can be avoided by withdrawal, deflected by resistance and transformed by assimilation.

Granted, for a moment, that the mass media play a comparatively minor role in shaping our society, why are they the object of so much popular concern and criticism? Why do so many become exercised by the "problems" of the radio and film and press and so few by the problems of, say, the automobile and the airplane? In addition to the sources of this concern which we have noted previously, there is an unwitting psychological basis for concern which derives from a socio-historical context.

Many make the mass media targets for hostile criticism because they feel themselves duped by the turn of events.

The social changes ascribable to "reform movements" may be slow and slight, but they do cumulate. The surface facts are familiar enough. The sixty-hour week has given way to the forty-hour week. Child labor has been progressively curtailed. With all its deficiencies, free universal education has become progressively institutionalized. These and other gains register a series of reform victories. And now, people have more leisure time. They have, ostensibly, greater access to the cultural heritage. And what use do they make of this unmortgaged time so painfully acquired for them? They listen to the radio and go to the movies. These mass media seem somehow to have cheated reformers of the fruits of their victories. The struggle for freedom for leisure and popular education and social security was carried on in the hope that, once freed of cramping shackles, people would avail themselves of major cultural products of our society, Shakespeare or Beethoven or perhaps Kant. Instead, they turn to Faith Baldwin or Johnny Mercer or Edgar Guest.

Many feel cheated of their prize. It is not unlike a young man's first experience in the difficult realm of puppy love. Deeply smitten with the charms of his lady love, he saves his allowance for weeks on end and finally manages to give her a beautiful bracelet. She finds it "simply divine." So much so, that then and there she makes a date with another boy in order to display her new trinket. Our social struggles have met with a similar denouement. For generations men fought to give people more leisure time and now they spend it with the Columbia Broadcasting System rather than with Columbia University.

However little this sense of betrayal may account for prevailing attitudes toward the mass media, it may again be noted that the sheer presence of these media may not affect our society so profoundly as it is widely supposed.

Some Social Functions of the Mass Media

In continuing our examination of the social role which can be ascribed to the mass media by virtue of their "sheer existence," we temporarily abstract from the social structure in which the media find their place. We do not, for example, consider the diverse effects of the mass media under varying systems of ownership and control, an important structural factor which will be discussed subsequently.

The mass media undoubtedly serve many social functions which might well become the object of sustained research. Of these functions, we have occasion to notice only three.

The Status Conferral Function

The mass media *confer* status on public issues, persons, organizations, and social movements.

Common experience as well as research testifies that the social standing of persons or social policies is raised when these command favorable attention in the mass media. In many quarters, for example, the support of a political candidate or a public policy by *The Times* is taken as significant, and this support is regarded as a distinct asset for the candidate or the policy. Why?

For some, the editorial views of *The Times* represent the considered judgment of a group of experts, thus calling for the respect of laymen. But this is only one element in the status conferral function of the mass media, for enhanced status accrues to those who merely receive attention in the media, quite apart from any editorial support.

The mass media bestow prestige and enhance the authority of individuals and groups by *legitimizing their status.* Recognition by the press or radio or magazines or newsreels testifies that one has arrived, that one is important enough to have been singled out from the large anonymous masses, that one's behavior and opinions are significant enough to require public notice. The operation of this status conferral function may be witnessed most vividly in the advertising pattern of testimonials to a product by "prominent people." Within wide circles of the population (though not within certain selected social strata), such testimonials not only enhance the prestige of the product but also reflect prestige on the person who provides the testimonials. They give public notice that the large and powerful world of commerce regards him as possessing sufficiently high status for his opinion to count with many people. In a word, his testimonial is a testimonial to his own status.

The ideal, if homely, embodiment of this circular prestige pattern is to be found in the Lord Calvert series of advertisements centered on "Men of Distinction." The commercial firm and the commercialized witness to the merit of the product engage in an unending series of reciprocal pats on the back. In effect, a distinguished man congratulates a distinguished whisky which, through the manufacturer, congratulates the man of distinction on his being so distinguished as to be sought out for a testimonial to the distinction of the product. The workings of this mutual admiration society may be as non-logical as they are effective. The audiences of mass media apparently subscribe to the circular belief: "If you really matter, you will be at the focus of mass attention and, if you *are* at the focus of mass attention, then surely you must really matter."

This status conferral function thus enters into organized social action by legitimizing selected policies, persons, and groups which receive the support of mass media. We shall have occasion to note the detailed operation of this function in connection with the conditions making for the maximal utilization of mass media for designated social ends. At the moment, having considered the "status conferral" function, we shall consider a second: the enforced application of social norms through the mass media.

The Enforcement of Social Norms

Such catch phrases as "the power of the press" (and other mass media) or "the bright glare of publicity" presumably refer to this function. The mass media may initiate organized social action by "exposing" conditions which are at variance with public moralities. But it need not be prematurely assumed that this pattern consists *simply* in making these deviations widely known. We have something to learn in this connection from Malinowski's observations among his beloved Trobriand Islanders. There, he reports, no organized social action is taken with respect to behavior deviant from a social norm unless there is *public* announcement of the deviation. This is not merely a matter of acquainting the individuals in the group with the facts of the case. Many may have known privately of these deviations—e.g., incest among the Trobrianders, as with political or business corruption, prostitution, gambling among ourselves—but they will not have pressed for public action. But once the behavioral deviations are made simultaneously public for all, this sets in train tensions between the "privately tolerable" and the "publicly acknowledgeable."

The mechanism of public exposure would seem to operate somewhat as follows. Many social norms prove inconvenient for individuals in the society. They militate against the gratification of wants and impulses. Since many find the norms burdensome, there is some measure of leniency in applying them, both to oneself and to others. Hence, the emergence of deviant behavior and private toleration in these deviations. But this can continue only so long as one is not in a situation where one must take a public stand for or against the norms. Publicity, the enforced acknowledgment by members of the group that these deviations have occurred, requires each individual to take such a stand. He must either range himself with the non-conformists, thus proclaiming his repudiation of the group norms, and thus asserting that he, too, is outside the moral framework or, regardless of his private predilections, he must fall into line by supporting the norm. *Publicity closes the gap between "private attitudes" and "public morality."* Publicity exerts pressure for a single rather than a dual morality by preventing continued evasion of the issue. It calls forth public reaffirmation and (however sporadic) application of the social norm.

In a mass society, this function of public exposure is institutionalized in the mass media of communication. Press, radio, and journals expose fairly well-known deviations to public view, and as a rule, this exposure forces some degree of public action against what has been privately tolerated. The mass media may, for example, introduce severe strains upon "polite ethnic discrimination" by calling public attention to these practices which are at odds with the norms of non-discrimination. At times, the media may organize exposure activities into a "crusade."

The study of crusades by mass media would go far toward answering basic questions about the relation of mass media to organized social action. It is essential to know, for example, the extent to which the crusade provides an organizational center for otherwise unorganized individuals. The crusade may operate diversely among the several sectors of the population. In some instances, its major effect may not be so much to arouse an indifferent citizenry as to alarm the culprits, leading them to extreme measures which in turn alienate the electorate. Publicity may so embarrass the malefactor as to send him into flight as was the case, for example, with some of the chief henchmen of the Tweed Ring following exposure by *The New York Times*. Or the directors of corruption may fear the crusade only because of the effect they anticipate it will have upon the electorate. Thus, with a startling realistic appraisal of the communications behavior of his constituency, Boss Tweed peevishly remarked of the biting cartoons of Thomas Nast in *Harper's Weekly:* "I don't care a straw for your newspaper articles: my constituents don't know how to read, but they can't help seeing them damned pictures (1)."

The crusade may affect the public directly. It may focus the attention of a hitherto lethargic citizenry, grown indifferent through familiarity to prevailing corruption, upon a few, dramatically simplified, issues. As Lawrence Lowell once observed in this general connection, complexities generally inhibit mass action. Public issues must be defined in simple alternatives, in terms of black and white, to permit of organized public action. And the presentation of simple alternatives is one of the chief functions of the crusade. The crusade may involve still other mechanisms. If a municipal government is not altogether pure of heart, it is seldom wholly corrupt. Some scrupulous members of the administration and judiciary are generally intermingled with their unprincipled colleagues. The crusade may strengthen the hand of the upright elements in the government, force the hand of the indifferent, and weaken the hand of the corrupt. Finally, it may well be that a successful crusade exemplifies a circular, self-sustaining process, in which the concern of the mass medium with the public interest coincides with its self-interest. The triumphant crusade may enhance the power and prestige of the mass medium, thus making it, in turn, more formidable in later crusades, which, if successful, may further advance its power and prestige.

Whatever the answer to these questions, mass media clearly serve to reaffirm social norms by exposing deviations from these norms to public view. Study of the particular range of norms thus reaffirmed would provide a clear index of the extent to which these media deal with peripheral or central problems of the structure of our society.

The Narcotizing Dysfunction

The functions of status conferral and of reaffirmation of social norms are evidently well recognized by the operators of mass media. Like other social and psychological mechanisms, these functions lend themselves to diverse forms of application. Knowledge of these functions is power, and power may be used for special interests or for the general interest.

A third social consequence of the mass media has gone largely unnoticed. At least, it has received little explicit comment and, apparently, has not been systematically put to use for furthering planned objectives. This may be called the narcotizing dysfunction of the mass media. It is termed *dys*functional rather than functional on the assumption that it is not in the interest of modern complex society to have large masses of the population politically apathetic and inert. How does this unplanned mechanism operate?

Scattered studies have shown that an increasing proportion of the time of Americans is devoted to the products of the mass media. With distinct variations in different regions and among different social strata, the outpourings of the media presumably enable the twentieth-century American to "keep abreast of the world." Yet, it is suggested, this vast supply of communications may elicit only a superficial concern with the problems of society, and this superficiality often cloaks mass apathy.

Exposure to this flood of information may serve to narcotize rather than to energize the average reader or listener. As an increasing meed of time is devoted to reading and listening, a decreasing share is available for organized action. The individual reads accounts of issues and problems and may even discuss alternative lines of action. But this rather intellectualized, rather remote connection with organized social action is not activated. The interested and informed citizen can congratulate himself on his lofty state of interest and information and neglect to see that he has abstained from decision and action. In short, he takes his secondary contact with the world of political reality, his reading and listening and thinking, as a vicarious performance. He comes to mistake *knowing* about problems of the day for *doing* something about them. His social conscience remains spotlessly clean. He *is* concerned. He *is* informed. And he has all sorts of ideas as to what should be done. But, after he has gotten through his dinner and after he has listened to his favored radio programs and after he has read his second newspaper of the day, it is really time for bed.

In this peculiar respect, mass communications may be included among the most respectable and efficient of social narcotics. They may be so fully effective as to keep the addict from recognizing his own malady.

That the mass media have lifted the level of information of large populations is evident. Yet, quite apart from intent, increasing dosages of mass communications may be inadvertently transforming the energies of men from active participation into passive knowledge.

The occurrence of this narcotizing dysfunction can scarcely be doubted, but the extent to which it operates has yet to be determined. Research on this problem remains one of the many tasks still confronting the student of mass communications.

The Structure of Ownership and Operation

To this point we have considered the mass media quite apart from their incorporation within a particular social and economic structure. But clearly, the social effects of the media will vary as the system of ownership and control varies. Thus to consider the social effects of American mass media is to deal only with the effects of these media as privately owned enterprises under profit-oriented management. It is general knowledge that this circumstance is not inherent in the technological nature of the mass media. In England, for example, to say nothing of Russia, the radio is to all intents and purposes owned, controlled, and operated by government.

The structure of control is altogether different in this country. Its salient characteristic stems from the fact that except for movies and books, it is not the magazine reader nor the radio listener nor, in large part, the reader of newspapers who supports the enterprise, but the advertiser. Big business finances the production and distribution of mass media. And, all intent aside, he who pays the piper generally calls the tune.

Social Conformism

Since the mass media are supported by great business concerns geared into the current social and economic system, the media contribute to the maintenance of that system. This contribution is not found merely in the effective advertisement of the sponsor's product. It arises, rather, from the typical presence in magazine stories, radio programs, and newspaper columns of some element of confirmation, some element of approval of the present structure of society. And this continuing reaffirmation underscores the duty to accept.

To the extent that the media of mass communication have had an influence upon their audiences, it has stemmed not only from what is said, but more significantly from what is not said. For these media not only continue to affirm the status quo but, in the same measure, they fail to raise essential questions about the structure of society. Hence by leading toward conformism and by providing little basis for a critical appraisal of society, the commercially sponsored mass media indirectly but effectively restrain the cogent development of a genuinely critical outlook.

This is not to ignore the occasionally critical journal article or radio program. But these exceptions are so few that they are lost in the overwhelming flood of conformist materials. . . .

Since our commercially sponsored mass media promote a largely unthinking allegiance to our social structure, they cannot be relied upon to work for changes, even minor changes, in that structure. It is possible to list some developments to the contrary, but upon close inspection they prove illusory. A community group, such as the PTA, may request the producer of a radio serial to inject the theme of tolerant race attitudes into the program. Should the producer feel that this theme is safe, that it will not antagonize any substantial part of his audience, he may agree, but at the first indication that it is a dangerous theme which may alienate potential consumers, he will refuse, or will soon abandon the experiment. Social objectives are consistently surrendered by commercialized media when they clash with economic gains. Minor tokens of "progressive" views are of slight importance since they are included only by the grace of the sponsors and only on the condition that they be sufficiently acceptable as not to alienate any appreciable part of the audience. Economic pressure makes for conformism by omission of sensitive issues.

Impact Upon Popular Taste

Since the largest part of our radio, movies, magazines, and a considerable part of our books and newspapers are devoted to "entertainment," this clearly requires us to consider the impact of the mass media upon popular taste.

Were we to ask the average American with some pretension to literary or esthetic cultivation if mass communications have had any effect upon popular taste, he would doubtlessly answer with a resounding affirmative.

And more, citing abundant instances, he would insist that esthetic and intellectual tastes have been depraved by the flow of trivial formula products from printing presses, radio stations, and movie studios. The columns of criticism abound with these complaints.

In one sense, this requires no further discussion. There can be no doubt that the women who are daily entranced for three or four hours by some twelve consecutive "soap operas," all cut to the same dismal pattern, exhibit an appalling lack of esthetic judgment. Nor is this impression altered by the contents of pulp and slick magazines, or by the depressing abundance of formula motion pictures replete with hero, heroine, and villain moving through a contrived atmosphere of sex, sin, and success.

Yet unless we locate these patterns in historical and sociological terms, we may find ourselves confusedly engaged in condemning without understanding, in criticism which is sound but largely irrelevant. What is the historical status of this notoriously low level of popular taste? Is it the poor remains of standards which were once significantly higher, a relatively new birth in the world of values, largely unrelated to the higher standards from which it has allegedly fallen, or a poor substitute blocking the way to the development of superior standards and the expression of high esthetic purpose?

If esthetic tastes are to be considered in their social setting, we must recognize that the effective audience for the arts has become historically transformed. Some centuries back, this audience was largely confined to a selected aristocratic elite. Relatively few were literate. And very few possessed the means to buy books, attend theaters, and travel to the urban centers of the arts. Not more than a slight fraction, possibly not more than one or two percent, of the population composed the effective audience for the arts. These happy few cultivated their esthetic tastes, and their selective demand left its mark in the form of relatively high artistic standards.

With the widesweeping spread of popular education and with the emergence of the new technologies of mass communication, there developed an enormously enlarged market for the arts. Some forms of music, drama, and literature now reach virtually everyone in our society. This is why, of course, we speak of *mass* media and of *mass* art. And the great audiences for the mass media, though in the main literate, are not highly cultivated. About half the population, in fact, have halted their formal education upon leaving grammar school.

With the rise of popular education, there has occurred a seeming decline of popular taste. Large numbers of people have acquired what might be termed "formal literacy," that is to say, a capacity to read, to grasp crude and superficial meanings, and a correlative incapacity for full understanding of what they read.* There has developed, in short, a marked gap between literacy and comprehension. People read more but understand less. More people read but proportionately fewer critically assimilate what they read.

Our formulation of the problem should now be plain. It is misleading to speak simply of the decline of esthetic tastes. Mass audiences probably include a larger number of persons with cultivated esthetic standards, but these are swallowed up by the large masses who constitute the new and untutored audience for the arts. Whereas yesterday the elite constituted virtually the whole of the audience, they are today a minute fraction of the whole. In consequence, the average level of esthetic standards and tastes of audiences has been depressed, although the tastes of some sectors of the population have undoubtedly been raised and the total number of people exposed to communication contents has been vastly increased.

But this analysis does not directly answer the question of the effects of the mass media upon public taste, a question which is as complex as it is unexplored. The answer can come only from disciplined research. One would want to know, for example, whether mass media have robbed the intellectual and artistic elite of the art forms which might otherwise have been accessible to them. And this involves inquiry into the pressure exerted by the mass audience upon creative individuals to cater to mass tastes. Literary hacks have existed in every age. But it would be important to learn if the electrification of the arts supplies power for a significantly greater proportion of dim literary lights. And, above all, it would be essential to determine if mass media and mass tastes are necessarily linked in a vicious circle of deteriorating standards or if appropriate action on the part of the directors of mass media could initiate a virtuous circle of cumulatively improving tastes among their audiences. More concretely, are the operators of commercialized mass media caught up in a situation in which they cannot, whatever their private preferences, radically raise the esthetic standards of their products?

---

*In *The American Commonwealth,* Part IV, Chapter LXXX, James Bryce perceived this with characteristic clarity: "That the education of the masses is nevertheless a superficial education goes without saying. It is sufficient to enable them to think they know something about the great problems of politics: insufficient to show them how little they know. The public elementary school gives everybody the key to knowledge in making reading and writing familiar, but it has not time to teach him how to use the key, whose use is in fact, by the pressure of daily work, almost confined to the newspaper and the magazine. So we may say that if the political education of the average American voter be compared with that of the average voter in Europe, it stands high; but if it be compared with the functions which the theory of the American government lays on him, which its spirit implies, which the methods of its party organization assume, its inadequacy is manifest." *Mutatis mutandis,* the same may be said of the gap between the theory of "superior" cultural content in the mass media and the current levels of popular education.

In passing, it should be noted that much remains to be learned concerning standards appropriate for mass art. It is possible that standards for art forms produced by a small band of creative talents for a small and selective audience are not applicable to art forms produced by a gigantic industry for the population at large. The beginnings of investigation on this problem are sufficiently suggestive to warrant further study.

Sporadic and consequently inconclusive experiments in the raising of standards have met with profound resistance from mass audiences. On occasion, radio stations and networks have attempted to supplant a soap opera with a program of classical music, or formula comedy skits with discussions of public issues. In general, the people supposed to benefit by this reformation of program have simply refused to be benefited. They cease listening. The audience dwindles. Researches have shown, for example, that radio programs of classical music tend to preserve rather than to create interest in classical music and that newly emerging interests are typically superficial. Most listeners to these programs have previously acquired an interest in classical music; the few whose interest is initiated by the programs are caught up by melodic compositions and come to think of classical music exclusively in terms of Tschaikowsky or Rimsky-Korsakov or Dvorak.

Proposed solutions to these problems are more likely to be born of faith than knowledge. The improvement of mass tastes through the improvement of mass art products is not as simple a matter as we should like to believe. It is possible, of course, that a conclusive effort has not been made. By a triumph of imagination over the current organization of mass media, one can conceive a rigorous censorship over all media, such that nothing was allowed in print or on the air or in the films save "the best that has been thought and said in the world." Whether a radical change in the supply of mass art would in due course reshape the tastes of mass audiences must remain a matter of speculation. Decades of experimentation and research are needed. At present, we know conspicuously little about the methods of improving esthetic tastes and we know that some of the suggested methods are ineffectual. We have a rich knowledge of failures. Should this discussion be reopened in 1976, we may, perhaps, report with equal confidence our knowledge of positive achievements.

At this point, we may pause to glance at the road we have traveled. By way of introduction, we considered the seeming sources of widespread concern with the place of mass media in our society. Thereafter, we first examined the social role ascribable to the sheer existence of the mass media and concluded that this may have been exaggerated. In this connection, however, we noted several consequences of the existence of mass media: their status conferral function, their function in inducing the application of social norms, and their narcotizing dysfunction. Secondly, we indicated the constraints placed by a structure of commercialized ownership and control upon the mass media as agencies of social criticism and as carriers of high esthetic standards.

We turn now to the third and last aspect of the social role of the mass media: the possibilities of utilizing them for moving toward designated types of social objectives.

Propaganda for Social Objectives

This final question is perhaps of more direct interest to you than the other questions we have discussed. It represents something of a challenge to us since it provides the means of resolving the apparent paradox to which we referred previously: the seeming paradox arising from the assertion that the significance of the sheer existence of the mass media has been exaggerated and the multiple indications that the media do exert influences upon their audiences.

What are the conditions for the effective use of mass media for what might be called "propaganda for social objectives"—the promotion, let us say, of non-discriminatory race relations, or of educational reforms, or of positive attitudes toward organized labor? Research indicates that, at least, one or more of three conditions must be satisfied if this propaganda is to prove effective. These conditions may be briefly designated as (1) monopolization, (2) canalization rather than change of basic values, and (3) supplementary face-to-face contact. Each of these conditions merits some discussion.

Monopolization

This situation obtains when there is little or no opposition in the mass media to the diffusion of values, policies, or public images. That is to say, monopolization of the mass media occurs in the absence of counter-propaganda.

In this restricted sense, monopolization of the mass media is found in diverse circumstances. It is, of course, indigenous to the political structure of authoritarian society, where access to the media of communication is wholly closed to those who oppose the official ideology. The evidence suggests that this monopoly played some part in enabling the Nazis to maintain their control of the German people.

But this same situation is approximated in other social systems. During the war, for example, our government utilized the radio, with some success, to promote and to maintain identification with the war effort. The effectiveness of these morale building efforts was in large measure due to the virtually complete absence of counterpropaganda.

Similar situations arise in the world of commercialized propaganda. The mass media create popular idols. The public images of the radio performer, Kate Smith, for example, picture her as a woman with unparalleled understanding of other American women, deeply sympathetic with ordinary men and women, a spiritual guide and mentor, a patriot whose views on public affairs should be taken seriously. Linked with the cardinal American virtues, the public images of Kate Smith are at no point subject to a counterpropaganda. Not that she has no competitors in the market of radio advertising. But there are none who set themselves systematically to question what she has said. In consequence, an unmarried radio entertainer with an annual income in six figures may be visualized by millions of American women as a hard-working mother who knows the recipe for managing life on fifteen hundred a year.

This image of a popular idol would have far less currency were it subjected to counterpropaganda. Such neutralization occurs, for example, as a result of preelection campaigns by Republicans and Democrats. By and large, as a recent study has shown, the propaganda issued by each of these parties neutralizes the effect of the other's propaganda. Were both parties to forgo their campaigning through the mass media entirely, it is altogether likely that the net effect would be to reproduce the present distribution of votes.

This general pattern has been described by Kenneth Burke in his *Attitudes Toward History* "... businessmen compete with one another by trying to *praise their own commodity* more persuasively than their rivals, whereas politicians compete by slandering the *opposition.* When you add it all up, you get a grand total of absolute praise for business and grand total of absolute slander for politics."

To the extent that opposing political propaganda in the mass media are balanced, the net effect is negligible. The virtual monopolization of the media for given social objectives, however, will produce discernible effects upon audiences.

Canalization

Prevailing beliefs in the enormous power of mass communications appear to stem from successful cases of monopolistic propaganda or from advertising. But the leap from efficacy of advertising to the assumed efficacy of propaganda aimed at deep-rooted attitudes and ego involved behavior is as unwarranted as it is dangerous. Advertising is typically directed toward the canalizing of preexisting behavior patterns or attitudes. It seldom seeks to instil new attitudes or to create significantly new behavior patterns. "Advertising pays" because it generally deals with a simple psychological situation. For Americans who have been socialized in the use of a toothbrush, it makes relatively little difference which brand of toothbrush they use. Once the gross pattern of behavior or the generic attitude has been established, it can be canalized in one direction or another. Resistance is slight. But mass propaganda typically meets a more complex situation. It may seek objectives which are at odds with deep-lying attitudes. It may seek to reshape rather than to canalize current systems of values. And the successes of advertising may only highlight the failures of propaganda. Much of the current propaganda which is aimed at abolishing deep-seated ethnic and racial prejudices, for example, seems to have had little effectiveness.

Media of mass communication, then, have been effectively used to canalize basic attitudes but there is little evidence of their having served to change these attitudes.

Supplementation

Mass propaganda which is neither monopolistic nor canalizing in character may, nonetheless, prove effective if it meets a third condition: supplementation through face-to-face contacts.

A case in point will illustrate the interplay between mass media and face-to-face influences. The seeming propagandistic success achieved some years ago by Father Coughlin does not appear, upon inspection, to have resulted primarily from the propaganda content of his radio talks. It was, rather, the product of these centralized propaganda talks *and* widespread local organizations which arranged for their members to listen to him, followed by discussions among themselves concerning the social views he had expressed. This combination of a central supply of propaganda (Coughlin's addresses on a nation-wide network), the coordinated distribution of newspapers and pamphlets and locally organized face-to-face discussions among relatively small groups—this complex of reciprocal reinforcement by mass media and personal relations proved spectacularly successful.

Students of mass movements have come to repudiate the view that mass propaganda in and of itself creates or maintains the movement. Naziism did not attain its brief moment of hegemony by capturing the mass media of communication. The media played an ancillary role, supplementing the use of organized violence, organized distribution of rewards for conformity, and organized centers of local indoctrination. The Soviet Union has also made large and impressive use of mass media for indoctrinating enormous populations with appropriate ideologies. But the organizers of indoctrination saw to it that the mass media did not operate alone. "Red corners," "reading huts," and "listening stations" comprised meeting places in which groups of citizens were exposed to the mass media in common. The 55,000 reading rooms and clubs which had come into being by 1933 enabled the local ideological elite to talk over with rank-and-file readers the content of what they read. The relative scarcity of radios in private homes again made for group listening and group discussions of what had been heard.

In these instances, the machinery of mass persuasion included face-to-face contact in local organizations as an adjunct to the mass media. The privatized individual response to the materials presented through the channels of mass communication was considered inadequate for transforming exposure to propaganda into effectiveness of propaganda. In a society such as our own, where the pattern of bureaucratization has not yet become so pervasive or, at least, not so clearly crystallized, it has likewise been found that mass media prove most effective in conjunction with local centers of organized face-to-face contact.

Several factors contribute to the enhanced effectiveness of this joining of mass media and direct personal contact. Most clearly, the local discussions serve to reinforce the content of mass propaganda. Such mutual confirmation produces a "clinching effect." Secondly, the central media lessen the task of the local organizer, and the personnel requirements for such subalterns need not be as rigorous in a popular movement. The subalterns need not set forth the propaganda content for themselves, but need only pilot potential converts to the radio where the doctrine is being expounded. Thirdly, the appearance of a representative of the movement on a nation-wide network, or his mention in the national press, serves to symbolize the legitimacy and significance of the movement. It is no powerless, inconsequential enterprise. The mass media, as we have seen, confer status. And the status of the national movement reflects back on the status of the local cells, thus consolidating the tentative decisions of its members. In this interlocking arrangement, the local organizer ensures an audience for the national speaker and the national speaker validates the status of the local organizer.

This brief summary of the situations in which the mass media achieve their maximum propaganda effect may resolve the seeming contradiction which arose at the outset of our discussion. The mass media prove most effective when they operate in a situation of virtual "psychological monopoly," or when the objective is one of canalizing rather than modifying basic attitudes or when they operate in conjunction with face-to-face contacts.

But these three conditions are rarely satisfied conjointly in propaganda for social objectives. To the degree that monopolization of attention is rare, opposing propagandas have free play in a democracy. And, by and large, basic social issues involve more than a mere canalizing of preexistent basic attitudes; they call, rather, for substantial changes in attitude and behavior. Finally, for the most obvious of reasons, the close collaboration of mass media and locally organized centers for face-to-face contact has seldom been achieved in groups striving for planned social change. Such programs are expensive. And it is precisely these groups which seldom have the large resources needed for these expensive programs. The forward looking groups at the edges of the power structure do not ordinarily have the large financial means of the contented groups at the center.

As a result of this threefold situation, the present role of media is largely confined to peripheral social concerns and the media do not exhibit the degree of social power commonly attributed to them.

By the same token, and in view of the present organization of business ownership and control of the mass media, they have served to cement the structure of our society. Organized business does approach a virtual "psychological monopoly" of the mass media. Radio commercials and newspaper advertisements are, of course, premised on a system which has been termed free enterprise. Moreover, the world of commerce is primarily concerned with canalizing rather than radically changing basic attitudes; it seeks only to create preferences for one rather than another brand of product. Face-to-face contacts with those who have been socialized in our culture serve primarily to reinforce the prevailing culture patterns.

Thus, the very conditions which make for the maximum effectiveness of the mass media of communication operate toward the maintenance of the going social and cultural structure rather than toward its change.

References

1. Bryce, James. *The American Commonwealth.* Vol. 2. New York: The Macmillan Company, 1910, 1914.

Fehl L. Shirley

Among the most interesting explorations of the influence of reading on people is this report of doctoral research by Fehl L. Shirley. Dr. Shirley believes reading does make a difference in the lives of young people and that they seek those materials which satisfy their needs for maturity.

The Influence of Reading on Concepts, Attitudes, and Behavior

The discovery of a favorite author, according to Lin Yutang, was like finding the reincarnation of the same soul. Although the author may have lived in another age, his thinking and feeling are so akin to the reader's that coming across them in the pages of a book is "like a person finding his own image"(5). George Eliot described her initial reading of Rousseau as an electric shock. Nietzsche felt the same way about Schopenhauer, although he later rebelled against his master. Others have reported that reading gave them a design for living purposefully or experiencing life more understandably. For some, reading was intellectual enlightenment; for others, intense empathic involvement.

This interaction between the reader and his book may be considered as a continuum from simple word recall to a dynamic reorganization of the self-image. In Russell's four levels of reading, the fourth is related to values that the reader takes "for his own" and which he may incorporate in his emerging life pattern (2). Strang maintains that, through identification with and imitation of characters in books, a reader achieves insight into the solution of personal problems. He develops a new self-image and a new concept of his own worth in the worldly scheme (4).

This investigation was concerned with the fourth level of reading, a road not taken by many researchers. While there has been considerable research on the deleterious effects of reading disability on personality, there is little research on the positive effects of reading. In this investigation, therefore, the individuals were asked to report any changes in concepts, attitudes, and behavior that they had experienced as a result of reading.

Reprinted with permission of Fehl L. Shirley and the International Reading Assoication.

Method of Study

A modified critical incident technique (1) was used as a basis for collecting the data. The aim of the technique was to obtain self-observations of internal behavior. Students were asked to tell specifically how books, poems or articles had affected their attitude (tendency to act in a certain way), their ideas, or behavior. A questionnaire was the major instrument used. This was supplemented and validated by interviews and case studies. The subjects were 420 sophomore, junior, and senior high school students in two public high schools in Tucson, Arizona.

In the analysis of the data from the questionnaires, the number of influences on concept, attitude, and behavior were correlated with age, intelligence, vocabulary, comprehension, grade level, and the number of materials reported as influential. The chi square of significance was used to test sex and grade level differences in the number of influences reported, as well as differences in the number of influences reported from voluntary and assigned readings and from fiction and nonfiction. Also obtained was the frequency of certain elements in the literature that the subjects reported had influenced them.

Intelligence and reading ability were measured by the Otis Beta group (Form DM) and the California Reading (Form W) Tests. A comparison was made of the influence reported by the 15 high ability students, who tended to be the best readers, and the 15 low ability students, who tended to be the poorest readers. Students whose questionnaire responses showed extreme patterns of high and low influence were selected for case study. Ten protocols representing the extremes in influence were chosen after quantitative and qualitative analyses of the protocols of the group selected for case study. The criteria for the selection of the five subjects of high influence were the following:

1. Evidence of a combination of concept, attitude, and behavior influence.
2. Statements disclosing development of:
    a. Self-understanding,
    b. Understanding of self in relation to others, and
    c. Understanding and empathy for others.
3. Statements revealing decisions formulated.
4. Statements revealing self-observed action taken by the subject regarding decisions formulated.

The criteria for the selection of the five cases of low influence were:

1. Assertion by the student that no specific book, story, poem or

article had influenced his point of view, attitude or behavior.
2. Vague, general statements about the influence of reading.

Data for studying these ten cases included information from counselors' records, teachers' observations and rating scales, written responses to the questionnaire, and free responses to the same questions asked a year later in interviews.

Qualitative Analysis

A qualitative analysis of the reported influences on concept, attitude, and behavior was made. To ascertain the percentage of agreement of classification, two independent analysts coded 20 protocols out of a total of 420. The percentage of agreement of the two analysts and the investigator are presented in Table 1.

TABLE 1

Percentage of Agreement on Classification
of Concepts, Attitudes, and Behavior
(N = 59)

Influence	Checked Items No.	Agreements No.	Agreements %
Concept	24	19	79.17
Attitude	17	10	58.82
Behavior	18	17	94.44
Total	59	46	77.97

The behavior response indicating action is more evident and easier to detect than the concept of attitude influence. However, a percentage of 77.97 for the check-coding of the total protocols is sufficiently high to indicate reasonable agreement for the classification procedure.

Influence on Concept

As used in this study, concept is defined as the overt, verbal representation of the common element distinguishing groups or classes and includes abstraction and generalization. Examples of responses classified as concepts are given below:

> *The Lord of the Flies,* W. Golding
> ... I gained insight into how civilization is a thin veneer and how people can change when away from it.
>
> *Death of a Salesman,* A. Miller
> ... it brought me to the realization of how very easy it is to get lost

The Influence of Reading on Concepts, Attitudes, and Behavior

in the shuffle of life and that once you get behind it's nearly impossible to find your place again.

Influence on Attitude

As used in this study, attitude is defined as the overt, verbal response indicating a tendency to act in a certain direction. Examples of responses classified as attitudes:

Catcher in the Rye, J. Salinger
Well when I was reading this book I put myself as the boy in the book. ... Everytime something he disliked I disliked.

Bible
When I feel depressed or angry at the whole world, or just plain useless my attitude can change a great deal by reading sections of the *Bible*.

Influence on Behavior

Behavior refers to change in the overt action of the individual as he has observed and reported it. This type of response is indicated by such comments as:

Karen, M. Killilea
I tried harder at the things I did, because of the way Karen fought and what little she had to fight for.

The Cross and the Switch Blade, D. Wilkerson
After I finished the article, I went into my room and prayed for these people and for myself. ... I help the people at a Continual Work Camp in Arizona.

Combinations of Related Influences

Many reported influences on concept, attitude, and behavior were not given separately or in isolated form but in combinations of two or three related elements:

None Dare Call It Treason, J. Stormer
This book made me aware of the threat of Communism in this country and in the world. Afterwards I wanted to join a youth political group and I did. I have become more aware of the current news and world events, and I do more reading in magazines, books, papers, etc. Reading this book has influenced me to take law in college. I feel that if I am trained in speaking and am learned in the laws and ways of my country, I can help and inform others in the future. (Concept + Attitude + Behavior)

Black Like Me, J. Griffin

Black Like Me definitely changed my attitude and point of view about the racial situation. It also enlarged my knowledge of the situation in the South. After reading the book, I felt as if I wanted to really do something to help the Negro in the South. I was shocked by some of the events that took place and surprised that one group of humans could possibly treat another group of humans so cruelly. . . . I try to instill better attitudes about the situation in the people close around me. I realize now when I know more about it, how much needs to be done to change the attitudes of some very prejudiced people. (Concept + Attitude + Behavior)

The responses were classified into areas influenced by reading, and seven areas in order of frequency emerged from the analysis of the data: Self Image, Philosophy of Life, Cultural Groups, Social Problems, Sensitivity to People, Political Science, and Miscellaneous. The reading materials reported by the students as having influenced them were classified under the foregoing areas. No two individuals were influenced in the same way, and one individual might be influenced in several areas by one book. The patterns of influence were complex and suggested wide individual variation.

Of 180 books the ten most frequently reported by the adolescents in this study as having influenced them are shown in Table 2.

TABLE 2
Ten Books Most Frequently Mentioned by Students

	Frequency in 708 Readings	
	No.	Percent
Black Like Me	43	6.07
Bible	25	3.53
To Kill a Mockingbird	12	1.69
Exodus	12	1.69
The Good Earth	12	1.69
Catcher in the Rye	9	1.27
The Ugly American	8	1.13
Animal Farm	7	0.99
Lord of the Flies	6	0.85
The Grapes of Wrath	6	0.85

Self-Involvement Reactions

The attempt was also made to classify responses into dimensions of self-involvement. The reactions of the adolescents of this study appeared to

The Influence of Reading on Concepts, Attitudes, and Behavior 51

fall into these dimensions: the indifferent, the observer, the participator, the synthesizer, and the decision-maker. Brief descriptions of the kinds of responses as well as examples from each category are given below:

The Indifferent

This reader exhibits apathy toward reading:

> I can't say there was any change in my behavior or attitude because of something I read. If there was, it lasted a very short time. I really don't enjoy reading in my free time very much. I'd much rather be out in the desert hunting. I get enough reading in school. If people read all the time, they'd dry up and blow away.

The Observer

The characteristic attitude of the observer is "based on external judgment rather than on empathic association with the feelings of a character" (3). In this investigation the classification of "observer" involves even less of the feeling response than suggested in Squire's definition:

> *The Lottery,* W. Woodward; *The Lord of the Flies,* W. Golding
> They affected me, not as a change in my attitude toward my behavior itself, but more or less as an outsider looking at the behavior of the whole human race in different situations.

The Participator

The reader who reacts as a participator may achieve identity with a character or characters, or he may become closely involved in the action. Two degrees of self-involvement as a participator were noted in the verbal reports: partial and intense. The "partial participator" is only tentatively involved in the action and is represented by such comments as:

> *Black Like Me,* J. Griffin
> Felt more sympathetic toward people of the Negro race, whereas before I had had a dislike for their violent demonstrations. I still don't condone these demonstrations but I understand the cause . . .

The "intense participator" shows a high degree of empathy or almost complete involvement:

> *The Grapes of Wrath* and *Of Mice and Men,* J. Steinbeck
> . . . taught me to see the plight of the poor common laborer and how

he is taken advantage of by better educated men. I felt sorry for them
. . . I felt depressed. I cried after reading *Of Mice and Men.*

The Synthesizer

The reports of the synthesizer reflect a new or reinforced construct or a new self-image. An individual who reacts as a synthesizer of impressions, ideas, feelings, and emotions may undergo a unique transformation of character in developing a new self-image or he may formulate new constructs.

The Self-Image Reaction

Crime and Punishment, F. Dostoevski

After reading the book I discovered how self-centered I was and how quick I was to form my opinions.

The Construct Reaction

Bible

. . . caused me to see that people are people and that the only way to happiness is love of my fellowmen.

The Decision Maker

The decision maker has made a decision and is acting upon it or plans to do so if circumstances warrant his action:

Magazine article on cancer

. . . the article made me stop smoking for fear of getting it. It helped me tremendously in many respects.

Combinations of Dimensions of Self-Involvement

As was evidenced by the reported influences on concept, attitude, and behavior, these self-involvement reactions were frequently combined into related dimensions:

Poems by Robert Frost

The poem *Stopping by Woods on a Snowy Evening* by Frost gave me the help I needed to get through some of the difficult periods of my life. When things were going badly I wanted to give up. Remembering that poem . . . I gained strength to carry on. The meaning of the words gave me strength to keep on working even though things looked bad. Once I started to read Frost, I found I enjoyed it so much I read a whole book of his poems. This one, *The Birches,* and *The Runaway* became my three favorite poems and gave me ideas to live by. (Synthesizer, Construct and Self-Image, + Decision Maker)

Two independent analysts coded 20 protocols out of 420 which represented all the dimensions of self-involvement. There was agreement by the two analysts and the investigator on 15 of the 25 items checked or a total percentage of agreement of 60 percent. There were so few frequencies in the indifferent and observer categories that only the total percentage of agreement is given for the classification.

The synthesizer reaction was the major type of self-involvement response reported; 13 percent reacted as construct synthesizers and 11 percent as self-image synthesizers although there was great variation in patterned reactions. It is to be expected that the synthesizer would be the major self-involvement reaction as the largest area of influence reported was self-image.

Findings of Main Study

Influence on Concepts, Attitude, and Behavior

The introspective and retrospective reports of 420 adolescents confirmed that reading influences concepts, attitudes, and behavior. Only 16 of the 420 students reported no personal influence from reading. Of the 1184 influences reported, 45 percent were concepts, 40 percent were attitudes, and 15 percent were behavioral responses. Of the responses reported, most were single items but about a third were combinations of concepts, attitudes, and behaviors, particularly combinations of concepts and attitudes.

Findings of Substudies

Influences Related to Certain Variables

Certain characteristics of the adolescents were associated with the number and kinds of influences reported. Among these were intelligence, general reading ability, age, grade level, and sex. For the entire group, a positive relationship (significant at the .01 level) existed between total influences and intelligence, vocabulary, and comprehension. There was also a significant relationship between total influences and number of materials read. The relationship between total influences and age and grade level was negative. The younger students in the lower grades tended to report high totals of influences. Female students who reported higher totals of influences tended to be more intelligent and better readers than the males who reported high totals of influences. Females also tended to read more materials that influenced them.

The characteristics of the adolescents varied somewhat with the separate totals of concepts, attitudes, and behavior. There was a very slight, positive relationship between total concepts and intelligence and vocabulary. A slight, negative relationship was suggested between total attitudes and total behaviors and intelligence, vocabulary, and comprehension.

Comparison of Influences Reported by Two Extreme Groups

In the comparison made of the influences reported by the 15 most intelligent students and the 15 least intelligent students, approximately the same number of influences were found in both groups. This relationship was supported by the case studies of students exhibiting maximal or minimal influence from reading, whose intelligence and reading ability varied, but was not confirmed by the findings for the entire group. The top group reported relatively more voluntary readings, although the number of voluntary readings reported by both groups was greater than the number of required readings. The low group reported relatively more non-fictional reading as having influenced them.

Voluntary and Assigned Readings

Of the reading reported, 77 percent were voluntary and 23 percent were assigned. Voluntary readings included, 1) readings specified by the student as voluntary, 2) those chosen from bibliographies furnished by the teacher, and 3) readings pertaining to research projects on topics chosen by the student. Assigned readings were on specific reading materials chosen by the teacher. Apparently, students were influenced more by voluntary reading than specifically assigned reading.

Fiction and Non-Fiction

Half of the total influences were reported from fiction (49.96 percent) and half from non-fiction (50.04 percent). The value of chi square for testing the difference between the total number of influences from fiction and non-fiction was small and not significant. Apparently, the number of influences was unaffected by the type of reading material.

Summary

The number of influences of reading on students' concepts, attitudes, and behavior is related to intelligence, reading proficiency, the number of books and articles read, and the situation in which the reading was done (voluntary and assigned) but not the type of material (fiction or non-fiction).

Implications

1. The case study method is recommended for the study of individual patterns of response. Dimensions of influence on concept, attitude, and behavior as well as dimensions of self-involvement might be studied further in idiographic research, which is concerned with the study of the individual case. Such studies might shed more light on the thinking processes involved in reading.
2. The finding that there appeared to be no significant difference in the number of influences reported from fiction and non-fiction might have implications for bibliotherapy. Non-fiction as well as fiction might aid in personality enhancement and serve a therapeutic purpose.
3. Since the reports of the adolescents in this study showed that reading can contribute to ideals and a philosophy of life, teachers might put more emphasis on the development of character and values through the reading program.
4. The influence of reading on the personality at different stages of child and adolescent development might be explored. Some of the case studies of this investigation showed more mature development when students were interviewed a year later.
5. Studies might be made of influences on reading and other variables, such as socio-economic class and other personality characteristics.
6. Negative influences from reading might be further investigated. The large majority of influences reported by the students of this study might be considered positive or beneficial. However, a few students reported books that had influenced them in an undesirable, antisocial way. There is need to know more about the elements in reading material that influence adolescents adversely.
7. Introspective reports might be used by teachers to ascertain the kind of reading materials that influence their students. In this way the teacher would become aware of reading interests and materials that influence students constructively or adversely. The students themselves might derive personal value and achieve insight and self-understanding from their introspective accounts. One student wrote on his questionnaire: "I'm glad I was given the opportunity for insight into something which had a favorable effect and caused a worthwhile change in me."

References

1. Flanagan, John C. "The Critical Incident Technique." *Psychological Bulletin* 51 (July 1954):327-58.
2. Russell, David H. "Contributions of Reading to Personal Development." *Teachers College Record* 61 (May 1960):435-42.
3. Squire, James. "The Responses of Adolescents to Literature Involving Selected Experiences of Personal Development." Unpublished Ph.D. dissertation, University of California, Berkeley, 1956.
4. Strang, Ruth. *The Adolescent Views Himself.* New York: McGraw-Hill Book Co., 1957.
5. Yutang, Lin. *The Importance of Living.* New York: Reynal and Hitchcock, 1937, pp. 380-87.

CHAPTER THREE

The Role of Reading in Youth Revolt

Just as reading and literacy play a role in the presentation of widely differing value systems, so are they participants in value conflicts. In their search for new adult models, adolescents and youth have always found that more antithetical and even heretical documents seem to speak especially to them. Every generation seems to discover and examine anew those authors who promise the Utopias most congruent with the value needs of the times. Today, a whole new galaxy of authors speak to these young people, presenting some startling new value constructs.

For many reasons, the latter half of the twentieth century has been the setting for a sharp reappraisal of values. Young adults of junior high school, high school, and college ages have carried the rebellious banners of conflicting values to a variety of strikes, stand-ins, sit-ins, lie-ins, tune-ins, and turn-ons. Peace and civil rights have most frequently been the chosen issues about which the battles are waged—and school grounds have often been the field of strife. Our part in this agonizing reexamination at Columbia and the University of California, at San Francisco State College and Kent State University is no more than one country's portion of a worldwide phenomenon. Thirty-seven students were shot in Mexico City, and Italian students held the police captive in their own barracks. The chant of *"Dubcheck! Svoboda!"* in Prague carried the same cadence as *"DeGaulle! Assassin!"* in Paris. While the conflict still rages, slowly the values as well as strategies of both sides are becoming modified. Standard Oil Company looks to new conservation-ecology techniques, and New York City's Police protest with a "sick-in."

Unfortunately, school programs have not often given attention to the interests of teen-agers. Whether it is because teachers are of the older

57

generation who feel threatened or whether it is because they typically come from social classes who would emulate established values is relatively unimportant. Most pertinent here is that schools have not chosen to regard the reading habits of young adults and, as a consequence, have not helped these students evaluate the materials they *do* read. By our ignorance of their concerns, we prevent a demonstration of the values of reading in the adolescents' terms. We ultimately prevent young adults from learning to use reading as a resource to "the good life."

Mario D. Fantini

Mario Fantini analyzes student rebellion today as a demand for humanism, a rejection of the mechanical way they are treated in schools. He considers, too, the shift in power away from previous "establishment" sources. Any change in school programs must affect the way reading is taught and learned, the way reading is regarded in the social fabric of the culture.

The Student Movement and School Reform

Unlike previous generations of students who have exhibited symptoms of rebelliousness, students of 1969 are not "getting over it," in the opinion of Mario Fantini. For, as Maxine Greene also stressed, the times are much different, and the nature and extent of dissent are much deeper and more fundamental in spirit and intent. Fantini supports Spender's point of view that the alienated student of today is trying to change values and consciousness. He is a revolutionary in spirit and action.

The school becomes the immediate target of this revolution, for it constitutes the community of the young. Moreover, the school, as a miniature of society, exhibits the same shams and distortions that the radical Left wants to uproot in the larger society.

Fantini sees great hope for basic educational reform in student movements of today. And basic changes in the program of education are, in his view, necessary. Our efforts at change in the past have been too narrow, attempting to reform the school by curriculum change without seeking a total transformation. The young generation is unique, and new kinds of schools must be established to serve this new body of students.

Drawing on a number of sources, Fantini presents some models and characteristics of these new schools, and describes several efforts now being made to develop different approaches to schooling. (J. Galen Saylor)

Adolescent rebellion has been tolerated, and even sanctioned, as a "normal" stage of human development. After all, "if you aren't a liberal when you're young, you have no heart, but if you aren't a middle-aged

---

From *Student Unrest: Threat or Promise?* edited by Richard L. Hart and J. Galen Saylor. Copyright © 1970 by the Association for Supervision and Curriculum Development. "The Student Movement and School Reform" by Mario D. Fantini. Reprinted with permission of the Association for Supervision and Curriculum Development and the author.

conservative, you have no head." "Idealist" and "dreamer" have been the timeless epithets for the young, and countless generations of parents have been amused and exasperated by their children's demands of the world. Parental frustration has been alleviated by the consensus of adult society: "Don't worry, all kids go through it, and yours will get over it!"

But these old rules are not working any more. The institutional and parental power base has been shaken by the sudden and volcanic force of the young. As recently as five years ago, an alienated youngster wondered what was wrong with *him* if he was uncomfortable with his environment. Now he knows his disaffection is shared by students all over the world, and that awareness nurtures his protest. Three out of five junior and senior high school principals in the United States report evidence of student activism (14). *The New York Times* has designated a segment of the front page to summarize student uprisings. The major television networks leap frantically from campus to campus on the evening news broadcasts. Students were a primary force in the mobilization of the French, and in the Czechoslovak resistance to Soviet repression.

The international student presence is neither a historical fluke nor the unified instrument of a political conspiracy. Parental, administrative, and governmental threats may diminish the visibility of the student movement, but they will not obliterate its roots; bandaging an ugly sore camouflages an infection, but it does not provide a cure. And the student movement, like the proverbial sore which refuses to heal, is only a symptom of a profound and pervasive illness. The students of 1969, unlike their ancestors, are not "getting over it," for the boundaries of their dissent are beyond politics, beyond institutions, beyond generations:

> [Stephen] Spender ... understands the cultural roots of student alienation, that they are trying to change values and consciousness rather than lay down a program and seize state power. He understands that they are trying to make *revolutionaries,* rather than make a *revolution,* that they are trying to make a "parallel world." ... [one must] see the personalities, confrontations, and dreams of the young Left in larger than just its surface political dimensions (12).

The school, as the immediate community of the young, is the most vulnerable target for reform. The Lemberg Center for the Study of Civil Disorders at Brandeis University reported that between January and April of 1968, 44 percent of the disturbances in six riot-prone cities involved schools—a threefold increase in one year. Recently the National Association of Secondary School Principals released a report based on a national survey of secondary school principals regarding the nature and extent of student activism. In this study nearly three out of five principals reported some form of active protest in their schools—whether junior or senior high, whether urban, suburban, or rural (14). The prevalent outrage against the sham of contemporary America is intensified toward the miniature society of the school. The appropriate instrument of a democratic system is a democratic school, yet we manifest diseased distortions of each. America's naïveté has begun to catch up with her; department stores are bombed despite civil rights legislation, heavy policing has not diminished the crime rate, and efficient schools have not produced a generation of patriots.

The age of expediency has nurtured an era of desperation, and the educator finds himself at an unprecedented crossroads. The first course, the more traditional and natural one, is to defend the existing institution by repressing its challengers. The less comfortable alternative is to utilize the energies of the "opposition" in an effort to redefine the school within the context of the principles of democracy.

Our frantic attempts at educational reform have been obstructed by a narrowness of purpose. We have concentrated on one educational component (for example, curriculum), and then waited breathlessly for a total transformation. If a scientist were to suggest modifying a Boeing-707 for space travel, he would be exiled from the laboratory. Yet the recent activity in educational research and development has involved a similar "tinkering" with the available mechanism. Just as a jet is simply not going to take us to the moon, so the present school is incapable of providing education.

The student movement offers a tremendous impetus and infinite resource for educational reform in the United States. Through the objectives and energies of American youngsters, we can and *must* construct a new institutional foundation. First, I will establish those cultural circumstances which make this generation unique, then examine the common and disparate qualities of American student groups, and, finally, describe our institutional obligations in view of those qualities. The angry voices of the young do not merely deserve new coverage. They also deserve responsible and responsive action.

Youth in a New Cultural Setting

Today's young people comprise the first generation weaned by the mass media. The effects of watching the world in the living room are now becoming manifest. In a recent psychological study, selected small children clearly demonstrated one horrifying aspect of television's impact. When told of death or illness in the family, these children immediately asked if their relatives had been assassinated. The ever-present television screen exposes even a three-year-old to the brutalities, realities, and fantasies of the world!

The adolescent easily perceives that thing which grown-ups call "the real world" as a chaotic phenomenon. Were it not for TV, today's youngster might consider his sense of isolation temporary:

> It's hard to remember sometimes that television is machinery—bits of equipment, consoles, cables, lenses, little hack boxes—and that when you turn it on one day (most days, in fact) and get *The Flying Nun,* you think of it as junk, as if the junk were somehow built into the equipment, and that when you turn it on another day and get, say, Dean Rusk and the gang down at the Foreign Relations Committee, or Bobby Kennedy announcing his reassessment, you think—well, what do you think! *The Flying Nun* is interrupting Dean Rusk? Dean Rusk is interrupting *The Flying Nun?* This country seems to include both, in some mysterious, lunatic balance, and television includes both, too, although commercial television has generally managed to push the balance so far out of whack that the country is barely recognizable to itself most of the time (1).

In addition to parading America's paradoxes, the whole realm of technology desensitizes the student to the bland stimuli in the classroom. Today's youngster is bombarded by strobe light shows, electrical guitar shrieks, pop culture, special effects movies, ad infinitum. His threshold for sensory stimulation has been elevated immeasurably; the same music which delights and relaxes him, appalls and unnerves his parents. The clinical and uninspired classroom cannot compel the attention of today's young Americans. The wonder is not so much that the young people "tune out," but that they even "tune in."

Contemporary students have acquired a certain level of sophistication through technological development. On the one hand, this worldliness expands the youngster's scope, but, on the other, it accelerates anxiety. Today's student, aware of the game which the world is playing, is in a position of choice. He can withdraw from the game entirely, play along with the rules of the kingdom until he is in a position to say that the emperor wears no clothes, or challenge the game itself. The "hippie" movement indicates the enormous appeal of withdrawal. At its original, most sophisticated moments, hippiedom sought to construct a social and economic alternative to the normative middle class game. Presuming that the values of Americana and happiness were mutually exclusive, the hippies adopted antithetical criteria in fringe communities. The three-piece suit became a haphazard costume, the studied coiffure was replaced by masses of curls, and the flower chased the dollar sign.

The hippie founders were not the 14-year-old runaways of Time-Life fame, but very serious young people longing for the promises of 18th century America. The hippies' staggering popularity has served to confirm their suspicions. Love beads and long hair are not accidental fashion trends; they are tacit nods of understanding toward the hippie movement.

If "dropping out" were an East Village peculiarity, the social import of the hippies would be minimal. However, evidence of drug use is not confined to the flower child's commune. *The New York Times* recently disclosed that 85 percent of the Columbia University undergraduate population has smoked marijuana at least once. Apparently marijuana is no longer the novocain of the poor but a fashionable, generally accepted pastime of the American middle class. Though heroin is still predominantly confined to impoverished neighborhoods, LSD is considered an elite intellectual adventure. The whole vocabulary attached to narcotics is based on the notion of mental seclusion: Timothy Leary's slogan, "tune in, turn on, drop out," "tripping out" on LSD, getting "high," "stoned," "wrecked," "destroyed" on marijuana, etc. The concept built into this extravagant use of drugs is the erasure of the "artificial" and complex considerations of society, and the substitution of the "real" world of the human mind.

"Dropping out" is frequently connected with professional decisions. The arts have never been more attractive to the politically conscious young, and the arts have rarely been more politically conscious. The Brontë sisters would be laughed off today's college lectern. The New Left demands political commitment from 20th century artists, and the Living Theatre, pop art, the films of Jean-Luc Godard fulfill that demand. Collections of modern poetry are steeped in Vietnam, racial discrimination, and international politics. One need not look beyond the recent National Book Awards for literary examples: Jonathan Kozol's *Death at an Early Age* (9), Norman Mailer's *The Armies of the Night* (10). Many young people feel they can vent their political dissatisfaction as movie critics, directors, playwrights, etc., without risking the moral corruption of the political and economic system. Others deem the possibilities of social change too remote to waste time manipulating the variables and prefer the more constant criteria of the arts.

The great majority of young people neither drop out nor challenge the system, but simply ride along with the institutional tides. This route, of course, is the safest and most accepted; dropouts and rebels invite censure. Some of this group are no doubt unaware that there is a game at all, but many fulfill society's expectations cynically. They intend to stand inconspicuously in the crowd until they are close enough to the emperor to expose his foolishness. These youngsters become Peace Corps volunteers, the politely persistent junior senators, the adamant young members of the Legal Aid Society. Their compliance with the system is often misinterpreted as proof that the system is viable. The young people who play the game do not disprove the presence of the game itself.

The Students' Movements

The public challengers of the schools not only represent an outspoken minority, but articulate the feelings of many less tenacious, yet similarly disaffected, young people. The so-called "student movement" does not present a unified program, for as Spender so perceptively indicates, the root of the uprising is beyond the realm of politics. All students are responding to their visions of themselves as victims—victims of an institution and a society-at-large which have repeatedly and undeniably refused to recognize them. Even the most disparate splinter groups are expressing common, and essentially emotional, grievances. All students, regardless of specific affiliations, want to be *seen;* they want to be acknowledged as thinking, feeling human beings. Second, they want to participate in the process of their education. How very obvious it seems—look, if this school is supposed to be for *me,* then let me tell you how I feel about it. Finally, students want their curriculum to be applicable to their individual lives—culturally, politically, socially, and personally. The cry for "relevance" is also painfully self-evident; who wants to study something he can't "relate" to? All three of these demands, though they have political translations like "democracy" and "freedom," stem from the most fundamental human needs, needs which the school has persisted in ignoring.

Because the student has been an anonymous face for so long, his desire to assert himself is now exaggerated. If one has been declared impotent, his exuberance in affirming his own power can lead him to point a machine gun at the dean, or destroy a private file, or paralyze the operation of an institution. The idea of recognition does not seem preposterous within the existing school system, yet consider the realities. The high school functions on a principle of adjustment: you will adjust, or you will suffer the consequences. The student is recognized *only* when he deviates from the norm, either negatively or positively. He is summoned to the principal's office if he cuts class, talks back to a teacher, is found in the hall without a pass. His chances of being summoned are slightly less if he excels academically, supports the policies of the school, or breaks up a fight in the gym. The undistinguished C student, however, graduates without ever having crossed the threshold of the principal's office.

The student is punished or rewarded according to his ability to adjust. If he cannot tell the difference between a predicate nominative and a predicate adjective, it is *his* fault—not the teacher's, or the book's, or the school's. Therefore, the D on the report card absolves the institution of responsibility, and the child is left to his own devices. The existing school, therefore, recognizes only its "idea" of what a student ought to be. He ought to be obedient, competent, and efficient, for these are the most expedient criteria for adult society. In perpetuating this notion of adaptation, the school denies itself the theoretical justification for an educational institution, the development of human potential. The existing school provides no mechanism for adjusting to the needs of the child, and, insofar as the school aims at preserving a smooth, unruffled operation, the student has to be a secondary consideration.

Need for Recognition

The concept of recognition—on an extremely personal level—is a theme for much of the student movement. Revolting against the societal tradition of judging an individual according to his extrinsic qualities, today's youngsters are interested only in intrinsic worth. They scorn definitions of people which deal with wealth, status, grade level, size of house, or number of television sets. Their language, like much of their behavior, is the language of confrontation. They admire those who talk "straight," those who seem to be authentic; credentials convince them of nothing. The student's value system has ousted society's normative psychology in favor of the individual's energy and growth; he is as interested in "becoming" as they are in "being," and he seeks environments which allow for individual development. An environment which maximizes a student's potential could never "fail" anyone.

The student's plea for participation in the classroom and the school community is not operational in the existing institution. Educational decision making is the business of the professional; he draws on his own experience, available information, and state requirements to design his school's academic and social framework. The professional, himself, is limited by restrictions which he cannot control; he is subject to a board of education, the judgment of his peer group, and the state government. It has been proposed in the United States Congress that the federal government deny financial subsidy to any school which tolerates student disturbances. The educational administrator is frequently powerless himself, but he participates in the professional hierarchy which deprives the student of an active voice in planning curriculum and establishing social rules in the school community. The student's voice is not only inaudible, but extraneous in the existing institution. The student is a mute subject in the kingdom of the professional, and the student is well aware of this.

Rejection of a Stale Curriculum

Aside from the student's subjection to social anachronisms, he is also plagued by a stale curriculum. He is the recipient of a wornout "line," a line which contradicts all his social experience. Built into contemporary curricula are the concepts of individuality ("How come I can't be *me* in school?"), virtue ("If I always told the truth I'd always be in detention."), American infallibility ("Why do Europeans hate the war in Vietnam?"), equal opportunity ("How come the maid is black?"), ad infinitum. Though he may acquire some general and ultimately helpful information in the process, the American public school student is fed a banquet of absolutes for a cafeteria of uncertainties.

Apart from the jolting discrepancy between the platitudes of the textbook and the realities of the world, the teacher rarely allows the world into the classroom. Little course content deals honestly (if at all) with the local community surrounding the school or with the community at large. The student may acquire the primitive tools of language, science, and mathematics, but he has no instruments for social action. He is not only deprived of a realistic view of the status quo, but is ignorant of the available or potential mechanisms for change.

The traditional underpinnings of American education do not provide those learning experiences which prepare people to be productive members of society.

The students' demands of their schools are as pragmatic as the American dream. They want to be prepared as future workers, with multiple options for professional achievement. It is interesting to note that vocational schools report fewer incidents of student unrest than their academic counterparts. They want to be provided with the tools for reconstructing the society which requires change. They want to be familiarized with the intricate workings of their society, a familiarity which requires *more* than the cherry tree saga or memorizing the Bill of Rights; they would also like to know about themselves as social creatures, to achieve a modicum of self-awareness through the interaction of the classroom. In short, today's students want a school in which they can learn.

These rather general descriptions of the student movement constitute the demands which transcend the specific stipulations of the various groups. It would be foolishly simplistic to imply that all young people have produced this single outline at an organized conference in the Midwest. Much of campus unrest is the result of intra-student dissension. The Students for a Democratic Society, the Students for Afro-American Studies, the Students for a Restructured University, are but a few splinter groups which run through the headlines, not to mention the hordes of students who are not officially affiliated, but who rally when circumstances are appropriate. The two significant factions of the contemporary student movement seem to be the white middle class and the black young people.

Need To Be a Person

White middle class youngsters are the disenchanted products of "things." They know, through firsthand experience, that those who demand their success are preparing them to be consumers, rather than people, and they also know that they want something more. Their fight against injustice is usually a vicarious one, for they are rarely victims of inequity themselves. Their parents have provided them with comfort, yet they crave the sensations of struggle. For them, the struggle is emotional and intellectual, not physical. They are frequently outraged by the complacency of their communities, and fight against falling into a similar trap. Many are exhilarated by the revolutionary game, for it provides them with the risks and rewards which suburban monotony has taken away.

This is not to minimize the sincerity of the white middle class youngster, for his complaints have no less urgency than those of his peers. His urgency, as a matter of fact, is often greater because of the vagueness of his ultimate aims. In the sterile, tree-lined, country club atmosphere, he longs for identity:

> The white students . . . had a problem of identity which they resolved first by being students, secondly, more emphatically by being rebellious students. . . . The neurosis of the white student is the fear that they have no identity, the passionate search to find one . . . (13).

Within the white middle class student movement are individuals who will go to various lengths to assert themselves. Thus, one side consists of a veto group which will go to any length, and whose demands are so outrageous that even they do not expect to be successful. These desperate youngsters often malign the honesty and intelligence of their more responsible peers, and eventually diminish their effectiveness. Those whose demands are preposterous and nonnegotiable may serve to initiate viable student protests, but fail miserably when they stand autonomously. The 1969 fiasco at Columbia University illustrates the susceptibility of the Students for a Democratic Society when it overstepped the bounds of reason; whereas most of the undergraduate population joined in the 1968 uprising, members of Students for a Democratic Society meekly cleared an administration building this spring, when they could not muster general student support.

The black students' movement has translated the students' general grievances into more specific terms. The quest for recognition becomes a plea for racial identity—a forthright, unrestrained awareness of color. The Negro is overwhelmingly aware of America's injustice, and he has achieved a plateau of historical consciousness which allows him to assess his oppression. Black students, cognizant of the instruments of oppression, have established a racial context which includes a new set of heroes and revised criteria for beauty, and they demand an institutional acknowledgment of these changes. Note for example, the expressed purpose of the Freedom School in Washington, D.C.:

> What we understand by education is the obtainment and application of all one's knowledge for the benefit of the group which in turn will benefit each individual within the collective. To this end what must constitute the basic part of one's education is the understanding of people more than things. We realize that when people understand themselves, their knowledge of things is facilitated, that the exclusive knowledge of things does not guarantee knowledge of people, and in fact contributes to the erosion, disintegration, and destruction of the creativity of man.
>
> Therefore our Freedom School must: (a) make Black People aware of who they are, (b) make Black People aware of who they must identify with, (c) enlighten Black People to the creative and scientific tools that are needed in order to obtain whatever we want to mean as freedom (6).

They, too, want to participate in their educational destiny, and the ubiquitous cry for black studies (Afro-American history, black poetry and painting, sociological courses on the American ghetto, etc.) is a particular way of vocalizing the need for potency through relevant curriculum. They want more black professionals; white teachers cannot possibly have appropriate expectations of black children. In describing the black students, Spender notes the following:

> Their behavior was maturer (perhaps because they accepted the advice of older people) and less neurotic than that of the improvising white students. . . . The black students, opposite here as in other respects, had a problem of losing their identity through segregation. Their identity is, of course, immensely real, in some ways the most real thing in America. . . . So if the neurosis of the white students is the fear that they have no identity, the passionate search to find one, that of the blacks is the fear that they will lose theirs, and beyond this the fear of actual extinction (13).

The youthful forces for institutional reform lack the cohesion which precludes optimal success. The black students often exclude the middle class whites from their activities, and the whites can neither comprehend nor adopt the focus of the black movement. The parents of black students are not only supportive, but frequently provocative regarding their children's protests. These adults have been victimized by societal inadequacies as well, and refuse to pass on a legacy of futility. They openly attack the schools, doubt the authority figures which represent institutions, and scorn those educational methods which have deprived their children of the tools of learning. These parents have been betrayed by the "democratic process," and want better things for their children. The adult fall guys of "the American nightmare" are as enraged as their offspring.

Need for Relevance and a New Model of Education

Among the middle and upper classes, parents are not nearly so sympathetic toward the student upsurgence. These adults, after all, "made it" according to the system's terms. Many of them surpassed the modest economic backgrounds of childhood, and view their children's challenge as ingratitude. For most Americans (and most people, in point of fact) that which exists is good by necessity—a normative value system. If it works, and if it has worked for generations, how bad can it be? Many Americans between the ages of 40 and 60 consider skepticism a flimsy indulgence; they had no time for intellectual exercises while they accumulated the wealth which has given their families security and comfort. They speak and think the language of the depression, of World War II, of breadlines and blackouts. They blame themselves for coddling their children, and bemoan the "insurrection." Having grown up in precarious times, many middle class parents prefer safety to justice, quiet to peace, and conformity to virtue. They are stunned by those who demand much more.

Notions of "the polite society," "the learned man," and "the joys of scholasticism" are whimsical vestiges in the United States. Perpetuating them in a 20th century school has contributed to the institution's demise. Education in an urban culture is not a luxury, but a necessity. Effective education must aim to produce a generation equipped to live with and control the elements of its environment.

Our schools are clinging to the nostalgic modes of an agricultural America, an America which has since been replaced by an entirely different ecological network. Students, no less than communities, in our urban ghettos are challenging the standard "model" of education; a model which was forged in another century, as Ira Gordon indicates (7):

Newtonian Model Man	*Einsteinian Model Man*
A mechanistic, fixed, closed system, characterized by:	An open-energy, self-organizing system, characterized by:
1. Fixed intelligence	1. Modifiable intelligence
2. Development as an orderly unfolding	2. Development as modifiable in both rate and sequence
3. Potential as fixed, although indeterminable	3. Potential as creatable through transaction with environment

Newtonian Model Man	Einsteinian Model Man
4. A telephone-switchboard brain	4. A computer brain
5. Steam-engine driven motor	5. A nuclear power-plant energy system
6. Homeostatic regulator (drive-reduction)	6. Inertial guidance and self-regulatory feedback-motivation system
7. Inactive until engine is stoked	7. Continuously active

The Reformation of Our Schools

The students are offering possible and invaluable contours for reforming the educational institution. They want to be potent adults—people who are capable of turning the United States into a participatory democracy. The schools, as an instrument for social change, can provide the first step toward achieving that larger end. We have a responsibility to give them the tools for social action, and can, simultaneously, create a healthy institution in the process (4).

The best way to learn about the democratic system is to participate in one. Yes, the students ought to have a voice in defining school policy, for they, presumably, are the very reason why the school exists at all. Students are clients, and the school's purpose is to serve them. They, along with the faculty and administration, can establish and preserve a composite idea of the classroom and the social complexion of the institution. The school seeks to foster the growth of a child, and a child grows through participation. The major thrust of the student movement consists of learning through doing that the intellect is significant insofar as it helps us act.

There is a fundamental difference between academic freedom and education. It is lovely to be uncensored in one's conversation, but chatter does not change things. The modern school must be *more* than talk, more than subject matter mastery. In a remarkable document issued by the Montgomery County Student Alliance, these points are made quite clear (11):

> Some of the county school system's announced goals are being met. County students on the whole are equipped with certain skills and facts, and test scores and grades show that the school system has by and large prepared them for college. ...
> The most significant effect of this emphasis on measurable, "acceptable" performance has been to subordinate greatly other basic goals of a desirable educational climate—goals which are less tangible but which, we feel and the county school system says (rhetorically) it agrees, are of

far greater and more lasting importance. It is these latter goals that have, practically speaking, been almost totally ignored by the county school system and the way it operates. Feedback to see whether these much more vital aims are being fulfilled has just not been sought by school officials; to our knowledge the county schools have shown little willingness to confront these questions and bring about the fundamental changes in attitude and organization that are necessary. . . .

It is becoming almost a cliché to say that the public schools are not relevant, yet very little positive action has been taken to do anything about it. Every student has things that interest him; but the sad fact is that the school system very rarely gives him an opportunity to explore these interests. In many cases the student is actually hindered by the pressures and restrictions of the school system. There is no provision for giving students the chance to explore different areas of interest and follow wherever this exploration may lead them. . . .

Very importantly, the individual student himself, what he feels, his concerns are ignored. How does he fit into all this? What is important to him? What does this mean to him and his life? These questions do not fit into the school system's equation. Assisted by experience and efficiency, the county public schools' operational equation seems simple: raw material (students) plus conditioning (classes, teachers, textbooks, discipline) equals products (graduates equipped to fill the necessary slots in society). The complexities of the individual, developing mind are passed over; the system is "successful," and, we are told, is among the best in the nation. . . .

Instead of the system's being built around the needs of the students, the students are being built around the needs of the system.

By acting out their opinions and feelings, students constantly test their own theories. The demand for relevance in the area of curriculum must consist of a similar interplay between thought and action. Work in the community can be just as accredited as a term paper, and course discussions must have something to do with the students' immediate and projected concerns. The school does not have to go beyond its students' present and future reality to develop a humanistic learning environment. Group encounter sessions, exchange programs with African countries are possibilities in a school which serves its students.

Reformed educational institutions, therefore, will have to alter at least three basic pillars:

1. *Governance.* There must be a shift from professional dominance to a meaningful parental and community role in the education process. Meaningful participation stands arm's length between professionally circumscribed participation on one hand and total control by students, parents, and community residents on the other. It calls for student, parent, and

community roles in the matters of budgeting, personnel, and curriculum. The vehicle of participation may be structures at the individual school level or elected bodies on a neighborhood basis. In either case, one of the chief criteria is proximity of educational decision makers to the affected schools. The chief political criterion is *accountability* of the professional and the school system to the students and community.

2. *Substance.* There must be an evolution to a humanistically-oriented curriculum and a modification of the skill-performance standard by which educational quality is primarily measured. The heavy emphasis on cognitive subject matter must be at least tempered with materials that bear some relevance to the students' lives and with newer kinds of content and procedures that help ghetto students answer deep personal concerns and often rediscover their own integrity. Curriculum that represents an alien, boring, and false culture must be abandoned (ghetto children *can* be well-educated without being robbed of their own subculture). Evaluative criteria, in particular, must be expanded to include ways of judging student abilities other than by the notoriously middle class-weighted verbal means.

3. *Personnel.* The educational system must be opened to a far broader base of talent than the conventionally prepared career educator. The staffs of schools must vary along a wide horizontal spectrum from the professional to the layman, the latter including parents, community residents, and students themselves. They must vary vertically as well, to include not only professional educators but also specialists from other disciplines and professions. Moreover, the training of teachers must be vis-à-vis and *in* the reality of community needs and expressions.

Moreover, there are other key bench marks differentiating the traditional from the reformed educational institutions [See Table 1(3)].

A viable school must also satisfy the following criteria:

1. Social reality and the school's curriculum have to be intrinsically connected.
   a. The school must acknowledge the realities by setting up a structure in which students are engaged in the examination of these realities.
   b. Students will learn the skills and behaviors needed to influence social realities.
   c. The skills and behaviors for social change will be applied by the students to the social realities.
2. Power, identity, and connectedness have to become a legitimized basis for curriculum development with the aim of expanding the repertoire of responses students have in dealing with these concerns.
3. Diversity, both cultural and individual, and its potential for cross-

TABLE 1
Characteristics of Traditional and Reformed School Systems

Distinguishing feature	Traditional system	Reformed system
Center of control	Professional monopoly	The public (the community)
Role of parents' organizations	To interpret the school to the community, for public relations	To participate as active agents in matters substantive to the educational process
Bureaucracy	Centralized authority, limiting flexibility and initiative to the professional at the individual school level	Decentralized decision making allowing for maximum local lay and professional initiative and flexibility, with central authority concentrating on technical assistance, long-range planning, and system-wide coordination
Educational objectives	Emphasis on grade-level performance, basic skills, cognitive achievement	Emphasis on both cognitive and affective development; humanistically oriented objectives; for example, identity, connectedness, powerlessness
Test of professional efficiency and promotion	Emphasis on grade-level and systematized skills, cognitive achievement	Emphasis on performance with students and with parent–community participants
Institutional philosophy	Negative self-fulfilling prophecy, student failure blamed on learner and his background	Positive self-fulfilling prophecy – no student failures, only program failures; accountable to learner and community
Basic learning unit	Classroom, credentialed teacher, school building	The community, various agents as teachers, including other students and paraprofessionals.

fertilization has to be encouraged and expanded through educational objectives and organization that allow and legitimize such an aim.

4. The school and the community it serves have to exist less as separate entities and instead develop responsibilities and lines of authority that are more integrated and shared (5).

The final bell rings at Eastern High School in Washington's Northeast ghetto (in the shadow of the Capitol dome, as editorial writers used to say), and a half-dozen students cross busy Maryland Avenue headed for a nearby Lutheran Church. Through a side alley, up a flight of iron outdoor stairs, and into a room littered with paper, they move, eventually settling down in some wooden folding chairs around a rickety table . . . (2).

Freedom Annex in Washington, D.C., is a different kind of high school. It has no grades, no desks for teachers, no bells to attend classes. The students choose the teachers and set the curriculum. They attend only if they choose, and they create hardly any disciplinary problems. Any that arise are handled by students, not teachers. Freedom Annex is, in fact, the first accredited student-run high school in the U.S. . . .

Freedom Annex now has a curriculum that many college black-studies departments would envy. Twelve salaried and accredited teachers offer 85 students courses in black history, Swahili, black literature, black art and drama, and community organization. Students spend half their day at Eastern High in the study of math and sciences, half at the Annex. Though the Annex gives no grades, just pass-fail ratings, the high school gives full credit for Annex classes, and Eastern's Principal William S. backs the student-run school enthusiastically. He is particularly impressed by the lack of disciplinary problems. "If all the students at Eastern High School brought me the kind of problems the students at the Annex do," says Mr. S., "my job would be a breeze and a source of continual challenge and excitement . . . (8)."

The Freedom Annex functionally illustrates the benefits in utilizing the students' energies in a positive way. These 85 youngsters are acting out their emotional concerns, not by occupying the principal's office, or ransacking a storeroom, but through the constructive and productive means of education. By providing an arena for options, the Annex has achieved a stability which few schools can approach. Where there is no basis for frustration, there is no reason for violence.

These young people are also involved in a curriculum which commands their immediate interest. They are learning about themselves and, simultaneously, acquiring the tools for learning about others. Through their student-directed, student-governed school they are establishing the social and academic confidence necessary for future mobility.

The Street Academies of the Greater New York Urban League implement the principle of community involvement in their mission of rescuing dropouts in ghetto areas. Mr. Harvey Oostdyk has overseen the contact of approximately 4,000 youths out of storefronts in Harlem. This contact is initiated by the students themselves, or "indigenous street workers," as they are called at the academies. Thus, the program perpetuates itself; prospective academy members trust the neighborhood figures who recruit them, and the former dropouts maintain a position at the school. The Street Academies have been so successful that ten former dropouts had been accepted at reputable colleges across the country at the time that the Ford Foundation offered its first grant to the project.

At the Parkway School in Philadelphia (popularly called The School Without Walls) the students and faculty air their concerns through a town meeting session each week. Through such a mechanism students are able to deal with such substantive issues as curriculum and personnel matters. The student movement, like all historical movements, is vulnerable to drastic change. I have selected the purest strains of the youthful rebellion for the purpose of discussing educational reform, and, at the present time, student criticisms and institutional inadequacies seem very close indeed. What a shame it would be to waste that proximity; yet we persist in polarizing the student and the school. Every time the police invade an institution of learning, we solidify the students. We also lead the institution further and further away from a healthy redefinition.

How often the students are criticized for their totalitarian tactics, their unwillingness to negotiate, their narrowness of purpose. In many ways, unfortunately, they have been bountifully trained; immediate suspension for cutting class on a clear autumn day, don't question my decision! and, now, using police to restore order in a playground. We, too, have been narrow, as well as antiquated in our purpose. If you read on grade level, punch your IBM answer sheet, and keep silent in class, you will succeed.

The student is a symptom, and the school is a glaring sore of the societal infection which threatens to erupt instantaneously. Allowing the student into the educational process may be the first remedy of a long cure.

Selected Items of Discussion

Question: I would like to inform the audience of an educational program known as Harlem Prep. Harlem Prep is an organization of private individuals who formed a private school in New York City. They hired black and white teachers who could not qualify as public school teachers because they did not have the correct credentials. The students were volunteers who had dropped out of school. This past year, 16 of the Prep graduates were accepted in the better Northeastern colleges. What are the implications of this success in reference to public schools?

Dr. Fantini: In a search for alternatives to existing educational programs, it is appealing to go to private schools, such as Harlem Prep, Street Academies, and other parallel institutions, where we do not have to put up with all the restraints in our public institutions. Financing of private institutions is a problem. When the fiscal aspects are worked out, as has been done in some instances, I believe we will see more of this type of parallel schools, unless something happens to public schools, which are our major option now.

Question: I am worried about the criteria we will use to evaluate the success of the alternative school systems which are being set up. I do not think we can evaluate their success or failure in terms of traditional criteria, such as the number of graduates entering colleges or their mean scores on reading achievement tests. I am not convinced this is the rationale for these schools. If they can survive and are able to govern themselves, then they are an absolute and utter success as far as I am concerned.

Dr. Fantini: I would say that, if there has been a transfer of power in organizing and running these schools, there has been a gain. The important thing is much more than a mere shift of power. The important thing is that the students, parents, and communities are saying that they want control so that they can make the educational program more relevant and responsible and join *with* the professionals in remaking the educational program. Unfortunately, those watching these experimental programs will use as their criterion of success, "What difference does it make to the traditional objectives of the school?" There will be tremendous pressure to evaluate these programs in terms of grade level achievement in a relatively short time.

Question: Do you feel that professional educational organizations are responsive to the kinds of questions that you are raising?

Dr. Fantini: Those who are really sincere about what is happening to society and education will have to work out means for reorienting professionals that are more than just talking. They must get at the level of interaction. They must interpret what may happen—collision or cooperation? This will mean a new type of leadership. If, and when, collisions take place, I hope they can become laboratories of education in which we all can learn.

References

1. Arlen, Michael J. *The Living Room War: Writings About Television.* New York: The Viking Press, 1969, p. 190.
2. Elsila, David. "A Student-Run Accredited School: D.C. Strivers Create Their Own Thing." *American Teacher* 53, no. 3 (November 1968):12.
3. Fantini, Mario D. "Community Control and Quality Education in Urban School Systems." In *Community Control of Schools,* edited by Harry M. Levin. Washington, D.C.: The Brookings Institution, 1970, p. 46.
4. Fantini, Mario, and Weinstein, Gerald. *The Disadvantaged: Challenge to Education.* New York: Harper and Row, Publishers, 1968.
5. ———. *Making Urban Schools Work: Social Realities and the Urban School.* New York: Holt, Rinehart and Winston, 1968, pp. 24-25.
6. Freedom School. *The Modern Strivers.* Brochure. Washington, D.C.: Eastern High School Freedom Annex.
7. Gordon, Ira J. "Task of the Teacher." *Studying the Child in the School.* New York: John Wiley and Sons, 1966, pp. 2-3.
8. "High Schools: Letting the Students Run Things." *Time* 92, no. 25 (December 20, 1968): 47-48. Copyright Time Inc. 1968.

The Student Movement and School Reform 77

9. Kozol, Jonathan. *Death at an Early Age.* Boston: Houghton Mifflin Co., 1967.
10. Mailer, Norman. *The Armies of the Night.* New York: The New American Library, 1968.
11. Montgomery County Student Alliance. "Wanted: A Humane Education. An Urgent Call for Reconciliation Between Rhetoric and Reality." A Study Report on the Montgomery County Public School System. P.O. Box 30204, Bethesda, Maryland, February 11, 1969.
12. Newfield, Jack. "The Year of the Young Rebels." Review of the book by Stephen Spender. *The New York Times Book Review* 118, no. 40,650 (May 11, 1969):5. Copyright © 1969 by the New York Times Co.
13. Spender, Stephen. *The Year of the Young Rebels.* New York: Random House, 1969, chapter 1.
14. Trump, J. Lloyd, and Hunt, Jane. *Report on a National Survey of Secondary School Principals on the Nature and Extent of Student Activism.* Washington D.C.: National Association of Secondary School Principals, 1969.

Bruce Cook

Hermann Hesse, author-idol of this generation demanding change, is here reviewed. Bruce Cook, the reviewer, does more than simply deal with Hesse, however; he reflects upon those qualities in Hesse that satisfy today's young people and, in so doing, reflects upon the qualities they share.

Hermann Hesse's Curious Appeal

Today's Young Embrace a German Writer From the Past

Nearly a century ago, in this Black Forest village of quaint gingerbread houses nestled in its storybook setting of wooded hills, a writer named Hermann Hesse was born. And although he emigrated to Switzerland in his 20s and did some traveling during his long lifetime, he never once went to America. Nevertheless, the enthusiasm for his books has grown so steadily among the American young that if a poll were taken today the Woodstock generation would probably discover that it had elected as its poet laureate this German author who has been dead now for about eight years.

A few statistics may prove the point. Although nearly all of Hermann Hesse's novels are now in print in hardback editions—Farrar, Straus & Giroux has been doing an especially fine job of bringing out good, new translations of his less-known works—it is in low-priced paperback editions that they are being bought and read today by college-age young people at such an astonishing rate. Hesse's *Siddhartha,* for instance, is New Directions' best-selling paperback to date: 1,000,000 copies are in print, and a quarter of these were sold just last year. When Bantam brought out the first paperback edition of *Steppenwolf,* it sold 360,000 copies the first month; a year later its total sales stand at 650,000. Another favorite, *Demian,* is also creeping up there; at last look, 750,000 copies had been sold—and the word on this one has just begun to spread.

Why? How to account for the particularly strong appeal of this German author whose works are in many ways so old-fashioned? Sometimes

---

Bruce Cook, "Hermann Hesse's Curious Appeal," *The National Observer,* September 14, 1970.

ponderously philosophical in the old, familiar German way, but more often in stark and simple parable style, Hesse's novels are all essentially religious in their intention—attempts to resolve the conflicts of flesh and spirit in a synthesis that will have some value for the individual. But they are religious works with few certainties and no dogma. This is my resolution, he tells the reader, and now you must do what you can to make your own.

To the degree that this translates as "do your own thing," it pleases his young readers and displeases the critics. Although a Nobel Prize-winner (1946) and an author of classic standing among the German-speaking peoples, he has always somehow put off English and American critics, who seem embarrassed by the sort of artless honesty and lack of guile that is so essentially Hesse's own. There is scarcely an ironic line in all his work. It is characterized by the sort of earnest Truth-seeking that went out with George Eliot.

For the most part the critics have ignored him. And when that has been impossible, as it was in Cambridge critic Ronald Gray's recent survey, *The German Tradition in Literature 1871-1945,* Hermann Hesse is given very short shrift indeed:

> His great reputation, continuing today and reflected in various popular editions, would be hard to account for, were it not for the unsure basis of so many reputations in this century, and not only in the German-speaking world. It is certainly due in part to the fact that his philosophical outlook taken in the abstract bears a resemblance to a good deal of the speculation that was going on in his time, and is presented in an easily assimilable form.

The best, finally, that Mr. Gray can say is that Hesse was an "outstanding popularizer." The implication—as well as the values behind it—should be quite clear: His work is too "easy" to be considered much good.

The Great Contemporary

Nevertheless, those American young who seem to value honesty above all other virtues and believe they have made Truth-seeking a way of life, find Hesse's work very much to their liking. Kurt Vonnegut, Jr., who is probably their favorite American writer, took a stab at accounting for Hesse's popularity in a recent essay. Devoting most of his space to a discussion of *Steppenwolf* as the most popular of all Hesse's books, he points out: "The politics espoused by the hero of *Steppenwolf* coincide with those of the American young, all right: He is against war. He hates armament manufacturers and superpatriots. No nations or political figures or historical events are investigated or praised or blamed. There are no daring schemes, no calls to action, nothing to make a radical's heart beat faster." In his curious, cryptic, oblique style Mr. Vonnegut keeps chipping away in this manner, and by the time he has finished, he has made a good case for Hermann Hesse as the great contemporary, a writer whose works have even greater relevance today than they did in the years they were written. This, he suggests, is the source of his appeal. Hesse's is a recognizable human voice that speaks to the contemporary young in gentle tones of things they can understand: "And I say again, what my daughters and sons are responding to in *Steppenwolf* is the homesickness of the author."

Nevertheless, there is another, darker explanation for Hesse's sudden popularity. Mr. Vonnegut touches on it just long enough to dismiss it, but it is worth dealing with directly. Ask some of the more far-out among the younger generation, and they will put it to you with assurance. "Sure," they will say, "Hesse was an early head. His books are about tripping, drugs, all that stuff."

And how do they get that idea? From none other than Dr. Timothy Leary, the guru of the psychedelic revolution, the former Harvard psychologist who put LSD on the map. As long ago as 1963, a year after Hesse's death and back when Dr. Leary still held a post on the Harvard faculty, an article of his appeared in the *Psychedelic Review* extolling Hermann Hesse as the "poet of the interior journey." It is a neat bit of business. Dr. Leary does some judicious quoting, makes a few rash insinuations, and then comes rather hastily to his conclusion: "So there it is. The saga of H.H. The critics tell us that Hesse is the master novelist. Well, maybe. But the novel is a social form, and the social in Hesse is exoteric. At another level Hesse is the master guide to the psychedelic experience and its application. Before your LSD session, read *Siddhartha* and *Steppenwolf*. The last part of *Steppenwolf* is a priceless manual."

Although elsewhere Dr. Leary admitted to his obvious consternation that Hermann Hesse had, according to one who would have known, never taken mescaline (the visionary drug whose effects he read into Hesse's writings), nevertheless he continued to promote him as the herald of the drug age. He even went so far as to name his independent center for psychedelic research, which he founded in Mexico after his dismissal from Harvard, "Castalia," after the beautiful Utopian city of the Twenty-fifth Century in Hesse's final work, *The Glass Bead Game*.

But face it: There is a long passage in *Steppenwolf* that does apparently deal with drug-taking. This is the last part, the one called "a priceless manual" by Dr. Leary. In it Harry Haller, the 50-year-old protagonist, is introduced by a young swinger to the joys of "long thin yellow cigarettes" and an "aromatic liquid" whose "effect was immeasurably enlivening and delightful—as though one were filled with gas and had no longer any gravity." What follows is a wild, phantasmagoric experience, the "Magic Theater," at once enlightening to Haller and confusing to the reader, wherein murders contemplated are committed, imagined orgies are made actual, and identities of the great are merged with the mean.

From the time *Steppenwolf* was published in 1927, Hermann Hesse found that people were enthusiastic for the book for what he thought were all the wrong reasons. From the beginning, it drew the attention of the revolution-sex-drug crowd of the 1920s and 1930s, so that by the time a Swiss edition of the work was being prepared during the war, he felt obliged to append a kind of disclaimer in which he complains that "of all my books *Steppenwolf* is the one that was more often and more violently misunderstood than any other."

As readers continued to write him about it, offering the wrong sort of praise or condemning the work for the wrong reasons, Hesse became increasingly annoyed and hurt. Soon this began to show in the letters he wrote. He replies to an acquaintance: "It was your question whether in *Steppenwolf* I intend anything serious or simply present a pleasant opium dream. With all my books and my life it has been a great personal disappointment to me—and a disappointment in principle—that my seriousness was not matched by success in being understood."

And so it went. Dr. Leary's enthusiasm for Hesse, and for this book in particular, is founded precisely on those misconceptions that the author so deplored. I found when I visited Hesse's German publishers, Suhrkamp, that they are aware of his reputation as a propagandist for the drug culture and are frankly disturbed.

I talked with Volker Michels, the young editor who is preparing a new, low-priced edition of the author's complete works, in the company's light, modern offices in downtown Frankfurt. Mr. Michels fell heir to his task because his great youthful enthusiasm for Hesse's work had led to a personal acquaintance with the author in his last years. The personal quality of the young editor's indignation is quite apparent as he denounces what he considers "a terrific misunderstanding." Says Mr. Michels: "He has been adopted by these people who smoke hashish and so forth. But Hesse himself wouldn't have had this. He would have denounced this tendency. You can be sure of it."

But Suhrkamp's problems in selling Hermann Hesse to West German youth are of a much different sort. To them Hesse has no glamorous reputation as a drug propagandist or revolutionary; he is rather the classic author who was the favorite of their fathers' generation. (Ah, kiss of death!) His works were assigned in school by war-weary teachers who urged Hesse on the students as a great dreamer, a writer of sweetness and light, a source of inspiration.

"But it was all a matter of emphasis," says Mr. Michels, who points out that Hesse was a dialectical writer, one who always sought to resolve the conflicts within himself, to contain the contradictory impulses that everyone feels. "The teachers can teach him any way they want to. The gentle side is certainly there. But they don't show the aggressive side that was most certainly there too. That is how he has been presented here in Germany. We want only to restore the balance, to show him as he was—interested in his times, always critical, always political."

The night before I left on my pilgrimage to Hesse's birthplace, I heard what Mr. Michels had said confirmed by a group of Goethe University students I met in Frankfurt's Jazz Keller. I mentioned to them that I was going to Calw because I was interested in seeing where Hermann Hesse had grown up. They couldn't understand why anyone should pursue such an outmoded writer. When I told them he was probably the favorite author of university students in America today, they were clearly amazed.

In America, of course, Hesse's young readers had no such prejudice to overcome. It is possible, of course, that his appeal to them is that of an exotic: After all, he speaks to American youth from another age and out of a different culture. Yet what he says must, to some extent at least, strike chords of response and give the young that shock of recognition that says, "This is it, the real thing. He felt what I feel."

"He's a Guy Who's Been There"

This is borne out, too, by what they say. The drug line is often quoted, of course, but when you ask others and get beyond the usual "he-knows-where-it's-at, he-tells-it-like-it-is" can't you hear something like this:

"What I get from Hesse is, you know, like a sense that he felt the same things I felt and experienced a lot of the same things too." So said a young Northwestern University student in Evanston, Ill., earlier this year. He added: "It's not like I really think of him as a German writer or anything. He's just a guy who's been there and tried to make sense out of things."

And a girl in New York—a *Siddhartha* reader on a Fifth Avenue bus —once said: "I think the good thing about him is that he doesn't give you a lot of set answers or anything. He says the answer is you should find your own answer." This she said, was the third time she had read the book.

The tentative quality of these responses would probably please Hesse, for he was undogmatic almost to a fault. And it is understandable, too, that so many young Americans would feel their own conflicts and troubles reflected in his writing, for Hesse—the most autobiographical of writers—wrote directly from his own experience. No matter how exotic the landscape he paints, familiar landmarks reveal it as a chart of his soul.

Hesse's parents had come here to Calw only a little before his birth in 1877. His father, a Protestant missionary in Mangalur, India, for four years, had been forced to return to Europe because of poor health. He had married and settled in Calw and was running the Calw Missionary Press when Hermann Hesse was born.

In later years the author always cited the strong Christian spirit of his family as one of the great positive influences in his life. Yet that didn't prevent him from fighting bitterly against it as he grew up. He was a very difficult child, rebellious to the extreme. Finally his father said he was "too nervous, too weak" to try to control his son any longer and shipped the lad off to a preparatory school *cum* seminary in Goeppingen.

What was it like? Hesse described it minutely and movingly in the novel of his adolescence, *Beneath the Wheel,* a kind of Black Forest *Catcher in the Rye,* a work infused with that sense of homesickness that Kurt Vonnegut, Jr., quite rightly said was so prominent in Hesse's novels. Hesse did brilliantly as a student in Goeppingen, and then suddenly fell into a kind of funk. The strict Teutonic discipline of the place simply became too much for him: "Thus the struggle between rule and spirit repeats itself year after year from school to school. The authorities go to infinite pains to nip the few profound or more valuable intellects in the bud."

Although Hesse did not come to the same sad end as his young hero, Hans Giebenrath, one of those who "waste away with quiet obstinacy and finally go under," he came home in disgrace, ran away from home only to be returned ignominiously after a single night by forest rangers who had found him sleeping in a haystack. Soon his parents were in utter despair over him. He had passed in and out of one school after another, had attempted suicide, and had been turned over to a clergyman with a reputation as an exorcist who tried quite literally to pray the devil out of him.

His First Book

Finally, at the age of 17 a change came over young Hesse. He dropped out of school completely, took a job in a local factory, and spent the next two years quietly filing gears. He then left his family and apprenticed himself to a book dealer in the university city of Tuebingen. There he read voraciously, found friends among the students, and began writing seriously. His first book, a collection of lyric poems, was published in 1899 when Hermann Hesse was 22.

It was for his novels, however, that he soon became well known throughout the German-speaking world. The success of his early books— *Peter Camenzind, Under the Wheel,* and *Gertrude*—gave him a certain financial freedom and the opportunity to travel first throughout Europe and then, in 1911, to India, on an extended trip that was to be of great importance to him.

Upon returning in 1912, he settled in Switzerland. He was there in 1914 when World War I broke out—and there he stayed. "I am a German," he wrote in an essay in 1914, explaining his position, "and my sympathies and wishes belong to Germany." But he was also by this time a convinced pacifist, and he refused either to serve in the Kaiser's armed forces or to support with his pen a war he felt was senseless. In this he was quite alone, for except for Hesse all German writers of the period gave enthusiastic support to the war, promoting it as a kind of holy crusade for *Deutsche Kultur.* Even Thomas Mann wrote impassioned nationalistic essays at the time that he later came to regret.

In Germany Hesse was denounced as a traitor. Book stores refused to sell his works. Editors declined his poems and stories. And although Hesse never for a moment doubted the rightness of his course, he was thrown into a deep personal crisis, torn by the conflict that he felt between his loyalty to Germany and his sense of individual duty. It was resolved, finally, through psychoanalysis. Through 1916 and 1917 he was treated in a sanitarium by an eminent disciple of Jung, Dr. Joseph B. Lang.

He emerged from psychoanalysis a much different sort of man and a much greater writer. Although they were fine works of their kind, the novels that Hermann Hesse wrote before World War I fit perhaps too neatly into categories. The thoughts and feelings expressed in them were predictable, expectable, generically similar to those that other writers of that time and in that place were themselves pouring into their poems, plays, and novels. But the intellectual and political sense of isolation that he had experienced during the war had thrown him back upon himself, and the experience of psychoanalysis had forced him to explore that *terra incognita* that every man fears—his own soul.

What Hesse found there he wrote down in *Demian,* a most unusual neo-Nietzschean work that, in the old form of the apprenticeship novel, presents the doctrine of a strong and totally ruthless young man named Max Demian. He acknowledges all the good and evil that is within him. He sees in himself the potentiality for all acts, and thereby derives from that potentiality an actual power that is equal to the sum of them all. Demian taught the lesson that Hesse himself had learned so painfully—that a man must live by the dictates of his own self.

Attractive as it may have sounded to some, this is a philosophy with some rather sinister overtones. There is something of the idealized storm trooper about Max Demian—in his nihilism and his contempt for the little man's notions of morality. Yet Hesse caught in him and his passionate individualism not only a resolution to his own internal conflict, but an expression of the spirit that was to grow in Germany and elsewhere in the coming decade. There is truly something prophetic about the book. Demian says, for instance: "Whether the workers kill the manufacturers or whether Germany makes war on Russia will merely mean a change of ownership. But it won't have been entirely in vain, it will reveal the bankruptcy of present-day ideals, there will be a sweeping away of Stone Age gods. The world as it is now wants to die, wants to perish—and it will." As rhetoric, that is a little frightening; as a prediction made in 1919, however, it was breath-takingly accurate.

Demian was a book that took the imagination of a whole generation of young Germans. They were sure it was by one of them, one who was speaking for them all, because Hesse, putting on the new man, had published the book under the pseudonym of its narrator, Emil Sinclair. *Demian* was even awarded a prize for the best first novel of the year before the identity of its author was discovered.

This and three subsequent novels are the major works of Hesse's lifetime. The remainder of his life was devoted to writing them. And it was in the act of literary creation that he was best able to resolve the many tensions of that lifetime.

Siddhartha, for instance, perhaps written in memory of his 1911 passage to India and published in 1922, is anything but the work extolling the Buddhist way to wisdom that many in the West have thought it to be. Prince Siddhartha's path to wisdom is devious indeed. Leaving his parents, he seeks out the Buddha and for a long period lives a life of meditation in his company—yet ultimately without finding satisfaction. And so he crosses over the broad river and seeks prosperity and sensual pleasure in the worldly city. Although he finds both in abundance, he does not find happiness. Yet he does, finally, manage to attain wisdom and true happiness as a ferryman on the boat that plies back and forth between the Buddha's land of meditation that lies on one shore and the worldly city on the other. It is only by touching in at both ports, in other words, that a balance can be preserved and real wisdom achieved.

Of *Steppenwolf* enough may have been said already to show that Hesse believed the problems it treated were best understood as those peculiar to a 50-year-old man. The precarious balance between the sensual and the spiritual achieved by Harry Haller was not one that Hesse urged as universally valid.

Curiously, Hermann Hesse came closest to achieving a real synthesis of the contending elements in his own soul in creating the character of Joseph Knecht, who is certainly the most sympathetic and in a way the most realistic to be found in any of his novels. Why curious? Because Knecht is the central figure of a Twenty-fifth Century Utopian fantasy dealing with life in a society and time as different as could be from the Europe that Hesse knew as he was writing the book.

Tranquility and Wisdom

The Glass Bead Game was the work of his maturity. He spent over a decade on it in the 1930s and '40s, working and reworking it, finally writing it several times over as he distilled into it those things in life that he felt he knew with some degree of certainty. The novel is most remarkable for its tranquility and wisdom. Far from ignoring the world that was crumbling around his mountain retreat in southern Switzerland, Hesse looked on and was deeply disturbed by the death of Europe that he had prophesied in *Demian*. Yet he transcended it, focusing his attention far into the future on a society in which the rule is service to all and the occupation of all is the playing of a mysterious game, a sort of cross between the *I Ching* and Herman Kahn's computer probability models, that somehow employs all the elements of human culture in configurations by which problems and theories of all sorts are worked out.

The Glass Bead Game is cast in the form of a biography of Joseph Knecht, a brilliant player of the game, who puts himself completely at the service of his state, Castalia. He rises steadily in the hierarchy there until, after service as ambassador to the monastery capital of Mariafels in a neighboring state dedicated to spiritual discovery, he is invited back to Castalia and elevated to the highest position in the realm, that of Magister Ludi (Master of the Game). But Knecht has been deeply affected by his stay at Mariafels. He feels that even the rational rule of social service must be tempered and guided by the spirit. He criticizes the state and the primacy of the purely intellectual pursuit of the Glass Bead Game. And he gives moral force to his objections by leaving Castalia for a martyrdom in exile. Eventually his criticisms are judged to be valid; changes are made; and the lesson is made clear: It is often only by opposing society that the individual can work real changes in it for the better.

This, of course, is a long way from the league of supermen Hesse posited in *Demian*. The responsibility between individual and society goes both ways here. It is the individual's duty to hold out for what he knows is right, and it is society's duty to listen to him.

A remarkably long journey it was for a man who had so little personal faith to sustain him. Just how little is indicated in this passage from a letter written in 1948, the year after he was awarded the Nobel Prize with a special citation of his novel, *The Glass Bead Game*. Hesse wrote: "Today we all live in despair, all awakened people, and are thus cast between God and

Nothingness. Between these poles we breathe, sway, and pendulate. Each day we are tempted to throw away our lives, but we are sustained by that within us which is suprapersonal and supratemporal. So our weakness—without our being heroes for that reason—becomes bravery, and we preserve a little of the faith that has been handed down from the past for those who will come after us."

Perhaps many of Hermann Hesse's young readers in America today find themselves between those two poles. Perhaps they learn from him that kind of bravery.

CHAPTER FOUR

The Impact of Institutionalized Education upon Reading

By its very size, education for all seems to create problems. As an instance of this, institutionalization, the large structure intended to serve masses of people, often seems to sterilize reading programs. Vitality seems to become wasted as programs and materials are chosen from more and more abstract models to serve a more and more anonymous student. Publishers and editors, to please the greatest market, produce dull and less relevant materials in their attempt to avoid controversy. Programs modelled to meet the assumed "average" of large groups sometimes seem to serve no one at all. In many ways institutionalization of education has seemed to have dire effects upon reading.

Reading teachers are concerned with the extent to which the avoidance of controversial materials is sponsored by selfish interests. First, of course, is the obligation of democratic citizenship with its peculiar relationship to publishers. Schools must participate in duties detailed by supreme court decisions surrounding First and Fourteenth Amendment cases. Simply said, schools must present wide varieties of attitudes and values if children are to grow to become democratic, choosing citizens. Restrictions placed upon materials of interest to youth may be seen to turn them from the use of reading as a valid part of the solution to their problems. Erroneous or misleading information (e.g., sexual or drug data that is more morality than science) drives students away from reading to more specious avenues of problem solution. The attitudes we sponsor by censorship are invariably harmful.

Primary offenders of relevant materials and the fair treatment of ideas have been schoolbooks. Textbooks and anthologies have consistently been reluctant to adopt unpopular stands in support of diverse opinion. Often they are accused of deliberate exclusion or distortion of data relevant to minority groups. And, it would be nearly heretical to suggest that students should *enjoy* reading their textbooks.

Finally, even the best materials continue to be poorly taught. Teachers are assigned courses of unfamiliar content and without time to prepare. Cover-to-cover reading assignments are made. Indiscriminate worksheets are handed out. And, in high school, the student is expected to know how to modify his reading technique to fit the purpose and the discipline he studies. These are the issues of institutionalized reading programs. Dull and unrelated materials, poorly taught, are sure to turn students away. One of the natural consequences of this institutionalization is boredom, *ennui,* a feeling that reading itself is of no value.

Frank G. Jennings

The wonder of relevant materials and why we read is extolled by Dr. Frank Jennings. The role of the teacher of such materials is that of the fine artist, not the simple purveyor of skills and drills. The dreariness that often accompanies the school book is reported, too.

Reading: A Search for Seeing Things Differently

Reading is a treacherous enterprise because writing is a most dangerous game. Words are very slippery; they do not always go where they are intended. Sometimes they refuse to mean what you want them to mean. There is a semantic play between the reader and the writer that confuses issues and intentions. I am immediately reminded of these lexical facts whenever anything I have written is published. I receive letters from my readers, sometimes complimenting me for something I did not write; sometimes chiding me for something I did not intend; sometimes scolding me for real or imagined lack of scholarship. In many of these confrontations between my readers and myself, I find that they are belaboring the irrelevancies of what I have said and losing sight of the important issue. Let it be made clear, then, at the outset that the important issue for all of us, whether we are teachers or librarians, should be the defense and improvement of the world of reading and the enhancement of the intellectual and aesthetic life of the citizens of that world; for the health of that world determines the quality of existence in all other aspects of the human condition.

For all of its power, reading is not now, nor has it ever been, universally regarded as good or even tolerable for the masses—which means all of us. The distrust of the reading man and the awareness of the social dangers in proliferating literacy has a long history. D. H. Lawrence was only half joking when he said, "Never teach the masses to read and write. Never, never!" Plato may have sparked this distrust, but it continues even today. Witness the view of Professor Floyd Zulli, that literary peacock of the

---

Reprinted by permission from the February 1968 issue of the *Wilson Library Bulletin.* Copyright © 1968 by The H. W. Wilson Company.

"Sunrise Semester," who, in an article in *The Villager,* decried the absolute degradation of literature in our mass society. He said he is all for literacy, but ". . . with moderation. Despite Jimmy Walker's gleeful maxim that no good girl was ever ruined by a book, literature and all the arts can be dangerous undertakings. They are too often fatal anodynes for frustration and day-dreaming, and I fear that that is what they are for many people, including professors and students." The poor, pallid professor is probably right. There is ancient precedent for his fears. Here is Charlotte Elizabeth Browne's confession of her childhood experience with *The Merchant of Venice.* The date is 1841:

> I drank a cup of intoxication under which my brain reeled for many a year. . . . I reveled in the terrible excitement that it gave rise to; page after page was stereotyped upon a most retentive memory; without effort, and during a sleepless night I feasted on the pernicious sweets thus hoarded in my brain. . . . Reality became insipid, almost hateful to me; conversation, except that of literary men . . . a burden; I imbibed a thorough contempt for women and children, and household affairs, entrenching myself behind invisible barriers that few, very few, could pass. Oh, how many wasted hours, how much of unprofitable labour, what wrong to my fellow-creatures, must I refer to that ensnaring book. . . . Parents know not what they do when from vanity, thoughtlessness, or over-indulgence, they foster in a young girl what is called poetical taste (1).

People who write are even more dangerous than people who read. We forget too easily that to take to the inkpot was to become "déclassé." The scrivener, the ink-stained wretch, the unhallowed grubbers in literary junkyards all spread seeds of sedition once they were allowed to become secular. They became purveyors of "intelligence," which to the members of the higher estates was the illegitimate child gotten off Dame Rumor by the nasty lust of the Levelers. In fact, well into the nineteenth century in England, the most disputed feature of popular education was the teaching of reading and writing to the masses. Many conservatives continued to regard this as rampant Jacobinism. It was not until 1833 that the first public funds in that country were allocated to education.

These are our ancestors, moilers in the dawn of our mass society, phrasemongers, sloganizers, and pamphleteers who declassified the printed page and tied education irrevocably to Gutenberg's machine. For them democracy of print made the acquisition of reading and writing a natural development in natural man, like breathing and walking and speaking. They had to savor life in all of its aspects. They knew that if you look upon life steadily you cannot see the whole of it. They could say, as many of them did, that "nothing that is human is alien to me." And none of them would understand what we are doing here today.

Now we are advised (*see Dec. 1966 issue of the* English Journal, *page 1233*) that "two concepts of English, almost diametrically opposed, are current in the present century. . . . On the one hand is the view that English is a discipline, that is, that it is a clearly developed branch of knowledge, characterized to include the study of language, literature, and composition. On the other hand is the view that English is a broad field embracing a range of competencies [oh, that degenerate word!] in reading, writing, speaking, and listening." At the beginning of this century English was looked upon as a discipline; later the "field theory" gained ascendency and along with it the notion that it consisted of a series of skills which properly acquired and reinforced would enhance the lives of students and improve the quality of the Commonwealth. Now, we are told, "the pendulum has swung back." The Commission on English in its 1965 report, *Freedom and Discipline in English,* has made us whole again.

Half a century of caucusing and conventioneering within NCTE, NEA, IRA, *et al.,* has gone down the drain. Most of the advanced degrees bought with so much anguish by so many of us have been devalued to parity with a union card—or enhanced to that level—it's a matter of scale and value. How our ink-stained ancestors would laugh. We had a warning two centuries ago from Dr. Samuel Johnson, and Boswell properly recorded it:

> Mr. Langton told us he was about to establish a school upon his estate, but it had been suggested to him that it might have a tendency to make the people less industrious. *Johnson:* "No, Sir. While learning to read and write is a distinction, the few who have that distinction may be the less inclined to work; but when everybody learns to read and write, it is no longer a distinction. A man who has a laced waistcoat is too fine a man to work; but if everybody had laced waistcoats, we should have people working in laced waistcoats. There are no people whatever more industrious, none who would work more, than our manufacturers; yet they have all learnt to read and write. Sir, you must not neglect doing a thing immediately good, from fear of remote evil—from fear of it being abused. A man who has candles may sit up too late, which he would not do if he had not candles; but nobody will deny that the art of making candles, by which light is continued to us beyond the time that the sun gives us light, is a valuable art, and ought to be preserved (4)."

Dr. Johnson would not have been troubled with the argument of field *vs.* discipline. He would have kicked the pedant's rump and called for a bowl of sack. He knew the difference between artist and artisan, and he would not have celebrated the former by demeaning the latter.

Reading and writing *are* rather low-order skills having the same kind of relation to literature that bricklaying and stonecutting have to the building of cathedrals. But just as the cathedral is more than a work of art, so too is literature more than cultural heritage. But what that *more* is is not susceptible to linguistic formulation. And it is that *more* imperfectly felt and understood, that results in the lifeless occasions during reading classes and English courses in which literature is denatured of its aesthetics.

Too many of us who are recruited and dragooned into this "field" or "discipline" of English begin our careers by being seduced by some sweet lady who truly truly believes that she loves both children and books and can tell the good ones in both categories by their covers. She in her own turn believes that she has had literary experiences that began at the "magic casements" or in a "hidden garden" illustrated by Maxfield Parrish, and she is absolutely certain that she can make these experiences available to her charges. I have no intention of demeaning her, but she is our archetypal problem. Listen to one of her voices:

> Our son discovered one day when he was about five years old that he could read—and came hurtling bumpity-bumpity-bump all the way down the stairs in his eagerness to tell me about it. He picked himself up, still clutching a book under his arm, gabbling in such a dither of excitement that I wondered momentarily if the bang on the head had loosened something vital. When he paused for breath I asked him if he had damaged himself. He looked at me blankly.
>
> "*Damaged* myself? I should think not! I tell you I suddenly *read* it, Mummy! I read it all by myself! I read *The Little House!*"
>
> Here was cause for rejoicing, to be sure, but little for surprise. We had known for a long time, from his diminishing satisfaction with an hour or two a day of being read aloud to, and his increasing impatience to "get at the *insides* of books for myself," that he felt a need—deep and strong and *right*—to learn to read. Now, all at once, he realized that he had made a beginning at satisfying that need, and his happiness was beautiful to behold (3).

This is so cloying, so redolent of cotton candy and hobbyhorses that it is almost self-insured against criticism—but not quite. For this report, which undoubtedly has a basis in family history, is the staple of those book-corner chats that have a rather poor grasp on reality.

In contrast, consider this recollection by Winifred Ellerman, who under the pen name of Bryher has written some of the finest historical novels, such as *The Gate to the Sea, The Fourteenth of October,* and *This January Tale.* I take the following from her autobiography *The Heart to Artemis:*

> I was just five when I was given a new and exciting picture book. Unfortunately I then had a disagreement with Ruth [her nurse] that ended again in my kicking her. Retribution was swift. "After being so naughty, nobody will read to you." I decided not to howl but took my present with

me to a favorite hassock in the shelter of the drawing room sofa. I opened the book at the picture of two girls and a small boy sitting around a tea table in a garden. There were a dog and cat in front of them and verses about them on the opposite page. I had some alphabet blocks with the symbols of "A is for Apple" and "Z is for Zebra" but I had never learned to put the syllables together. Full of fury, I sat and struggled. Dog and tea were easy, but there were some longer words that were very baffling and difficult.

"What can she be up to?" I heard, "She is so very quiet." It was such a wet afternoon that for wonder I had not been dragged out for a walk. Teatime came, I wasn't even hungry, "Come along, darling, whatever are you doing?"

"I am reading my book," I replied proudly. There were the usual incredulous smiles so I read a poem out to them, slowly, stammering a little over one or two long words but without making any mistakes. I can still hear my mother's astonished words, "She has taught herself to read!" (2)

The difference between these two reports is not substantive, but rather one of voice, stance, and style. Two women can wear the same dress. One will look like a frump, the other will embody Robert Herrick's Julia, who wore silks with "liquefaction" knowing that when art is too precise it cannot tell the truth.

Each of us has a private recollection of how it was that we learned to read, and that recollection is embroidered by years and circumstance. Some I am sure do announce with flushed face and dancing eyes, "I can read, Mummy, I can truly read." Others keep the magic secret from the enemy lest it be put to dull work too soon. For most of us, however, for whom the printed page is a badge of employment, there is no precise memory of that primal achievement. There was a time when we could not read very well and then, somehow, it was not difficult any more. We could get on with the profitable business of using books for all of our growing purposes, untrammeled by pseudointellectual shackles and the distortions of the basal reader view of life.

The practicing teacher, however, cannot afford the luxury of memory over the reading process, sentimental or otherwise; as between the saccharine romanticism of Annis Duff's recollection of her child's first encounter with books and the tough-minded artistry of Bryher recalling her victory over the printed page, the teacher is caught at the bottom of an unbridgeable abyss. His dilemma is compounded even further by the powerful philosophical insights that educators generate to assess problems of education, as when, for example, Lawrence Cremin of Columbia University speaks of education as being tested by its performance, both with the most gifted and the least well-endowed. To use his own phrase, educational practices "are tested at the extremes." This is probably true, but for the classroom teacher, his point is irrelevant. The teacher rarely has either extreme in the classroom. He almost always has the group that Walt Whitman called "the divine average." And strategies that are appropriate and effective with the extremes are either too powerful or too specific to make much sense in the ordinary schoolroom.

Yet in all classrooms in any school, at any level, or within any subject, nothing can be carried on effectively or with any intellectual legitimacy unless primary attention is given to the continual teaching of reading. And reading, in its broadest definition, includes quite literally every bit of considered information that the human organism takes in through its senses. Within this definition the specific act of reading which involves the printed page is a very specialized enterprise, which can be described analogically at its most primitive level as a playback function not very different from that of phonograph pickup, and at its most sophisticated level as an aesthetic response.

Reading is not a "mechanic trade," nor should teachers of reading be thought of as mere tinkers, patching up the pots and kettles of their students' understanding with the solder of syntax. We who teach children, though we may have earned the title or have been cursed with the label of "reading specialist" or librarian, we are teachers, and as such are committed to enlarging the child's experience, even as we help him develop richer skills to make use of that experience. We are often, because of our calling, driven from sentiment into sentimentality and then into behavior that does no honor to adulthood and no service to the child. I'm thinking of those practitioners of "early childhood education" who used to instruct student teachers in ways of becoming more child-like as they taught younger and younger children, or of the proponents of the doctrine of t.l.c., always pronounced with a lilt as "tender loving care," which doctrine was offered as a sovereign shield against shame and guilt and reality itself.

But I have no intention of scoring cheap points off the teachers of yesterday. They were more valiant than any of us can really appreciate, and if they erred on the side of sentimentality in their concern for the child, theirs was a most generous fault, for, just behind them in time was a period when the public schools in our great cities were used mainly as a form of riot control, when children were kept off the streets in filthy, ill-ventilated loft rooms, seated for long periods like prisoners in stocks, subjected to mindless drill of words and numbers, and to equally mindless punishment for any display of childishness. No historian of education, to my knowledge, has adequately celebrated the worth of these valiant people, most of them women, who fought not only for the rights of children to appropriate education, but for the rights of adults to general enfranchisement, and who, despite their own limited access to higher education, were primarily responsible for the democratization of the schools. I, myself, was taught by many such women and most of them were trained—and the accent is on training, not on education generously conceived—in normal schools; a few even got their certification after high school by virtue of on-the-job apprenticeship. At their best they brought a healthy pragmatism to the problems of the school. But in the community of scholars, they always suffered from second-class citizenship, and to this day most of us who are or have been teachers or librarians are looked upon as less than full-fledged members in the community of scholars. I suppose by most of the obvious markers, this second-class citizenship is proven. Though we teach reading and writing, though we serve as the child's initiators into our cultural heritage, few of us are scholars. And few even are members of the intelligentsia. I should add that some of us mightn't be interested in joining those country clubs. And yet this is an odd pass that we have come to.

I said at the beginning that we often forget that the makers of literature in the modern world, many of whom were literary hacks, were not very highly regarded in their own societies. And if they were motivated by anything beyond their necessary money-grabbing, it was by vague pedagogical feelings that the masses should be enlightened. What has happened in the subsequent centuries, however, has been a divorce of their commitment to enlightenment and their desire to instruct; and a confusion about the relationship between both impulses.

Can it be that we are all of us confused, still, about the relationship between love of children and love of books? Can we be still haunted by ancient myths, by word magic? Is it perhaps because we rarely examine the aims of education that we are not very secure about the value of what we do in the classroom? Is it because we are self-conscious about the always impending possibility of scornful criticism from the world of higher scholarship that we imitate some of the less attractive characteristics of the citizens of that world, and forget that the teacher of children has a primary task of unlocking doors, opening gateways, and allowing discovery to happen? We are only incidentally, sometimes by accident, literary scholars, social critics, historians, and philosophers.

I suspect that sometimes we are blinded by the image of the book *writ large,* the book as the special repository of wisdom and power, and we forget that with the dazzling exception of the poet's work, the book is merely a data storage and retrieval system. (By "poet," I mean novelist, dramatist, storyteller, philosopher, or anyone who refuses to allow mere facts to stand in the way of truth.) I think I can explain this point best with a comment from the Nobel laureate Albert Szent-Gyorgyi:

> ... There is a widely spread misconception about the nature of books which contain knowledge. It is thought that such books are something, the contents of which have to be crammed into our heads. I think the opposite is closer to the truth. Books are there to keep the knowledge in while we use our heads for something better. Books may also be a better *place* for such knowledge. In my own head any book-knowledge has a half-life of a very few weeks. So, I leave knowledge, for safekeeping, to books and libraries and go fishing, sometimes for fish, sometimes for new knowledge (5).

I like that image of going fishing because that, too, is what reading is all about, because what is fishing if it is not a search for surprise? And what is reading if it is not a search for seeing things differently?

I am fully aware that the housekeeping requirements of the classroom and library make most adventure messy, if not downright dangerous, because most classroom work, whether in kindergarten or in a graduate seminar, mainly involves avoiding disorder. That is why the basal readers are so effective, not as teaching and learning instruments, but as housekeeping tools. They are insurance that children will not get out of hand, that they will not be amazed or enchanted or frightened. That is why the canned anthologies have for so long held sway throughout so much of the elementary and secondary curriculum. They have the same virtues as teflon-coated cookware, so easy to keep clean, and, more important, nothing ever sticks. Literature, by which I mean good writing, by which I mean words so arranged as to surprise, to please, to terrify, even as they instruct—this literature is like a well-seasoned black iron pot. You have to learn how to use it; you've got to control the fire, or it will burn the vittles; but if you tend it properly and treat it with respect, it will nourish you and last a lifetime.

I like what Daniel Fader of the University of Michigan has to say about textbooks. You know him as the author of that marvelously provocative little volume *Hooked on Books*. I quote from an unpublished paper of his describing his project called "English in Every Classroom":

> An acceptable text can be negatively defined as one that is not an anthology and does not have hard covers, for the hard-bound text and the anthology have a number of serious defects in common.
>
> First of all, both are symbols of the world of scholastic failure, and both are to some degree causes of that failure. No hard-bound text was ever thrust into a child's pocket, and no anthology was ever 'read' in any meaningful sense of that word by anybody. The student fed upon a steady diet of highly selected collections is not being encouraged to read, so much as he is to survey, to mine, and to collect shining nuggets of precious literature. ... Generations of students have grown to scholastic

maturity nurtured almost solely on anthologized and authorized classics, and have become parents of new generations, who, like themselves, are quite without the habit of reading because the typical school program neither stimulates nor breeds in the average student a normative, rewarding relationship to reading.

We mean so well, and we do so badly in the business of bringing children and real books together. We always suffer a failure of nerve at the thought of allowing a child to confront an author unadorned by footnotes, study helps, sample questions, and "things to do."

I recall talking with the English teachers at one of New Jersey's better high schools. I was told that they, brave souls, had gotten rid of *Silas Marner*, that quintessential exemplar of nineteenth-century literary hackwork, and they replaced it with *The Catcher in the Rye*—to which they attached a study guide, vocabulary list, and a set of mimeographed work sheets with suggestions to their fellow teachers on how to develop a six-week unit on this little novel. You see, it is not necessary to ban a book from the school or public library; if you do not want the kids to be exposed to its infections, stretch the thing upon the rack of a lesson plan and all of its juices will dry out in a week.

Let me suggest a parlor game from which you might draw some professional instruction; take some bestseller, or other book that a significant number of your colleagues are known to be reading, and ask them the kinds of questions you demand of children. You may lose a few friends, but, who knows, you may discover something about an aesthetic bill of rights for readers.

At its best the American schoolbook is a marvelously effective instrument, but it is a book because its pages have been gathered, sewn, and bound, and because in its general production it has met the textbook specifications of the several states. We can be certain that there will always be textbooks of some kind, for they are relatively simple to operate. You don't have to worry about blowing a fuse or tearing the tape. But there are other data storage and retrieval systems that are more sophisticated and more flexible. There are other ways of storing the information and making it accessible in manners more appropriate to the material. You need only to look at the catalogs of many audiovisual concerns to see what can be done on tape, on film, on records, on transparencies, with overhead projectors, with programmed material, etc. I don't intend here to celebrate the achievements of the audiovisual field, for considering the fact that audiovisual aids have been with us in schools for almost three-quarters of a century, its achievement in education is something less than world-shattering.

The greatest audiovisual system ever devised is still in production, and was marketed as nearly as I can tell some five thousand years ago in the ancient city of Sumer when the scribes started to push the clay tablet business. In its present form that model is a sensitive, well-educated, alert, and interested teacher standing before or among children she knows very well, talking about things that concern them, and making connections between them and the things and the rest of the universe. This teacher functions well in an automated classroom or in a one-room shack. She functions well with the rich resources of a central library, or with nothing but her bare hands and imagination. She may complain about the absence of materials appropriate to the needs of her class, but since she knows what they need, if she can't get it, she'll make it. If she has available to her all of the riches of our affluent society, all of the great new gifts of science and technology, she will govern herself by the most puritan laws of parsimony and use only what is necessary, while at the same time she will make the wealth available to her children in such a way that each may go as far as his capacities, his talents, and his interests can be urged to go, under the gentle urgings of her own professional skill and commitment.

I'm sure you can detect some not very carefully hidden biases here, involving such things as individualized instruction. I am persuaded that Jeannette Veatch is absolutely right in this matter. Her book *Reading in the Elementary School,* published by the Ronald Press, is, in my judgment, the best description and demonstration of that kind of a reading program which makes the fullest possible use of what is now available to the teacher. Dr. Veatch doesn't urge revolution, although her language sometimes sounds that way. She does insist that from the very beginning we must use the children's own language in helping them to learn to read, and that every child, meaning each child, should be taught to read with books he chooses himself. She believes that there must be frequent and private individual conferences between child and teacher, especially in the beginning of reading, and that beyond this there are certain tasks that require small group instruction.

I want to elaborate briefly on Dr. Veatch's point: the importance of using the child's own language in teaching him how to read. This holds true whether the child comes from the most favored circumstances, or from the most deprived and disabling environment, whether the child comes from a home where books are treasured, where language is cherished, or from a home where words are rarely used, and then more often to hurt than to love. You see, it is too easy to forget in our work-oriented society that the child who does not speak well is not as disabled in the learning process as he appears to be. Although we learn to speak long before we learn to read, we learn to see long before we can speak. In childhood we have more experience in making fine visual discriminations than we have in making fine auditory discrimination. And I suspect that, if we're not prejudiced to the contrary, much of the difficulty experienced by both teachers and children in slum schools would be dispensed with very quickly, could the teachers but accept the child and his language as they are and help him build on the riches he already possesses, rather than confront him with his comparative poverty in a language he cannot yet call his own.

There is instruction for us here in some of the work, so far not formally reported, done by Peace Corps Volunteers, as well as by some Head Start programs, most especially in the Deep South, in the use of the children's language as it is and the environment they are actually familiar with in producing reading materials which violate every grammatical and literary standard, but enable the child to communicate with the printed and the spoken word.

One of my old and revered teachers used to say, very simply, that if you dare to teach, and most especially if you dare to teach English, you must begin with respect for the words in the mouth of a child.

References

1. Browne, Charlotte Elizabeth. Quoted in Altick, Richard. *The English Common Reader.* Chicago: The University of Chicago Press, 1947, pp.112-13.
2. Bryher, Winifred pseud. *The Heart to Artemis.* New York: Harcourt, Brace and World, 1962, p. 14.
3. Duff, Annis. *Longer Flight.* New York: The Viking Press, 1955, p. 67.
4. Johnson, Dr. Samuel. Quoted in Fuess, Claude M., and Bosford, Emory S., eds. *Unseen Harvests: A Treasury of Teaching.* New York: The Macmillan Co., 1947, p. 116.
5. Szent-Gyorgyi, Albert. "Teaching and the Knowledge Explosion." *Science* 126 (December 4, 1964):2378.
6. Zulli, Floyd. *New York University Alumni Bulletin,* January 12, 1967.

Herbert C. Rudman

In this classic study, Herbert Rudman rather graphically demonstrated how perishable the reading interests of children are. Some authors have seen this modification of book use as developing "socialization," a sometimes positive force. Others see it as stifling. The implications here are clear: at an early age, children are turned away from reading as a resource to their own needs.

The Informational Needs and Reading Interests of Children in Grades IV Through VIII*

The primary objective of this study was to find out what children want to read about, what they want to find out about, and what they are looking up in books. A secondary objective was to learn whether parents, teachers, and librarians have the same desires for children with respect to reading and informational needs that the children have for themselves.

Method

Questionnaires were sent to children, their parents, and their teachers in 270 communities. Another 270 questionnaires went to librarians in or near these communities. Care was taken to select equally from the nine census regions of the United States; from rural, urban, and metropolitan communities; and from Grades IV through VIII. A representative sampling with respect to socioeconomic status was also obtained for the whole group.

A total of 73 percent of the questionnaires from among the four samples were completed and returned. In all, 6,313 pupils in Grades IV through VIII, 4,531 parents of these pupils, 212 teachers, and 169 librarians re-

---

*This study was made possible by a research grant provided by Spencer Press, Inc.

All material used in this article was taken from the author's doctoral dissertation, "Interrelationships among Various Aspects of Children's Interests and Informational Needs and Expectations of Teachers, Parents, and Librarians," completed at the University of Illinois in June, 1954. This is the first article based on this dissertation that has been released by the author.

Herbert C. Rudman, "The Informational Needs and Reading Interests of Children in Grades IV Through VIII," *Elementary School Journal,* Vol. 55, No. 9, May 1955, University of Chicago Press. Copyright © 1955 by the University of Chicago. All rights reserved. Reprinted with permission.

turned usable questionnaires. The distribution of the returns closely approximated the original sampling plan.

The questionnaires sent to the four groups (children, parents, teachers, and librarians) were constructed as parallel instruments. The following three questions taken from the questionnaire sent to children illustrate the information elicited:

1. If someone were to give you a book as a present, what would you want it to be about?

2. If a very good friend could answer any question you asked, what would you ask about?

3. When you went to a book (not a dictionary) not long ago to find out something, what did you want to find out about?

Twelve major classifications were set up to contain the responses given and thus do not conform to a logical organization of content and are only generally suggestive of the data classified within each. The percent of responses made by each group to each question was calculated, and the differences obtained between groups were tested for statistical significance by the formula for the standard error between two proportions (1). The differences mentioned in the following pages were found to be statistically significant.

Read-About Interests

Table 1 shows the reading interests that the pupils mentioned and the interests that parents, teachers, and librarians would like children to have.

1. When subcategories reflecting science responses are combined, science is among the top three categories of children's reading interests.

2. Children as a group choose mystery, adventure, children, horses, and dogs to read about. As children progress through Grades IV-VIII, they show increasing interest in mystery stories and decreasing interest in cowboy stories and fairy tales. As children reach Grades VII and VIII, they are increasingly interested in reading about teen-agers and children. Children show strong interest in animal stories through Grades IV-VIII. As children move toward the upper elementary grades, they show a greater interest in reading about sports and recreational activities.

3. There appears to be little difference in the reading interests of children from rural, urban, and metropolitan centers.

4. Contrary to the findings of other studies, few sharp sex differences are found. More than girls, boys want to read about astronomy, geology and physical geography, space travel, Indians, science, airplanes, jets and rockets, boats, and sports. More than boys, girls want to read about animals,

TABLE 1

Reading Interests Reported by 6,313 Pupils and Choices of Reading for Children Reported by 4,531 Parents, 212 Teachers, and 169 Librarians, Ranked by Frequency of Mention

Children's Reading Interests	Parent Choices for Children	Teacher Choices for Children	Librarian Choices for Children
Literature (34.0%) *	*Literature (31.0%)*	*Literature (19.5%)*	*Famous people (19.5%)*
1. Mystery	1. Reference books	1. Adventure and travel	1. Famous people
2. Adventure and travel	2. Adventure and travel	2. Teen-agers and children	
3. Teen-agers and children	3. Teen-agers and children	3. Literature	
4. Cowboys and western	4. Literature		
5. Fairy tales and mythology	5. Mystery		
Animals (20.8%)	*Miscellaneous (17.3%)*	*Other school subjects (19.4%)*	*Literature (18.3%)*
1. Horses	1. Religion	1. Science	1. Adventure and travel
2. Dogs	2. Ethics and values	2. History	2. Literature
3. Birds	3. School	3. Geography	3. Fairy tales and mythology
4. Other wild animals	4. Miscellaneous	4. Social Science	4. Teen-agers and children
Sports and recreation (8.4%)	*Animals (10.4%)*	*Social studies (15.4%)*	*Other school subjects (14.8%)*
1. Sports	1. Animals	1. Foreign countries	1. History
2. Baseball	2. Horses	2. Current events and social problems	2. Science
	3. Dogs	3. U.S.A.	
Social studies (7.9%)	*Sports and recreation (6.6%)*	*Miscellaneous (12.9%)*	*Social studies (11.6%)*
1. Foreign countries	1. Sports	1. Ethics and values	1. Foreign countries
2. Opening of the West	2. Hunting and camping	2. Miscellaneous	2. U.S.A.
3. Indians	3. Crafts	3. Religion	3. Current events and social problems
	4. Baseball		
	5. Hobbies		
Machines and applied science (5.5%)	*Other school subjects (6.5%)*	*Famous people (5.0%)*	*Miscellaneous (10.0%)*
1. Airplanes, jets, rockets	1. Science	1. Famous people	1. Miscellaneous
	2. History	2. Historical U.S.	2. Ethics and values
			3. Religion
Famous people (5.4%)	*Social studies (5.7%)*	*Animals (5.8%)*	*Animals (7.5%)*
1. Famous people	1. Foreign countries	1. Animals	1. Animals
	2. U.S.A.		2. Horses
			3. Dogs
Other school subjects (4.1%)	*Famous people (5.0%)*	*Biological science (5.6%)*	*Sports and recreation (5.7%)*
1. Science	1. Famous people	1. Nature	1. Sports
2. History	2. Historical U.S.	2. Flowers and plants	2. Hobbies
			3. Crafts
Miscellaneous (3.6%)	*Personal problems (4.0%)*	*Personal problems (4.2%)*	*Biological science (5.5%)*
1. Miscellaneous	1. Getting along with others	1. Vocations	1. Nature
2. Religion	2. Vocations	2. Getting along with others	
Physical science (2.9%)	*Biological science (3.5%)*	*Sports and recreation (4.0%)*	*Personal problems (3.2%)*
1. Physical geography	1. Nature	1. Sports	1. Getting along with others
2. Astronomy			2. Family relations
3. Space travel			
Biological science (2.2%)	*Machines and applied science (2.0%)*	*Fine and applied arts (2.6%)*	*Fine and applied arts (3.1%)*
1. Flowers and plants	1. Airplanes, jets, rockets	1. Poetry	1. Art
2. Nature		2. Art	2. Poetry
Personal problems (2.0%)	*Fine and applied arts (2.3%)*	*Machines and applied science (2.4%)*	*Physical science†*
1. Vocations	1. Art	1. Cars and trucks	1. Technology
	2. Music	2. Machinery	
	3. Poetry	3. Boats	
Fine and applied arts (1.2%)	*Physical science (1.5%)*	*Physical science (1.5%)*	*Machines and applied science †*
1. Art	1. Astronomy	1. Astronomy	1. Airplanes, jets, rockets
	2. Geology and physical geography		

*The per cent of total responses to the question.
†Fewer than 0.5 per cent of responses fell in major categories without percentage figures.

literature, fairy tales and mythology, mystery, teen-agers and children, famous people, boy-girl relationships, and school.

5. Parents, more than any other of the adult groups, want children to choose reference books to read.

6. Adults, especially parents, indicate a strong desire for children to read about ethics and religion.

7. Librarians, more than the other two adult groups, want children to read biographies of famous people.

8. In general, adult wishes for children's reading choices do not show the same trends through the grades as do the expressed reading choices of children.

9. Unlike the children's choices, parents' reading choices for their children show many population-center differences. Rural parents choose for their children books from the social studies more consistently than do urban parents. In the major category of "Literature," the book choices that rural parents make for their children are the same as the choices of metropolitan parents. Urban parents choose books for their children more often from this area than do either rural or metropolitan parents. In general, metropolitan parents choose books for their children from the area of the formal school subjects more often than do either rural or urban parents. Metropolitan parents seem to be more concerned about personal problems of children than are either rural or urban parents. Urban parents show more desire for their children to read books dealing with religion than do either rural or metropolitan parents.

10. Children as a group are reading about the same types of things that parents, teachers, and librarians want them to read about.

11. Generally speaking, the choices of parents, teachers, and librarians for children's reading are in closer agreement with each other than they are with children's own reports of what they want to read about.

Ask-About Interests

In Table 2 are shown the interests that children would like to ask about and the interests that adults would like children to want to ask about.

1. When the subcategories reflecting science responses are combined, science is among the top three categories of children's ask-about concerns.

2. Children indicate a strong interest in questions related to ethics, values, and religion and become increasingly concerned with these types of questions as they progress through the upper elementary-school grades.

3. As children progress through Grades IV-VIII, they want to ask fewer questions about animals.

4. Children's concerns with their personal problems increase dramati-

TABLE 2

Ask-about Interests Reported by 6,313 Pupils and Ask-about Choices for Children Reported by 4,531 Parents, 212 Teachers, and 169 Librarians, Ranked by Frequency of Mention

Children's Ask-about Interests	Parent Choices for Children	Teacher Choices for Children	Librarian Choices for Children
Miscellaneous (19.9%)*	*Miscellaneous (34.1%)*	*Miscellaneous (31.7%)*	*Miscellaneous (27.0%)*
1. Miscellaneous	1. School	1. Miscellaneous	1. Miscellaneous
2. Ethics and values	2. Ethics and values	2. Ethics and values	2. Ethics and values
3. School	3. Religion	3. School	3. Religion
4. Religion	4. Miscellaneous	4. Religion	
Physical science (12.3%)	*Personal problems (16.5%)*	*Social studies (22.4%)*	*Social studies (22.5%)*
1. Astronomy	1. Vocations	1. Foreign countries	1. Current events and social problems
2. Geology and physical geography	2. Getting along with others	2. U.S.A.	2. Foreign countries
3. Space travel	3. Self-improvement	3. Current events and social problems	3. U.S.A.
Other school subjects (12.3%)	*Social studies (10.9%)*	*Other school subjects (14.1%)*	*Personal problems (13.5%)*
1. Reading	1. Current events and social problems	1. Reading	1. Getting along with others
2. Mathematics	2. Foreign countries	2. Science	2. Others' perception of self
3. Science	3. U.S.A.	3. History	3. Vocations
4. History	4. War and peace	4. Geography	4. Boy-girl relationships
		5. Social science	
Social studies (11.4%)	*Other school subjects (9.9%)*	*Personal problems (13.2%)*	*Other school subjects (13.0%)*
1. Foreign countries	1. History	1. Getting along with others	1. Science
2. U.S.A.	2. Science	2. Vocations	2. Reading
3. War and peace	3. Reading	3. Self-improvement	3. History
4. State history	4. Mathematics		
5. Current events and social problems			
Animals (9.9%)	*Sports and recreation (6.6%)*	*Biological science (7.6%)*	*Biological science (7.5%)*
1. Horses	1. Sports	1. Nature	1. Nature
2. Animals	2. Hobbies	2. Plants	2. Physiology and anatomy
3. Dogs	3. Crafts	3. Health	3. Health
4. Birds		4. Physiology and anatomy	
Personal problems (8.7%)	*Biological science (4.9%)*	*Machines and applied science (4.0%)*	*Sports and recreation (5.0%)*
1. Vocations	1. Nature	1. Mass communication	1. Hobbies
2. Boy-girl relationships	2. Physiology and anatomy	2. Airplanes, jets, rockets	2. Sports
3. Future for me			3. Crafts
Sports and recreation (6.4%)	*Machines and applied science (3.5%)*	*Sports and recreation (3.9%)*	*Literature (3.5%)*
1. Sports	1. Airplanes, jets, rockets	1. Sports	1. Literature
2. Baseball		2. Hobbies	2. Teen-agers and children
			3. Adventure and travel
Machines and applied science (5.8%)	*Animals (3.5%)*	*Literature (3.2%)*	*Fine and applied arts (3.0%)*
1. Airplanes, jets, rockets	1. Animals	1. Adventure and travel	1. Music
2. Cars and trucks	2. Horses		2. Poetry
Famous people (4.7%)	*Physical science (3.3%)*	*Animals (3.1%)*	*Animals (2.5%)*
1. Historical U.S.	1. Astronomy	1. Animals	1. Animals
2. Famous people		2. Other wild animals	2. Horses
Literature (4.3%)	*Fine and applied arts (3.0%)*	*Famous people (3.1%)*	*Famous people (2.5%)*
1. Mystery	1. Music	1. Famous people	1. Famous people
2. Adventure and travel			
3. Literature			
Biological science (3.1%)	*Literature (2.0%)*	*Physical science (3.0%)*	*Physical science (1.0%)*
1. Flowers and plants	1. Adventure and travel	1. Atomic fission	1. Astronomy
			2. Space travel
Fine and applied arts (1.5%)	*Famous people (1.3%)*	*Fine and applied arts†*	*Machines and applied science (0.5%)*
1. Music	1. Famous people		1. Machinery

*The per cent of total responses to the question.
†Fewer than 0.5 per cent of responses fell in major categories without percentage figures.

cally as they approach puberty. Interest in this area centers in vocations and boy-girl relationships.

5. Unlike their responses to the question dealing with reading choices, children's responses show a great number of population center differences when they are discussing questions they would ask an omniscient person. There is usually no difference in the number of questions asked by rural and metropolitan children in the major categories of "Physical Science" and "Famous People." Rural children ask questions characterized by the major category "Miscellaneous" more often than do urban or metropolitan children. On the other hand, metropolitan children ask more questions which fall in the subcategory "Ethics and values" than do rural or urban children.

6. More frequently than girls, boys indicate a desire to ask about things dealing with the history of the United States, airplanes, rockets, and baseball. Girls, more frequently than boys, want to ask about horses, dogs, vocations, boy-girl relationships, ethics, values, and religion.

7. Adults want children to ask about ethics, values, and religion. They are in close agreement with children in this respect.

8. Parents show a strong desire for children to ask about personal problems at all grade levels (but especially in the upper grades) and a particularly strong desire for children to ask questions about vocations.

9. Although parents want their children to ask questions related to sports activities, they do not indicate the strong interest in baseball that their children do.

10. Parents of upper-grade children indicate a strong desire for their children to become familiar with current events and social problems.

11. Upper-grade teachers have a strong desire for children to ask questions concerning their personal problems, particularly questions about how to get along with others.

12. There appears to be little difference between rural, urban, and metropolitan parents concerning what they want children to ask about.

13. Children, in general, are asking about the same types of things that parents, teachers, and librarians want them to ask about.

14. In general, children do not want to ask about the same things that they want to read about, nor do parents, teachers, and librarians want children to ask about the same things that they want children to read about.

15. Adults are generally in close agreement concerning the topics that they want children to ask about.

Look-Up Behavior

The topics that the children looked up as reported by the pupils and by parents, teachers, and librarians are presented in Table 3 in order of frequency of mention.

TABLE 3

Topics Looked Up in Books as Reported by 6,313 Pupils, 4,531 Parents, 212 Teachers, and 169 Librarians, Ranked by Frequency of Mention

Reported by Children	Reported by Parents	Reported by Teachers	Reported by Librarians
Social studies (22.9%)*	*Social studies (23.3%)*	*Social studies (21.3%)*	*Animals (16.5%)*
1. Foreign countries	1. Foreign countries	1. Foreign countries	1. Animals
2. State history	2. State history	2. U.S.A.	2. Birds
3. U.S.A.	3. U.S.A.	3. State history	3. Other wild animals
4. Ancient history		4. Current events and social problems	4. Snakes and reptiles
Animals (14.2%)	*Other school subjects (14.0%)*	*Animals (14.0%)*	*Social studies (16.3%)*
1. Animals	1. History	1. Animals	1. Foreign countries
2. Birds	2. Science	2. Birds	2. State history
3. Horses	3. Geography	3. Fish	3. Local history
4. Other wild animals	4. Reading	4. Other wild animals	4. Indians
Other school subjects (12.5%)	*Animals (12.1%)*	*Physical science (13.9%)*	*Other school subjects (12.8%)*
1. Reading	1. Animals	1. Astronomy	1. Science
2. Science	2. Birds	2. Geology and physical geography	2. History
3. Language	3. Horses	3. Technology	3. Geography
4. History		4. Volcanoes	4. Social science
5. Geography			
Famous people (12.2%)	*Famous people (10.7%)*	*Other school subjects (13.6%)*	*Miscellaneous (10.3%)*
1. Historical U.S.	1. Historical U.S.	1. Science	1. Miscellaneous
2. Authors and artists	2. Authors and artists	2. Geography	2. Children's organizations
3. Famous people	3. Famous people	3. History	3. School
4. Inventors and explorers			
Physical science (7.9%)	*Miscellaneous (10.4%)*	*Famous people (10.7%)*	*Sports and recreation (10.2%)*
1. Geology and physical geography	1. Miscellaneous	1. Famous people	1. Hobbies
2. Astronomy	2. School	2. Authors and artists	2. Crafts
3. Technology	3. Religion	3. Historical U.S.	3. Collections
	4. Children's organizations	4. Inventors and explorers	4. Sports
Biological science (6.5%)	*Physical science (7.3%)*	*Biological science (6.6%)*	*Famous people (10.0%)*
1. Plants	1. Geology and physical geography	1. Insects	1. Famous people
2. Insects	2. Astronomy	2. Agricultural	2. Authors and artists
3. Agricultural		3. Trees	3. Historical U.S.
4. Health			
Miscellaneous (6.4%)	*Machines and applied science (5.6%)*	*Miscellaneous (6.6%)*	*Biological science (7.0%)*
1. Miscellaneous	1. Airplanes, jets, rockets	1. Miscellaneous	1. Nature
	2. Mass communication	2. Buildings	2. Flowers and plants
			3. Health
Machines and applied science (5.9%)	*Biological science (5.4%)*	*Machines and applied science (3.7%)*	*Machines and applied science (6.6%)*
1. Airplanes, jets, rockets	1. Insects	1. Airplanes, jets, rockets	1. Airplanes, jets, rockets
2. Weapons	2. Flowers and plants	2. Applied science	2. Applied science
			3. Boats
Literature (4.4%)	*Sports and recreation (4.8%)*	*Fine and applied arts (3.6%)*	*Physical science (6.6%)*
1. Literature	1. Crafts	1. Poetry	1. Geology and physical geography
	2. Sports		2. Astronomy
Sports and recreation (3.8%)	*Literature (3.5%)*	*Sports and recreation (3.4%)*	*Literature (2.4%)*
1. Baseball	1. Literature	1. Sports	1. Literature
Fine and applied arts (2.3%)	*Fine and applied arts (2.9%)*	*Literature (2.8%)*	*Fine and applied arts (2.2%)*
1. Poetry	1. Poetry	1. Fairy tales	1. Poetry
	2. Music	2. Reference	
Personal problems (1.1%)	*Personal problems (0.7%)*	*Personal problems†*	*Personal problems†*
1. Vocations	1. Vocations		1. Vocations
			2. Getting along with others

*The per cent of total responses to the question.
†Fewer than 0.5 per cent of responses fell in major categories without percentage figures.

1. When the subcategories reflecting science responses are combined, science is the largest area of look-up behavior of children.
2. Children look up information about animals in decreasing amounts as they advance through the upper elementary grades.
3. Children look up much information about formal school subjects at all grade levels.
4. Children look up information about famous people increasingly through the grades.
5. Although the data show many population-center differences in the look-up behavior of children, no consistent pattern can be established.
6. Boys tend to look up more often than do girls information about geology, physical geography, airplanes, rockets, boats, and sports. Girls tend to look up more often than do boys information about foreign countries, history of the United States, mathematics, and famous people.
7. In general, parents and teachers report that children look up the same things that the children themselves report. Parents seem to agree more closely with their children than do either teachers or librarians.
8. More frequently than any of the other three groups, librarians place children's look-up behavior in the areas of hobbies, crafts, and collections.
9. In general, children do not look up the same things that they want to read about.
10. There seems to be a slightly closer relation between what children look up and what they want to ask about than between what children look up and what they want to read about.
11. Rural and urban parents report that their children look up material described with the names of the formal school subjects more often than do metropolitan parents.

Conclusions

1. The results of this study seem to bear out one of its assumptions, namely, that children are not necessarily interested in reading about the same things that they want to ask about. There are a number of reasons which may explain this.

Books have to deal in generalities, while the individual child's questions may be very specific. The question, "How can I get along with Johnny, Sue, or Tommy?" is much more specific than, "How do I get along with people?" Children probably realize this difference and make a distinction when indicating what they would ask about rather than what they would choose a book about.

Another consideration is the nature of the question itself. The fact that a child has one question of great import to him does not mean that he wants to own or read a complete book in this area.

Other possibilities may be that (*a*) the material at present in print may not meet children's informational needs, (*b*) the printed material that is suitable may not be readily available in home or school libraries, (*c*) talking about a problem rather than reading about it may have mental-hygiene values.

These results suggest that authors and publishers of printed material for children might re-examine their material in light of these findings and write new material to meet better some of the informational needs of children; that school personnel, parents, and librarians should gain a better knowledge of the available materials that meet the interests and needs of children and should see that these materials are placed in school and home libraries; that parents and teachers might profit from the realization that children's questions about some topics can never be suitably answered in print and that these call for the kind of rapport with children which will provide an adequate basis for counseling.

2. As children progress through the grades, they show increasing interest in mystery stories and decreasing interest in cowboy stories and fairy tales. Children want books of action and adventure at all grade levels. There is a change, however, in children's preferences for the kinds of stories which express this action and adventure. This change may be due, in part, to the complexity of the plot and action. Older children, better able to follow the involved plots and to appreciate the subtleness of action in mystery stories, may prefer them to the more simple plots and the direct action in fairy tales and cowboy stories.

The apparently close correlation between increase in grade level and interest in reading about other children is notable. This may be explained, at least in part, by evidence concerning child development. As children approach the age of puberty, interest in peer groups reaches a peak.

As children advance through the elementary grades, they are increasingly interested in books about sports and recreational activities—an interest which reflects, perhaps, their increasing participation in these activities.

Teachers at various grade levels can use information about the clusters of interests that children in particular grades have expressed. With this information, teachers can provide books to meet these interests and books to encourage new interests.

3. Children show few population-center differences in reading choices but many population-center differences in the questions they ask. It may be that there are greater similarities in the books available to these population centers or in the books with which children are generally acquainted than there are in their immediate environments, which are probably the seedbeds

of their questions. This line of reasoning might argue for changes in the school programs so as to include the informational needs of children. It may be that printed materials somewhat common to all communities do not satisfy the informational needs of children in any one community. It might also suggest that needs related to the local community might be given more attention in the school and that there might be advantages to the child in gaining realistic understandings of communities different from his own.

4. The fact that parents, more than any of the other three groups questioned, choose reference books for their children would indicate that teachers and librarians ought to discuss with parents the relative values of reference books in the teaching-learning process. In this manner parents would be given an opportunity to see the values of reference books as teachers and librarians do. If parents view these books as a cure-all for inadequate progress in school, teachers and librarians might encourage a closer examination of reference books as a material of learning.

5. The strong interest in religion, ethics, and values displayed by children and adults may indicate that they are sensitive to a need for more consideration of moral and ethical values in the school program than is now provided.

6. Librarians place great stress on biography as a desirable reading choice for children. The fact that librarians, more frequently than any other group, place children's look-up behavior in the area of hobbies, crafts, and collections may indicate that the public library serves the informational needs of children in this area better than do school or home libraries.

7. In general, children are reading about and asking about what adults want them to read about and ask about. There is also close agreement between what adults say children are looking up and what children themselves report that they look up. What children look up may be largely determined by adult choices and especially by the school situation. If this is true, teachers and others concerned with the education of children might want to attempt to develop a learning environment which not only meets the teachers' goals for children but which also encourages, and provides opportunity for, children to use reference materials for their own purposes.

8. Although both parents and teachers want children to ask about and read about their personal problems, parents are more concerned that children get information concerning vocations, while teachers are more concerned with the social skills. This difference may be due to the fact that parents, seeing their children in the perspective of the family group, take for granted their social skills but are more anxious about the vocational future of their children. Teachers, on the other hand, see the development of desirable social skills as one of their primary responsibilities. Dealing with large groups of children, teachers are probably more sensitive than are

parents to the necessity for good working relationships among children. Teachers may also see the elementary-school years as an inappropriate age for serious concern with vocations.

9. Parents show a keen sensitivity to the problems confronting our contemporary society. In particular, parents of upper-grade pupils want their children to ask about problems of war, peace, segregation, housing, and conservation. The schools might consider this type of finding in revisions of the upper-grade curriculum in social studies.

10. Of all the areas examined, science was the most persistent interest of pupils, parents, teachers, and librarians, appearing as a top interest in reading choices, in questions to be asked, and in look-up behavior. Examination of existing elementary school curriculums would probably indicate that science needs are not met as fully as they could be and that science interests are not well utilized. The findings in this area might prove useful in curriculum revisions.

Limitations

As this study was being designed and during the period when the data were gathered, several limitations were apparent.

First, an erroneous picture of the importance of science interests may have been developed by breaking the science area into major categories called "Physical Science," "Biological Science," and "Machines and Applied Science," and into a minor category of "Science" under "Other School Subjects."

Second, some of the responses were unspecific and general or were given in one word. The difficulty of analyzing these replies lessened somewhat the accuracy of the categorization of the data.

Also, because the questionnaires were administered just once during the academic year, it was difficult to determine accurately the extent to which the responses were influenced by the season of the year.

Again, because the children's questionnaires were administered in classrooms, the possibility exists that the responses were somewhat influenced by the school setting.

Finally, the inherent limitations of the questionnaire method of gathering data were, of course, still present. There is, however, always the unanswered question whether another technique would elicit the same or similar results.

References

1. McNemar, Quinn. *Psychological Statistics.* New York: John Wiley and Sons, 1949, p. 76.

PART TWO

Reading for Personal Needs

CHAPTER FIVE

In Search of Self

Ultimately we seek reading which satisfies that unique set of emotions and intellect, attitudes and values, we call our "self." It is true that reading contributes some influences to understanding the environment, a confrontation of old and new information, but it is also true that we choose reading that supports our own point of view. We choose to read about ourselves, materials of similarities and complements that are pleasurable to us. Thus, reading, as most human activities, may be seen to be an extension of self.

Because reading is communication, the reader subtly projecting his own interpretation upon the materials, it can be a valuable resource to adolescents who want to know who they are. They can use fiction as well as nonfiction to discover more about themselves. A particularly heroic character from fiction may help adolescent boys to accept their own qualities of tenderness or chivalry. The young man may seek the biography of a famous person to learn about his own "differences." Girls read love stories as much to learn about love as to dote upon their fancies. Books of horoscope information can be rewarding as an introduction to discussions about personality, and everything from career choices to etiquette can be explored in pamphlets. In all of this, the young person is comparing, testing, questioning his own values alongside those about which he reads.

It is a mistake to assume that reading is a passive pursuit carried out in isolation. No real reading is done in quiet isolation for the reader is engaged in active dialogue with the author. Some researchers claim that we can predict some of the stages children go through in this interaction between reader and author. These supposed "phases" of reading development (cf. Robert G. Carlson, *Books and the Teen-Age Reader.*) represent a reflection of the young reader's growth. Whether such patterns follow predictable steps or not, from comic books to fantasy, book choices follow the needs of the reader's most personal life. The reader's responses to the books he chooses seem to be predicated upon his personality, too. He interprets what he reads in ways that are least threatening to him. As an adolescent, he will see admirable characters in fiction behaving in ways that support his views. As an adult he will distort the opinions of his favorite politicians in order to make them acceptable.

The precise role that reading plays in the developing individual is delicate and subtle. Sometimes we may directly see the influence of books upon adolescent self-concept as they "try-on" a role, mimic a character from fiction, espouse the heretical values of George Bernard Shaw, or adopt manners from King Arthur's Court. On the other hand, the reader often unfairly imposes his values upon the reading he does. In addition to selecting supportive, reinforcing materials, he may draw unjustified conclusions or misconstrue facts in the reading he does do. In nearly the same fashion that we identify with and choose our friends, we can be expected to learn from the behavior of our fictional heroes. As we grow and mature, so does our reading interest. We select materials of greater depth and allow the author greater freedom to impose upon our thought.

Louise M. Rosenblatt

Beginning with reading as creative experience, Professor Rosenblatt defines reading from the context of the reader. What is reading must lie in the unique event that is the interaction of reader with text. This process would differ only in degree for materials as diverse as a poem and a kitchen recipe.

Towards a Transactional Theory of Reading

The task assigned to me in this Seminar on Reading Theory grows out of my interest in the interpretation of literary works of art. The effort to develop a "model" for the kind of reading thought of as aesthetic has led to a view that seems relevant to the whole reading spectrum, aesthetic and non-aesthetic, advanced and elementary. Reversing the usual procedure of beginning at the simpler level, I shall attempt to sketch some emphases that result from consideration of the interpretation of fairly complex literary works of art. This will provide the basis for clarifying resemblances and differences between aesthetic and non-aesthetic reading processes. Some implications may emerge for the dynamics of the reading process in general.

Materials drawn from a study by Rosenblatt (15) of the responses of a group of men and women to four lines of verse may serve as a springboard for discussion. It should be pointed out that these materials do not offer introspective evidence, about which there is justified skepticism. Before being given the text, the readers were told that they would remain anonymous and were asked simply to start writing as soon as possible after beginning to read. They were to jot down whatever came to them as they read. These notes turned out to be analogous to "stills" at various stages in a slow-motion picture. Thus it was possible to reconstruct some of the kinds of responses and stages involved in the process of arriving at an interpretation. The quatrain (without the name of the author, Robert Frost) and a sampling of the responses follow:

Reprinted with permission of Louise Rosenblatt and the National Reading Conference, Inc.

It Bids Pretty Fair

The play seems out for an almost infinite run.
Don't mind a little thing like the actors fighting.
The only thing I worry about is the sun.
We'll be all right if nothing goes wrong with the lighting.

Typical opening notes in two commentaries reflect a rudimentary literary response, yet they already represent a very high level of organization:

> This seems to me to be bits of conversation between people who are interested in moviemaking or legitimate play.
> Sounds as if it could be producer of a play giving encouragement to backers.

The effort here is to find a framework into which to fit the meanings of the individual words and sentences. *Who is speaking? Under what circumstances? To whom?* are questions already assumed in these first tentative comments.

The following note reveals another step or kind of awareness; it starts like the others, but quickly makes articulate the realization that this text is to be read as a poem: "This seems to be bits of conversation between people who are interested in moviemaking or a legitimate play. On second thought, the rhymes show it is a poem." This led to a rereading of the text for the purpose of paying attention to rhythm; the lines had evidently first been read as simple conversation, with no effort to sense a rhythmic pattern.

Some of the readers became involved with ideas called up by the first two lines, and neglected the rest. But for most, the third line, with its reference to the sun, created the necessity for a revision in some way of the tentative response to the first two lines. In comment after comment, there occurs a phrase such as "on second thought," "a second look," "another idea." One reader spells out the problem: "The third line seems most confusing. If I stick to my theory of producer talking to backers it really makes no sense."

Many of the readers, having called up such a vivid notion of a director or producer talking about a play, immediately attempted to adapt this to a situation in which there might reasonably be a concern about the sun: "I am reminded of the Elizabethan theatre open to the skies, which indeed was dependent upon the sun (good weather)"; "Seems to be about life in a summer stock theatre"; "Is it a summer theatre? But then there would be worry about the rain, rather than the sun."

Within the brief time given for reading and comment, a number of the readers never freed themselves from the problem of finding such a practical explanation for a play's success being dependent on the sun. One comment ends on this realization: "I'm afraid this is a very literal reading."

Others more quickly became aware of the need for another level of interpretation: "However, after a moment or two, the implied stage begins clearly to represent the world, and the actors, the world's population"; "On second thought, play metaphor—'all the world's a stage'—Life goes on in spite of quarreling, but it won't if the 'lighting' (moral? spiritual?) fails.... Anyway, war, disagreement, etc., don't matter so much—so long as we still have the 'light' (sun—source of light—nature? God?)."

Several readers were alerted, evidently, by the contrast between the word "infinite" and the colloquial tone of the rest of the line. When they were led to wonder about the kind of play for which the sun provides lighting, the notion of infinity had prepared them to think of the great drama being played out through the ages by mankind on this planet. Some tried unsuccessfully to merge with this another level of meaning for the sun.

A few readers sensed the Olympian remoteness of the "I" who could find it possible to view man's life on this planet in the light, almost, of eternity, and who was thus able to see as "little things" such momentous episodes as wars.

For another reader, the reference to something happening to the sun awakened a recollection of Burns', "Till a' the seas gang dry" as another image of boundless time. This led to a feeling that the persona's "worry" was ironic, a belittling of human conflicts when viewed against the background of the life of the sun.

The following notes illustrate the range covered in one commentary: "Sounds as if it could be producer of a play giving encouragement to backers.... I just got another idea: First line—the world will always be here. Second line—there will always be fighting. We shouldn't worry too much about it. Third line—worries about H-bomb." (Here we see how the reader's fears of an atomic catastrophe were activated by the reference to "worry" about the sun.)

Even these few excerpts demonstrate the need to insist that the reader is *active*. He is not a blank tape registering a ready-made message. He is actively involved in building up a poem for himself out of the lines. He selects from the various referents that occur to him in response to the verbal symbols. He finds some context within which these referents can be related. He reinterprets earlier parts of the poem in the light of later parts. Actually, he has not fully read the first line until he has read the last, and interrelated them. There seems to be a kind of shuttling back and forth as one synthesis —one context, one persona, etc.—after another suggests itself to him.

Moreover, we see that even in these rudimentary responses the reader is paying attention to the images, feelings, attitudes, associations that the words evoke *in him*. It is true that what looks like a certain amount of reasoning went on in the effort to fix on a kind of "play" that would depend on the sun. Actually, however, the notes indicate that, for example, the feeling for the "play" as metaphoric for the life of mankind, and the "sun" as suggesting the backdrop of space and time against which to view it, seems to have been arrived at, not by reasoning, but by paying attention to qualities of feeling due to such things as tonal variations created by the diction, juxtaposed associations, or literary analogies. Notions of mankind as a whole, war, or astronomical time were part of the readers' contribution to the "meaning."

The preceding discussion may point up the need to eliminate a widespread semantic confusion, the tendency to use the words *poem* and *text* interchangeably. Teachers tell students to "read the poem"; contemporary critics make no distinction between "the poem itself," "the work itself," and "the text itself." This reflects a failure to distinguish between the linguistic symbols (the sounded words, the written or printed marks on the page) and what a listener or reader makes of them. Perhaps it is utopian to hope to change such entrenched confusions in literary or critical usage, but at least in a consideration of the reading process such as the present one, there will be an effort to maintain a semantic distinction: *Text* will designate a set or series of signs interpretable as linguistic symbols; thus, in a reading situation, *text* will refer to the inked marks on the page. *Poem* (or *literary work of art,* and terms such as *lyric, novel, play*) will designate an involvement of both reader and text, i.e., what a reader evokes from a text.

The idea that a *poem* presupposes a *reader* actively involved with a *text* is particularly shocking to those seeking to emphasize the objectivity of their interpretations. Afraid that recognition of the importance of the reader will lead to an irresponsible impressionism, critical theorists such as Wellek and Warren have tended to talk about "the poem itself," "the concrete work of art," or even the ideal and unattainable "real" poem. Yet all that they can point to is an interpretation that has been arrived at by a reader in response to a given text. We cannot simply look at the text and predict the poem. The text is a necessary, but not a sufficient, condition of the poem. For this, a reader or readers with particular cultural and individual attributes must be postulated. The author, at the time of its creation, is the first reader. At a later time, even the author himself has a different relationship with the text; there are many stories about this. So it is with a potentially infinite series of other readers of the text. We may postulate a contemporary of the author with similar education and literary and life experience; a contemporary of the author with different background and experience; other individual readers in specific places and times and at a particular point in their lives, bringing to bear on the text specific linguistic, literary, and social experience.

Always each of the readers has before him only black marks on the page, the text by means of which a poem is to be called forth. These readings may be compared, generalizations may be made about them, some may be considered more generally acceptable by a body of critics, but ultimately specific individual readings must be assumed. Fortunately, the whole problem of the "mode of existence" of the poem need not be debated here, since our concern is necessarily with individual readers in an active relationship with individual texts. To speak of an ideal reading is simply to postulate a relationship between the text and a reader possessing "ideal" attributes, which will need to be specified.

Some critical theorists set up the author as the ideal reader of the text and, especially if it was produced at some remote time, or in another society, use many scholarly aids in order to approximate to the author's hypothetical reading. Yet it is clear that the scholar-reader brings another component to the reading, namely his awareness of the difference between what he brings to the text and what the author or his contemporaries presumably did. (Santayana somewhere tells about the man who built a perfect reconstruction of an eighteenth-century house. There was only one anachronism in it: himself.) Part of the interest of reading any literary work is the sense of participating in another "world."

Wimsatt and Beardsley (19) and Wimsatt (18) illustrate how twentieth-century criticism has sought to dissociate the interpretation of the text from the author's intention. The author, it is true, may state his intention, or there may be biographical or historical evidence that would indicate his intention. Yet the question still remains, *Did the author succeed in carrying out his intention in the text?* The author may test his creation in the light of his intention, but all that the reader has to fall back on is the text. Any intention of the author's which is not capable of being called forth from the text, or justified by the text, is a matter of the author's biography. Knowledge of the author's intention drawn from other sources may aid in the reading of the text, but only by alerting the reader to verbal cues that he might otherwise overlook. The interpretation, however, cannot validly be "of" anything other than the text itself. The effort to avoid "the intentional fallacy" did not, however, lead to a systematic understanding of the reader's contribution.

The familiar information theory diagram may help us to further clarify the relationship of the reader to the author and the text:

Speaker—encoding—message—decoding—hearer

There is a temptation to substitute *author* for *speaker* and to think of the *reader* simply as seeking to decode the message in a way parallel to the *hearer* decoding the message. But in any actual reading, there is only the text and the reader. The speaker, we know, offers many clues to the listener, through emphasis, pitch, rhythm, pauses—and, if face-to-face, facial expression and gesture. The reader finds it necessary to construct the "speaker"—the "voice," the "persona," the "tone"—*as part of* what he decodes from the text.

Contemporary critical theory has recognized this, but has primarily developed its implications for the author's need to select elements that will produce the effect he desires. Thus T. S. Eliot (9) developed the notion of the "objective correlative" to refer to elements in the text that would possess the same emotional impact for the author and the reader. There is, however, a tendency to think of the "objective correlative"—whether the structure of a play or the metaphors embedded in it—as somehow eliciting an automatic reponse from the presumably passive reader. If that were true, the reading of a poem or of a Shakespeare play would be analogous to responding to a red traffic light. Any reading is far more complex than such a simple stimulus-response situation.

In information theory, the listener is said to have "decoded" the "message" when he has reconstructed the sounds and has recognized the patterns of words. This view is understandable when it is recalled that information theory is concerned with such matters as the transmission of utterances over, for example, the telephone. But, of course, workers in this field are quite ready to admit that in any actual communication, the process must be carried through to an interpretation of meaning. And even on the level of recognizing the sounds, evidence exists to demonstrate that the listener's present expectations and past experience are important. For example, Cherry (6) reports experiments which reveal that once a listener is aware of the general subject matter of an utterance, he is more likely to recognize the words in spite of distorting interference or "noise."

If what the listener brings to even this simple level of listening is important, how much more necessary is recognition of the importance of what the reader brings to a text. The matrix of past experience and present preoccupations that the reader brings to the reading makes possible not only a recognition of shapes of letters and words but also their linkage with sounds, which are further linked to what these sounds point to as verbal symbols. This requires the sorting out of past experiences with the words and the verbal patterns in different contexts.

The readers of the quatrain demonstrated very clearly that, whatever the "model," the reading of a poem is not a simple stimulus-response situation. There was not a simple additive process, one word-meaning added to another. There was an active, trial-and-error, tentative structuring of the responses elicited by the text, the building up of a context which was modified or rejected as more and more of the text was deciphered.

The fact that a reader of the quatrain might be able to assign "meaning" to each of the verbal symbols and to each of the separate lines did not guarantee that he would be able to organize these into a significant structure of idea and feeling. The reader had to pay attention to much more than the "meanings" of individual words or their syntax before he could relate the four lines meaningfully. He had to respond to many elements, of diction, rhythm, association, possible figures of speech or levels of meaning. In order to sense the particular way of voicing the last line to himself, he had to select a particular implied persona with a particular point of view or tone or attitude toward the subject about which the poem might center.

Thus the text, a pattern of signs, is interpreted as a set of linguistic symbols. But the text serves as more than a set of stimuli or a pattern of stimuli; it is also a guide or continuing control during the process by which the reader selects, organizes and synthesizes—in short, interprets—what has emerged from his relationship with the verbal symbols. The text is not simply a fuse that sets off a series of responses. As a pattern of linguistic symbols derived from the signs on the page, the "text" also underwent a series of transformations during the process of arriving at the *poem*.

Moreover, the readers of the quatrain were creating a poem through paying attention to what the stimulus of the text was calling forth within them: attention to the sound of the words in the inner ear, attention to the residue of past experiences with these words in different contexts, attention to the overtones of feeling and the blendings of attitude and mood. All of these were needed before even a tentative organization of an interpretation was possible. Hence my [Rosenblatt (14)] continuing insistence on the idea that the *poem* is what the reader lives through under the guidance of the text and experiences as relevant to the text.

The question remains: Although this view of reading may be important in counteracting the neglect of the reader's contribution and the excessive emphasis on the text of the literary work of art in current criticism and teaching, *What light does this throw on the reading process in general?* How much of what has been said about "the reading of a poem" applies to the reading of other kinds of texts that do not give rise to works of art but that provide, say, information, logical analysis, scientific formulae, or directions for action?

This question leads into the general realm of reading theory where many dangers await the unwary amateur. Having cast discretion to the winds, I shall venture the hypothesis that the reading of a poem probably provides a better basis for a general "model" of the reading process than does the reading of a scientific formula or a recipe for cooking. The tendency of the layman is to assume that the latter forms are simpler modes of reading, and that in the reading that results in a poem, something more has been added. Actually, are not both the aesthetic and non-aesthetic readings different versions of the same basic process? The difference between these two kinds of reading derives ultimately, it seems to me, from a difference in the aspect of the reading process that the reader holds in the focus of his attention.

In a reading that results in a work of art, the reader is concerned with the quality of the experience that he is living through under the stimulus and guidance of the text. No one else can read the poem or the novel or the play for him. To ask someone else to experience a work of art for him would be tantamount to seeking nourishment by asking someone else to eat his dinner for him.

The non-aesthetic mode of reading is primarily instrumental. The differentiating factor is that the reader is not primarily concerned with the actual experience during the time of his relationship with the text. His primary purpose is something that will remain as a residue *after* the actual reading event—e.g., the information to be acquired, the operations referred to or implied in a scientific experiment, or the actions to be carried out in some practical situation.

An illustration of this instrumental type of reading might be a woman who has just discovered a fire in her kitchen, has picked up a fire extinguisher of a type that she has never used, and is frantically reading the directions for its use. Her attention, her whole muscular set, will be directed toward the actions to be performed as soon as she has finished interpreting, i.e., reading, the text. She is not paying attention to the sound of the words, nor to the particular associations that they might evoke. Whether the directions refer to "fire" or "flames" or "combustion" is quite unimportant to her, so long as she grasps what the word points to. The sound, the associations, the relationship of the overtones of these words to those of the rest of the verbal context, would be very important if she were paying attention to this aspect of the reading while evoking a poem; in this instrumental reading they are ignored, are not allowed into the center of attention. The response to the text will be the actual operations to be performed. It would not matter if someone else read the directions and rephrased them for her, so long as the required actions were made clear.

The same text may even provide the occasion for both of these two kinds of reading, depending on the focus of the reader's attention. The young American tourist discovered this when she finished reading the *London Times* weather report, with its "high over Iceland" and its talk of the "Gulf Stream" and found her head full of sonorous phrases and images of snow-peaked mountains and waving tropical palms. She had been paying attention to the sounds and the associations evoked rather than to the practical indications as to whether or not she should carry her umbrella that day. The current "pop" poets who take a sentence from a newspaper article and break it up into free verse are, similarly, inviting the reader to pay attention to the experience evoked even by these seemingly banal words rather than to pay attention primarily to their practical reference. Contrast with this the third-grade textbook in which a poem about a cow in a meadow is headed with the question: "What facts does this poem teach you?" Clearly, the pupil is being instructed to direct his attention to what is farthest from the possibilities of a poetic experience.

The preceding instance undoubtedly spells trouble for that third-grader, since he needs to learn that the visual patterning of the verbal symbols in lines of verse is one of the ways in which the reader is alerted to direct his attention toward the quality of what he evokes from the text. There are, of course, many ways in which the text alerts the reader to adopt one or another stance in his relationship with the text. Courses in poetry are largely concerned with sensitizing the reader to such cues. The more such past experience he brings to the text, it is assumed, the better able he will be to select the appropriate attitude and the more successful he will be in evoking an experience that does justice to the text.

At the other extreme, the mathematical or logical text that is written in a special system of symbols quickly alerts the reader to the fact that he must focus his attention on the operations pointed to by the text and must disregard his senuous or emotionally-colored responses. The reader is further assisted in this by the fact that the special mathematical language is free of irrelevant associations that accrue to ordinary words encountered in a wide range of contexts. But even here the experiential attitude may creep in—as when the mathematician responds to the "elegance" of a proof that he has encountered through a text.

Of course, in much of what we read, both kinds of attitude are brought into play. Our primary purpose may be to gain information, but at the same time we may be aware of the rhythm or the qualitative responses aroused in us by the text, its sound in the inner ear, its appeals to memories involving the senses and the emotions. In fact, it seems not unlikely that such responses are operating even when they are not in the focus of attention. The experienced reader learns to adopt the appropriate stance, and to attend to the aspects of the reading process that are appropriate both to the text and to his own purposes.

The reading process seems to represent a continuum of potential attitudes. A complex literary work of art, such as *Hamlet* or a lyric by Blake, can be placed at one end of the continuum, where the reader's attention is focused squarely on what he is living through in his relationship with the text. Toward the other end of the continuum, would be placed the reading of a text with the attention directed toward its instrumental value in terms of information to be assimilated or operations to be performed. The phrasing here is designed to avoid the implication that texts possess absolute "poetic" or "scientific" values, and to suggest a relationship between the reader and the text resulting in one or another kind of reading event. Thus there is not a break between these kinds of reading, but rather a continuum. Any particular reading is situated at a point between these extremes that reflects the nature of the activity and the focus of attention that the conjunction of the reader and text have produced.

Borderline cases, involving both instrumental and "literary" attitudes, illuminate, on the one hand, the importance of the text and, on the other, the fallacy of assuming an absolute character in words themselves. Words, it is usually said, point to sensations, images, ideas, objects, concepts. But this conventional formulation is not a description of the actual way in which these referents are crystallized out. Linguists and psychologists have recognized the existence of this matrix of inner experience or consciousness out of which our common language is ultimately carved. But usually in discussion of reading this matrix has not been sufficiently emphasized. Critics and linguists have been eager to move on to the more easily-studied public manifestations of external linguistic behavior, as in analysis of spoken or printed texts.

The problem of the nature of experienced "meaning" is indeed complex and only now beginning to interest the psycholinguists and linguistic philosophers. Some of the entrenched and misleading notions about how we think about the meaning of words are being dispelled. For example, the "picture" theory of meaning is being discarded, as indeed is the idea that the word *think* points to a single activity (12,16,20). Such questions are mentioned here only to indicate awareness of the complexity of the process involved when one talks, as I have so blandly, of the reader focusing his attention "on what the linguistic symbols have called forth within him." Still, is it not becoming generally accepted that when we speak of the reader's sensing the meaning of words from their context, we must broaden the scope of that term? Usually it is the verbal context that is referred to —the lexicographical clues present in the text that indicate which of the alternative dictionary meanings of the words should be selected. And of course the verbal context functions also to indicate to the reader what should be his appropriate stance in relation to this text.

But the context is not limited simply to the interlocking pattern of verbal symbols. The reading even of initial cues, we have seen, is a function of the reader as well as of the text, the result of a two-way process. We can say that the text leads the reader to order segments of his past experience; but it is equally necessary to say that the reader is dependent on past experience, both linguistic and life experience, for the sense of possible modes of order that he brings to the text. (Consider the implications of even so simple an illustration as the following: the sign *pain* will be made a different linguistic symbol by the English and the French reader. Within a common culture and language, individual differences, no matter how subtle, still enter into the process of interpretation.)

Hence we cannot even assume that the pattern of linguistic signs in the text gives us knowledge of the exact nature of the stimuli acting upon a given reader. The living organism, Dewey (7) pointed out decades ago, to a certain extent selects from its environment the stimuli to which it will respond, and seeks to organize them according to already-acquired principles, assumptions, and expectations. Hence the "meaning" of any element in the system of signs in the text is conditioned not only by its verbal context, but also by the context provided by the reader's past experience and present expectations and purpose. Out of this emerges the new experience generated by the encounter with the text. Thus, the coming together of a particular text and a particular reader creates the possibility of a unique process, a unique work.

In discussion of the reading process, as in other disciplines undergoing revision, we need to free ourselves from unscrutinized assumptions implicit in the usual terminology. The usual phrasing makes it difficult to attempt to do justice to the dynamic nature of the actual reading event. The reader, we can say, interprets the text. (The reader acts on the text.) Or we can say, the text produces a response in the reader. (The text acts on the reader.) Each of these phrasings, because it implies a single line of action by one separate element on another separate element, distorts the actual reading process. This is not a linear relation, but a situation, an event at a particular time and place in which each element conditions the other.

The "transactional" terminology developed by John Dewey and Arthur F. Bentley (8,4,13) seems most appropriate for the view of the dynamics of the reading process that I have attempted to suggest. This philosophic approach, for which Dewey developed various phrasings during his long career, has had repercussions in many areas of twentieth-century thought. Dewey and Bentley sought to counteract the nineteenth-century phrasing of phenomena as an *interaction* between different factors, as of two separate, self-contained, and already defined entities acting on one another—in a matter, if one may use a homely example, of two billiard balls colliding. They offered the term *transaction* to designate situations in which the elements or factors are, one might say, aspects of the total situation in an ongoing process. Thus a *known* assumes a *knower,* and vice versa. A "knowing" is the transaction between a particular individual and a particular environment.

The transactional view of the reading process not only frees us from notions of the impact of distinct and fixed entities, but also underlines the essential importance of both elements, reader and text, in the dynamic reading transaction. A person becomes a *reader* by virtue of his activity in relationship to a text, which he organizes as a set of verbal symbols. A physical text, a set of marks on a page, becomes the text of a poem or of a scientific formula by virtue of its relationship with a reader who thus interprets it. The transaction is perhaps similar to the electric circuit set up between a negative and positive pole, each of which is inert without the other.

The transactional view is especially reinforced by the frequent observation of psychologists that interest, expectations, anxieties, and other patterns based on past experience affect what an individual perceives. Dewey rejected the simple stimulus-response notion in which the organism passively receives the stimulus, and pointed out that to some extent the organism selects out the stimulus to which it will respond. This is not limited to situations in which, for example, the perceiver projects his interpretation upon a formless or "unstructured" stimulus as in the projection of meanings onto the blots of ink of the Rorschach Test. Experiments have demonstrated that the perceiver "sees" even a structured environment in the way that his past experience has led him to interpret it. Cantril and Livingston (5) report that this transactional view of human behavior is reinforced by recent experiments dealing with the selecting and policing activities of the central nervous system.

The transactional point of view has been systematically developed by a group by psychologists mainly through experiments in perception (1,2,3,10). For example, in one of the Ames-Cantril experiments, the viewer "sees" a room as rectangular although it is in actuality trapezoidal or otherwise distorted. Here, the observer is confronted with a definitely structured stimulus, but the cues are selected and organized or interpreted according to past experience of a room. Simple information that the room is distorted has not necessarily been sufficient to enable the observer to see the room as distorted. Often a disturbing period of readjustment is required. The observer hits walls which he sees or interprets as being elsewhere; he flails about with a stick at non-existent walls. Ultimately, a new set of sensitivities and assumptions is built up, and he learns to respond to or organize those cues that can be interpreted as a room distorted in certain ways. Without the effort at testing his perception, the observer would not have realized that what he saw was largely a projection from past experience. Yet only through such criticism of his own perception could he build up the equipment with which to achieve a more adequate perception. In both instances, what was perceived involved both the perceiver's contribution and the environmental stimulus.

The view of the reading process presented here has not been derived from such experiments. Rather, these offer reinforcement and confirmation for the transactional as a conceptual model. This seems to do greatest justice to the results of prolonged observation of readers encountering texts, and to provide a solution for current confusions in literary theory. Thus, a reader revising his interpretation may be considered analogous to the person looking at the distorted room. In the light of what he brings to the transaction, the reader arrives at a tentative interpretation and then tests it by further study of the text or by comparison with others' interpretations of it. He seeks to find in the verbal symbols the source of his and others' interpretations. He may discover that he ignored some elements or that he projected on it responses irrelevant to the text. Out of this may come a reinterpretation of the text, that is, the structuring of a new kind of experience in relation to it. This simply is a further development of the transactional process that begins with the first effort to derive even the simplest level of meaning from the text.

The transaction involving a reader and a printed text thus can be viewed as an event occurring at a particular time in a particular environment at a particular moment in the life history of the reader. The transaction will involve not only the past experience but also the present state and present interests or preoccupations of the reader. It stresses the possibility that printed marks on a page will become different linguistic symbols by virtue of transactions with different readers.

There is always some kind of selecting out from a matrix of past experiences of language as a phenomenon in particular contexts. Thus the reader draws on this experiential reservoir in even the simplest reading. When only the simplest phonological experience is drawn on, someone has said that the child "barks at the page." As soon as meaning enters, there is not only a recognition of shapes of letters and a linkage with sounds; there is also a sorting out of past experiences with the sounds as symbols or words, and with what the words pointed to in different contexts. "Interpretation," a selective and synthesizing activity, is thus engaged in by the reader even in the most elementary kind of reading.

Does not the transactional point of view suggest that we should pay more attention to the experiential framework of any reading transaction? Is it not extraordinary that major social upheavals seem to have been required to disclose the fact that schools have consistently attempted to teach reading without looking at the language and life experience, the cognitive habits, that the child brought to the text? And should not this same concern be brought to bear on more than the problem of the language or dialect that the child brings? Should not a similar concern for reading as an event in a particular cultural and life situation be recognized as pertinent to all reading, for all children at all phases of their development as readers, from the simplest to the most sophisticated levels?

Nothing that has been said thus far should be interpreted as denying that there must be highly specialized research on many facets of the reading process. But should not both basic and applied research make much more explicit the assumptions concerning the total transaction within which any one element in the reading event may function? The experimenter who is concerned with determining the physical conditions under which spoken utterances may be transmitted by telephone is quite ready to recognize that the physical, linguistic, and general cultural and life equipment that the hearer brings to his listening will condition what he hears, as well as what he interprets. Difficulties arise when these contexts or frameworks are forgotten and the results of narrow experiment are looked upon as significant in isolation. Can it be that many of the efforts to compare various techniques of inducting the child into reading have yielded indeterminate results because elements were being studied without sufficient concern for how these elements fit into the particular reading transactions being studied?

The transactional approach would particularly redress the balance so far as what seems to be a tendency to concentrate on what is most easily measured and analyzed—namely, the signs or, at a somewhat higher level of complexity, the linguistic symbols to which the reader is exposed. This is reflected not only in current controversies about beginning reading, but can also be seen in the zest with which some linguists are applying their particular systems of linguistic analysis to the texts of poems. Such analysis often yields interesting results. But it leaves untouched the question concerning how an individual reader becomes sensitive to the particular linguistic patterns, the parallelisms, the variations from ordinary usage, that often are found to characterize the verbal structure. Statistical analysis of literary styles, for example, must be translated back into terms of sensitivities of the reader in the transaction with a particular text. The difference between statistical or syntactic analysis of a text and the mode of perception of differences within a reading process especially should be recognized.

The importance of the reader in the transaction once established, certain questions become more insistent. What, for example, is the function of the reader's *purpose* in the reading transaction? What are the ways in which the reader develops habits of paying attention to one or another aspect of the highly complex operations generated within this transaction? How, for example, does he develop the habits that enable him to build up from the inked symbols on the page a context within which not only the word order but also the inflections and meaningful cues of the spoken language are embedded (11)? How does he learn when and how to pay attention to the qualitative responses generated by the designated rhythmic patterns and to the past associations with the elements of experience designated by the text? How does he learn when and how to adopt a scientific attitude and pay attention only to the completely public referents of the printed signs? A transactional model of the reading process would not permit neglect of the experiential matrix within which spoken and written language functions. Perhaps this would generate cumulatively meaningful questions, and would provide a framework within which the experimental treatment of aspects of the reading process can be fruitfully carried out.

References

1. Allport, Floyd H. *Theories of Perception and the Concept of Structure.* New York: John Wiley, 1955, p. 271 ff.
2. Ames, Adelbert, Jr. "Reconsideration of the Origin and Nature of Perception." *Vision and Action.* Edited by Sidney Ratner. New Brunswick, New Jersey: Rutgers University Press, 1953.
3. Ames, Adelbert, Jr. *The Nature of Our Perceptions, Prehensions and Behavior: An Interpretative Manual for the Demonstrations in the Psychology Research Center, Princeton University.* Princeton: Princeton University Press, 1955.
4. Bentley, A. F. "Kennetic Inquiry." *Science* 112 (December 29, 1950):775-83.
5. Cantril, Hadley, and Livingston, William K. "The Concept of Transaction in Psychology and Neurology." *Journal of Individual Psychology* 19 (May 1963):3-16.
6. Cherry, Colin. *On Human Communication.* New York: John Wiley, 1957, p. 276.
7. Dewey, John. "The Reflex Arc Concept in Psychology." *Psychological Review* 3 (July 1896):357-70.
8. Dewey, John, and Bentley, Arthur F. *Knowing and the Known.* Boston: Beacon Press, 1949.
9. Eliot, T. S. "Hamlet and His Problems." *Selected Essays.* New York: Harcourt-Brace, 1932, pp. 124-5.
10. Kilpatrick, Franklin P. Ed. *Human Behavior from the Transactional Point of View.* Hanover, New Hampshire: Institute for Associated Research, 1952.
11. Lefevre, Carl A. *Linguistics and the Teaching of Reading.* New York: McGraw-Hill Book Co., 1964.
12. Quine, Willard V. "Speaking of Objects" and "Meaning and Translation." *The Structure of Language.* Edited by Jerry A. Fodor and Jerrold J. Katz. Englewood Cliffs, New Jersey: Prentice-Hall, 1964.
13. Ratner, Sidney, *et. al.* eds. *The Philosophical Correspondence of John Dewey and Arthur F. Bentley.* New Brunswick, New Jersey: Rutgers University Press, 1964.
14. Rosenblatt, Louise M. *Literature as Exploration.* New York: Appleton-Century, 1938; Revised edition, New York: Noble and Noble, 1968. (See Part One for discussion of the problem of the relative validity of different interpretations).
15. Rosenblatt, Louise M. "The Poem as Event." *College English* 26 (November 1964): 123-25.
16. Ryle, Gilbert. "Thinking and Language." *Proceedings of the Aristotelian Society,* Supplement 25 (1951):65-82.
17. Wellek, Rene, and Warren, Austin. *Theory of Literature.* 3rd ed. New York: Harcourt, Brace and World (1956):146-47 and *passim.*
18. Wimsatt, W. K., Jr. *"The Intentional Fallacy." The Verbal Icon.* Lexington, Kentucky: University of Kentucky Press, 1954, pp. 3-18.
19 Wimsatt, W. K., Jr., and Beardsley, Monroe C. *"Intention." Dictionary of World Literature.* Edited by J. T. Shipley. New York: *Philosophical Library,* 1943, pp. 326-29.
20. Wittgenstein, Ludwig. *Philosophical Investigations.* Translated by G. E. M. Anscombe. New York: Macmillan, 1953, p. 175 ff.

David H. Russell

The depth of comprehension or interpretation we bring to reading quite obviously varies from time to time. For many reasons—our skills, internal needs, and overt purposes—we read at differing levels. The definition of just what you think reading is may determine how much you depend on each of the levels discussed in the following article.

Contributions of Reading to Personal Development

In his autobiography, *Safe Conduct,* Boris Pasternak says that the biography of a poet is found in what happens to those who read him. What *does* happen to a reader?

We read at four levels. At the first level we are largely concerned with the association of printed words with their sounds. In some school situations children are drilled in word-calling—"barking at words" without much attention to meaning. At the second level we read for literal meanings. We get the facts or we follow explicit directions. Such reading may have many functional values for the child finding out about India or for the suburbanite engaged in a week-end do-it-yourself project.

The other two levels of reading are more complex. At the third level we interpret what we read. That is, we go beyond the literal comprehension of the fact or the main idea to read between the lines. We draw some conclusion of our own from the passage—we envisage or predict or infer. Sometimes we reflect on the author's point of view or the relation of the material to other things we know—we evaluate or analyze critically. But we also read at a fourth level or depth. Sometimes the passage takes us beyond thoughtful analysis or critical review to a more stirring experience. We feel "the shock of recognition." We recognize a new or an important idea in the actions, characters, or values described. The impact of the material is such that we receive fresh insight into our own or others' lives. In our reading we are changed, a little, as persons.

David Russell, "Contributions of Reading to Personal Development," *Teachers College Record,* Vol. 61, No. 8, May 1960.

Contributions of Reading to Personal Development

Most reading is done at the second, literal level, and most of the writing and research in the field of reading have had to do with the first two levels. We know a lot about word perception, the teaching of phonics, and ways of developing comprehension of the printed page. Such activities make many contributions to the individual. The young child enjoys his new-found skill of working out new words, and the world's work and its week-end hobbies involve the use of much factual reading matter contributing to knowledge and skill. Reading has always been one of the individual's most important resources for gaining knowledge. Granted a modicum of reading skill in the individual, books and libraries are storehouses of information for him. Thus, reading at the second level may have many influences on personal development, as in increasing skill in making model airplanes or in preparing a traveler in Spain to get the most out of direct experiences in a foreign country. The main branch of the Berkeley Public Library has approximately 375 books whose titles begin with the words "How to—," starting with *How to Abandon Ship* and including *How to Live with Children.* Reading at the second level can be a big help to us!

At the third level, we are not so sure of our ground as we are when concerned with word recognition or literal comprehension. A feature of recent research, however, has been considerable work on critical and creative reading abilities. In a recent study at the University of California, for example, Clark (4) developed twenty-three lessons in reading to predict beyond the given facts and tested some ways of teaching these in the classroom. He found that tests of reading to predict were relatively independent of vocabularly and comprehension. In going from literal comprehension to personal interpretation as in prediction a reader puts more of himself into his reading. He thinks beyond the line of print. The perceptual process is the stimulus to many kinds of thinking—to drawing analogies, to checking a writer's point of view, or to beginning an attack on a personal problem. As suggested below, more work needs to be done in exploring this process of thoughtful reaction to an author's ideas.

It is at the fourth level, however, that our knowledge is slight and our needs are great, and so it is with effects of reading on individuals that this discussion is chiefly concerned. Can Pasternak or other poets influence us deeply? Do we really have *Books That Changed the World,* as the optimistic title of one publication suggests? Can a book, story, or poem change one person, much less the world? Can reading have the effect Lincoln believed it could have when he first met Harriet Beecher Stowe? On that occasion he said, "Is this the little woman whose book made such a great war?" In a world of television, radio, comic books, parents, and teachers, can a book be an experience which changes the nature of reality for the young reader? In the words of Ciardi, can it make him "quietly passionate" about an idea or a cause? Or can a book help a person to the self-insight attributed to a man who, seeing his neighbor going by in a new pink Cadillac, said, "There, but for me, go I!" Can a book fill a boy with courage or help him find himself? Or is this too much to ask, even of great literature? Reading may be useful at all four levels, but somehow this fourth level seems the most tantalizing and important of all.

Some Possible Effects of Reading

The kind of reading that we do affects the contribution of the reading matter to our development. In the primary school grades so much of the effort goes into the first level—into the mechanics of reading, into getting the words right, toward following the sequence of the writer's thought—that the chance of added dividends is unlikely. Similarly, in the later grades, the poor reader, or the child deciphering material much too difficult for him, has little opportunity or stimulus to interpret a story or to find materials meaningful to his larger concerns or problems. Piekarz (11) has shown that when children are unable to read a passage with reasonable ease they have fewer reactions to it, with many more responses at the literal-meaning level than at the implied-meaning or evaluation level.

Accordingly, the time and effort given to the making of fluent, skillful readers at the elementary and secondary school levels may be worth while, not only in terms of specific aspects of reading skill but also because such reading is a basis for operation at the two higher levels of reading. Children need word-attack skills and ability to follow directions, not because they are merely going to read words or to follow directions blindly, but so that, having clearly recognized words or accurately interpreted directions, they can then go to the meanings behind the words and, if necessary, to questions about the validity of the directions.

Such an interpretation of reading is not a derogation of reading skills. Many children and adolescents work very hard to attain word recognition skills and the ability to grasp the literal meaning of a paragraph, passage, or chapter. Indeed, success in these matters may make a contribution to personal development beyond that of the facts read because of the "nothing succeeds like success" formula. The child who learns to read skillfully not only pleases his parents but contributes positively to his self-concept. The converse is even clearer. The child who has reading difficulties at the first two levels may have emotional and personality problems associated with his reading. The primary causation may not be so important as the *fact* that reading difficulties are affecting his total development adversely.

When poor readers have not achieved fluency in reading they must have help. For these pupils various types of remedial programs have been developed in schools.

For young children, one aid to fluency is to have their parents and teachers read stories to them, more complex stories than they can read for themselves. For their own first reading practice there seems no reason why children should not begin on easy, graded materials developed in light of many of the things we know about the psychology of learning. In the preschool and early primary years, children can be challenged and helped to reach higher levels of reading by the ideas in the stories read to them.

An example of such reading-listening situations affecting total development is given in a recent master's thesis by Webster (21). She found in a group of eighty first-graders that thirty-five expressed fear of the dark and five indicated fear of dogs. Accordingly, in groups of seven children, she read to and discussed with the children five stories dealing positively with the dark and with dogs—stories such as Margaret Wise Brown's *A Child's Good Night Book* and Ruth Dixon's *Three Little Puppies.* Three months later, an impartial judge agreed with Webster's analysis of interviews: twenty-nine out of the thirty-five children had, it seemed, reduced their fear of the dark and all five of the children had lost most of their fear of dogs. Such a study needs verification with more careful controls, but it suggests that, for young children, the "read-to" situation may affect a child's emotional development.

As a child develops the ability to read for himself some books and stories of merit, the second level of reading flourishes. He finds out not only the secret of the lost treasure but something of the lives of early Americans or something about woolgrowing in Patagonia or in Queensland. The purpose of many books, newspapers, and magazines is to inform. We live in a difficult period of man's history, and the problems which beset us demand our best knowledge and efforts. Therefore, we read for main ideas, for facts, for following a sequence of events, for seeing relationships, and for arriving at conclusions.

Teachers of English at the secondary school and college level have not always considered such reading part of their domain. Of course they must also be concerned with the third and fourth reading levels of interpretation and with the impact of great literature. The value of the information contained in a book has little or nothing to do with its value as literature. One level is concerned with getting a fact right and clear, the other is concerned with some basic human expression or need. One makes for grasp of the immediate, the other, as Bernard Berenson remarked of great pictures, makes for the enhancement of life. Most of our school texts are written and should be used at the level of accurate comprehension. I believe the problem is not "either-or" and that the teacher of English must be concerned with both kinds of reading. Skill at the first two levels seems to be basic to achievement at the third and fourth levels. But it is in the realm of imaginative literature that we usually get to the third and fourth levels of reading. It is here that writing is intrepid in its approach to problems, ingenious in its solution of difficulties, in a way that the child or adolescent cannot achieve by himself. It is at these levels that reading can operate in depth and make its greatest contribution to individual development.

Fortunately, some research evidence is beginning to be accumulated about reading at the third level of interpretation of printed materials. May I quickly suggest a variety of findings. *(a)* Most children do not seem to respond to some of the commoner literary devices such as metaphor or personification before they are in their teens (23). *(b)* Children's interpretations are influenced by their attitudes and expectancies toward what they are reading, by their previous "set" in the reading situation (5). *(c)* When asked to respond to short stories, adolescents give interpretational reactions as a dominant type of response; other categories of response, in order of frequency, are narrational, associational, self-involvement, literary judgment, and prescriptive judgment (19). *(d)* Responses to a piece of literature are largely an individual matter. Children and youth with different experiences, personalities, and needs see different things in the same character, story, or poem—and one interpretation may be just as "true" or "honest" as the other. Consequently, teachers of reading and literature should beware of looking for the one "correct" interpretation (14). *(e)* With adolescents, literary judgments and emotional involvements vary inversely. In other words, children and adolescents tend to suspend objectivity when emotionally involved (19). *(f)* The most common emotional involvements of adolescents in fiction seem to be "happiness binding" (the desire for a happy ending) and insistence upon certainty in interpretation (19). These half-dozen statements can be extended in a consideration of the process of interpretation. Perhaps the samples are enough to show that we are beginning to accumulate some research evidence about some of the psychological factors which are involved in interpretation, whether of a good story in a third reader, a chapter or poem in a high school anthology, or an individual example of an author's work.

Unfortunately, the evidence about effects at the fourth level of reading is sparse. Perhaps it will always be shaky in the scientific sense and we shall always have to rely in part on individual testimony regarding the effects of books or literature. Down through the generations great and good men have testified to the influence of a book or books in their lives. The Greeks believed in the effect of literature on the growing boy, and Plato wrote in

The Republic, "... we should do our utmost that the first stories that they hear should be so composed as to bring the fairest lessons of virtue to their ears." Much later, Stephen Vincent Benet wrote, "Books are not men and yet they are alive." Luther Burbank, the great horticulturist, testified that his whole life was changed by reading one book, *The Origin of the Species.* But the testimony of these and other men and women, interesting in itself, does not constitute evidence in the scientific sense. What about the individual's readiness for change? What about other supporting or conflicting influences in classroom, home, or community? Can a biography of sacrifice and social service influence a twelve-year-old girl for whose parents the good life consists of cocktail parties and Las Vegas week ends? If we as teachers are trying to influence the ideas and lives of young people through literature, we need to know much more about the role of the individual himself, the content of the materials, the total situation in which the reading takes place, and the overt reactions to be expected in speaking, writing, and action (14).

To some teachers such analysis of the four factors influencing the impact of reading on the individual makes the whole process needlessly complex. Not every teacher of reading in the fourth grade or of literature in the tenth grade can take time to know individual children and materials in such intimate fashion, nor can they easily arrange maximum environmental conditions for reading to affect individual development. Perhaps the problem is still one for research rather than classroom practice, and yet somehow the two must be combined. All elementary and secondary teachers of literature know that some pieces are more effective than others with a group but may not have tried to discover the reason. Why does one story "hit" a group of ten-year-olds or another, a group of fifteen-year-olds "just right"? What kind of matching of material and reader can a teacher accomplish? How can this be individualized at the secondary as well as the elementary school level? What are maximal conditions when "boy meets book"?

The evidence that reading affects lives is largely confined to the subjective, individual testimony illustrated above and to some reports of bibliotherapy in individual case studies (8,15,17,24). Studies by Russell (12), Smith (18), and Weingarten (22) have attempted to get at the effects of reading by requesting direct reports of them from teachers and from elementary and secondary school students. Such reports may all be too optimistic because of the desire of students to give congenial answers but they do suggest that the effects of reading may be widespread and sometimes profound. The present scattered findings can be substantiated or refuted by further research. Perhaps at the moment the teacher can only adopt the optimistic view that there are certain things that are true even if not experimentally verified. Perhaps such a faith is needed if one is to teach literature well. The possibilities are so vast that this article concludes with a few more examples of research explorations in unmapped territory.

Research on Interpretation

In addition to the investigation by Squire cited above and the studies supporting the six conclusions stated earlier, some careful investigations have been made of the interpretive process in reading. These date back at least to 1917, when Thorndike (20) published his classical study of ways children misinterpret paragraphs. One reason for flagrant errors in interpreting a factual passage he attributed to the overpotency of certain words. He said, "The mind is assailed as it were by every word in the paragraph. It must select, repress, soften, emphasize, correlate and organize, all under the influence of the right mental set or purpose or demand." This statement was explored further by Hinze (9) in a recent doctoral study at the University of California. She was interested in the cluster of associations the reader may have with certain words as explored by Jenkins, by Osgood and others. She first selected two passages, one factual (about scientific discoveries) and one emotionally charged (part of a Kafka story). Before the students saw these passages they were asked, in interview, to associate all the words they could with certain individual words from the two selections and to rate the words as positive or negative associations. Later, the students read each passage and interpreted its meaning. Hinze found clear evidence that when students had consistent emotional responses to the words in the passage, that is, all positive or all negative reactions, they tended to interpret the paragraphs objectively or "correctly," but when some of their emotional responses to the individual words were opposed to the dominant association, that is, when they had "conflict words," they had trouble giving a clear interpretation of the passage. Conflict words, in contrast to unidirectional words, caused significantly greater misinterpretation of the affective materials.

Some other investigations have given clues to the kinds of interpretation a teacher can expect. In a study (23) in England, the subject of the work was found to be most important for young children. Before they were twelve they made judgments about the ethical intention of the writer, and after twelve there emerged some feeling for "literary quality" as shown in structure and the aptness of simile or metaphor. In an American study, Harris (6) analyzed students' responses to literature into four types: translating; summarizing; inferring tone, mood, and intent; and relating technique and meaning. He devised tests of seven specific recognition skills but found on factor analysis of results that one general factor was adequate to account for the intercorrelations of the test results. This suggested that comprehension of literary materials may be a general function.

A study by Groff (5), however, emphasized the factors of individuality and attitude in interpreting paragraphs. He found that as a child reads critically, his interpretations are influenced by his attitude toward the content type of material read and his attitude toward reading as a school activity. In a factor analysis of scores on twenty-seven variables Bauer (2) found that achievement in reading was positively related to two variables, "self-expressiveness" and "drive for achievement," but negatively related to social adjustment and absence of excessive fears. Personality factors may influence reading behavior.

Another unpublished study of interpretation is that of Scribner (16), who found wide differences in the interpretation of poems by students, teachers of English, and literary critics. These differences are not great in the interpretation of relatively clear-cut poems such as Robert Frost's "The Road Not Taken." Even here, however, in a group of eighteen-year-olds, Scribner got such divergent interpretations of the main theme as

> The necessity of making decisions in life.
> The idea that one road may be better than the other.
> The idea that it is important to think for yourself and make your own decisions.
> He took the less travelled road.

These may seem varied responses from a group of eighteen-year-olds to a relatively simple poem, but Scribner found that variety in interpretation becomes much greater for the more "difficult" or ambiguous poem such as Blake's "Tiger," both in the student group itself and in terms of differences among students, teachers, and critics.

Why do students interpret a poem, story, or novel differently? We have already suggested one group of causes in the student or reader—his reading ability, his background of experience, his attitude and expectancies, his needs perhaps. The second group of causes lies in the piece of literature itself. As Hinze found, an overlap in these two occurs in the reader's associations with the individual words. It also occurs in the pupil's sensory perception of a poem or other piece of imaginative writing—his response to images in seeing, hearing, feeling, or even smelling. The piece of literature itself may affect the reader's interpretation through the arrangement or pattern; for example, the rhyme scheme or the use of onomatopoeia.

Finally, there is the symbolization in the story or poem. At the elementary level the lion is the symbol of courage, a flag of nationality, and Loki of trouble and mischief among the gods. With older children, we begin to get values attached to symbols. Some things are true and good, as motherhood, and some wrong or unworthy, as cowardice. Studies of school reading texts by Anderson (1) and by Child (3), of children's biographies by McConnell (10), and of best-selling fiction by Harvey (7) are examples of analyses of content of reading materials which *may* influence a reader. Thus the reader himself and the content of the material, particularly the symbolic content, may influence interpretation.

This research report is sketchy, and necessarily so. Most of it consists of spot checks instead of long-term studies of the effects of reading. We need to know much more about both cross-sectional and longitudinal aspects of each of the four factors influencing interpretation and personal development through reading. Since the days of the *New England Primer* we have had the feeling that, somehow, reading can help create a virtuous life. Almost three hundred years after the *Primer* perhaps the goal is still a good one.

References

1. Anderson, Paul S. "McGuffey *vs.* the Moderns in Character Training." *Phi Delta Kappan* 38 (November 1956):53-58.
2. Bauer, Edith B. "The Interrelatedness of Personality and Achievement in Reading." Ph.D. dissertation, University of California, Berkeley, 1956.
3. Child, Irwin L. *et al.* "Children's Textbooks and Personality Development: An Exploration in the Social Psychology of Education." *Psychological Monographs* 60, no. 3 (1946):54.
4. Clark, Charles M. "Teaching Sixth-Grade Students to Make Predictions from Reading Materials." Ph.D. dissertation, University of California, Berkeley, 1958.
5. Groff, Patrick J. "Children's Attitudes Toward Reading and Their Critical Reading Abilities in Four Content-Type Materials." Ph.D. dissertation, University of California, Berkeley, 1955.
6. Harris, Chester W. "Measurement of Comprehension of Literature." *School Review* 56 (May, June 1948):280-89, 332-43.
7. Harvey, John. "The Content Characteristics of Best-Selling Novels." *Public Opinion Quarterly* 17 (1953):91-114.
8. Herminghaus, Earl G. "The Effect of Bibliotherapy on the Attitudes and Personal and Social Adjustment of a Group of Elementary School Children." Ph.D. dissertation, Washington University, 1954.
9. Hinze, Helen A. "The Individual's Word Associations and His Interpretation of Prose Paragraphs." Ph.D. dissertation, University of California, Berkeley, 1959.
10. McConnell, Gaither A. "An Analysis of Biographical Literature for Children." Ph.D. dissertation, University of California, Berkeley, 1952.
11. Piekarz, Josephine A. "Getting Meaning from Reading." *Elementary School Journal* 56 (March 1956):303-9.
12. Russell, David H. "Teachers' Memories and Opinions of Children's Literature." *Elementary English* 26 (December 1949):475-82.
13. ———. "Personal Values in Reading." *The Reading Teacher* 12 (October 1958):3-9.
14. ———. "Some Research on the Impact of Reading." *English Journal* 47 (October 1958):398-413.

15. Russell, David H., and Shrodes, Caroline. "Contributions of Research in Bibliotherapy to the Language Arts Program." *School Review* 58 (September, October 1950):335-42, 411-20.
16. Scribner, Marion. "Responses of Students, Teachers and Critics to Selected Poems." In manuscript, University of California, Berkeley.
17. Shrodes, Caroline. "Bibliotherapy: A Theoretical and Clinical-Experimental Study." Ph.D. dissertation, University of California, Berkeley, 1949.
18. Smith, Nila B. "Some Effects of Reading on Children." *Elementary English* 25 (May 1948):271-78.
19. Squire, James R. "The Responses of Adolescents to Literature Involving Selected Experiences in Personal Development." Ph.D. dissertation, University of California, Berkeley, 1956.
20. Thorndike, Edward L. "Reading as Reasoning: A Study of Mistakes in Paragraph Reading." *Journal of Educational Psychology* 8 (June 1917):323-32.
21. Webster, W. Jane. "Some Effects of Stories on the Reduction of Fears of First Grade Children." M.A. Seminar Study, University of California, Berkeley, 1960.
22. Weingarten, Samuel. "Developmental Values in Voluntary Reading." *School Review* 62 (April 1954):222-30.
23. Williams. E. D.; Winter, L.; and Woods, J. K. "Tests of Literary Appreciation." *British Journal of Educational Psychology* 8 (November 1938):265-84.
24. Witty, Paul A. "Promoting Growth and Development Through Reading." *Elementary English* 27 (December 1950):493-500.

Richard S. Alm

Reading programs that do not emphasize the creative experience assiduously turn young people from reading. This author discusses five ways in which schools fail to encourage lifetime reading habits.

Goose Flesh and Glimpses of Glory

Every three years in Hawaii a large group of us who are devoted to the cause of bringing books and children together restore our souls and our faith in this cause by devoting countless hours and considerable effort to stage a book fair. Our fair is a simple one. We place on tables, in a colorful setting with beautiful art work, 3,000 new books—titles old and new—for youngsters, preschool age through junior high school and for interested adults, to see, to handle, to read, to enjoy. The fair is not a commercial event, but it is one in which the whole community gets involved, from janitors to Junior Leaguers.

The devotion to this project of a corps of volunteers and the willingness of several hundred members of the community to lend a hand have startled and puzzled observers. What do these people get out of the book fair? No money, no glory, no tangible return—except for one thing: appreciating the magic that occurs when child and book meet.

In acknowledging the Caldecott Medal, given to him in 1941, Robert Lawson voiced a plea which is really our motivation in Hawaii in having children's book fairs.

> ... We must give ... [our children] BOOKS. Books that will become tattered and grimy from use, not books too handsome to grovel with. Books that will make them weep, books that will rock them with hearty laughter. Books that absorb them so that they will have to be shaken loose from them. Books that they will put under their pillows at night. Books that give them goose flesh and glimpses of glory (7).

Richard S. Alm, "Goose Flesh and Glimpses of Glory," *English Journal.* Copyright © 1963 by the National Council of Teachers of English. Reprinted by permission of the publisher and Richard S. Alm.

Robert Lawson is talking obviously about the wonder that young children find in books, the wonder which for one reason or another dissipates as youngsters grow older. By the time they reach our high school English classrooms, most of them are rather jaded in their approach to literature.

Most of us, I assume, want our students to develop lifetime reading habits, to become, insofar as possible, *literary* men. All could not be, but surely more could be than the few who are now.

Have you read C. S. Lewis' definition of the literary man (8)? He notes that this kind of man is few in number. First, he is unlike the un-literary man who thinks the remark " 'I've read it already,' to be a conclusive argument against reading a work." Second, these literary men "are always looking for leisure and silence in which to read and do so with their whole attention. When they are denied such attentive and undisturbed reading even for a few days they feel impoverished." A third characteristic is that "the first reading of some literary work is often an experience so momentous that only experiences of love, religion or bereavement can furnish a standard of comparison. Their whole consciousness is changed. They have become what they were not before." And, finally, for those with this literary bent, "what they read is constantly and prominently present . . . they mouth over their favourite lines and stanzas in solitude. Scenes and characters from books provide them with a sort of iconography by which they interpret or sum up their own experience. They talk to one another about books, often and at length."

We English teachers would readily agree that the company of literary men seems to be a small one. At the same time we are aware of the riches in the world of books. Why, relatively, is such scant attention paid to these riches? I should like to focus on the *why* of this situation and then to offer a few observations.

Factors in Student Attitude

The change in our students' attitude toward books—from wonder to jadedness—is in part our doing. Let me note five factors:

1. *A primary difficulty is that we too often select the wrong books.* Last year I made a study of the classics being read as class assignments all over the country. The more than 500 responses to a questionnaire came from more than 400 communities. Here are some of the findings: 1. One of the great masterpieces of American literature, *Moby-Dick,* is taught as a class reading-in-common in every grade, seven through twelve. Surely there is a

good deal of *wrongness* in this selection in most of these schools. 2. The list of classics most commonly read by entire classes today does not differ markedly from the list read most commonly in 1900: *Julius Caesar, Macbeth, Silas Marner, A Tale of Two Cities, Hamlet, The Scarlet Letter, Idylls of the King, Merchant of Venice, The Odyssey, Ivanhoe.* Although we surely would not quarrel with all of these classics, we might object to the narrowness of the list. 3. Adaptations of the classics are used by twenty-five percent of the teachers who responded to the questionnaire. Ten percent use classic comics as an aid. Anyone who must resort to the use of an adaptation or a comic book to teach a literary selection is teaching the wrong selection to that group of students.

In this context I differ strongly with former Harvard president Conant's sympathetic point of view toward the use of adaptations of classics for the slow reader (2). Why prostitute literary masterpieces for such students when there are so many books—straightforward and honest—available for readers at all levels of reading performance today?

My point here is that we should teach those books which are best for a class. The teacher must, therefore, take on a greater responsibility than most teachers have or have sought. We are aiming for literary men. We want the best books that a group, or individuals within the group, can read with pleasure and profit. Literary excellence is one criterion; the capabilities of a class are another, a too-often neglected criterion.

2. *A related factor is that we sometimes expect too much of our students.* I believe that we must expect *all* that our students can give, but at this point I am saying that often our expectations are beyond what our students *can* give.

In *Longer Flight,* Annis Duff describes the reactions of her adolescent daughter and her classmates when a young, insensitive teacher began a study of "The Rime of the Ancient Mariner."

> Simply read through as the wonderful adventure of a ghostly ship and its crew, it would probably have been well liked. But discussion of its mystical and metaphysical aspects went against the grain because it was neither understandable nor interesting to eighth graders, and they refused to take it seriously. Inexperience betrayed the teacher into the further blunder of mistaking his students' perfectly legitimate—if ineptly expressed—protest for rebellion against his authority, and perhaps for a flouting of a poem he particularly admired. As a corrective measure he required every one of them to memorize all twenty stanzas of Part I! Nothing could have quenched more thoroughly any latent spark of response, and it was hard to know whom to feel sorrier for, the young man who had spoiled his honest intention of teaching the meaning of a magnificent poem, or the youngsters who unwillingly learned the words alone as a penalty for showing their own honest feeling (4).

That young teacher erred in the selection and the teaching of this literary piece. He made demands upon these youngsters which they could not meet.

3. *We expect the same book to be the same things to all readers.* Each person takes to a reading situation *his* intellect, the accumulation of *his* experiences, *his* emotions, *his* biases, *his* dreams, and all these determine what—the extent, the depth—he will understand and interpret. And yet, most teachers ignore this basic fact about reading by regimenting instruction. Literature is taught as if all students can and do read with the same understanding, insight, maturity.

Often, a teacher presents his own interpretation of literature as if by merely presenting it, he has actually made possible similar interpretations for his students. This, as Thomas Clark Pollock has pointed out, is the didactic error commonly found in English teaching.

4. *We get in the way of the book.* The literary artist tries to communicate directly to his readers, but often we teach as if what the writer has to say must be strained through our consciousness. Here certainly the teacher must learn to *shut up*—that is, admittedly, a difficult role for any teacher to play, but it is almost an absolute.

Janet M. Cotter has recently described her teaching of *The Old Man and the Sea.* Her guide is Carlos Baker's statement that Hemingway's novel is an example of open—rather than closed—literature. A characteristic of such literature is that it suggests, rather than dictates. Mrs. Cotter concludes her article:

> It is good for students to know that they, like the critics, have the right to let the book touch them as it will, to let it suggest rather than dictate its wider meanings. They will respond of their own accord to the beauty of this book, its power, its universal applications, and its memorable portrait of a humble and heroic man. It is the teacher's function to stand in the wings, allowing the book itself to occupy center stage (3).

To stand in the wings, however, is not to leave the theater. The teacher must be present to help the reader develop his own awareness. Kahlil Gibran describes this responsibility of teachers precisely: to lead the child to the threshold of his own mind. We want our students to gain as much as is reasonably possible, in knowledge, sensitivity, understanding, appreciation in reading any literary work, but we do not want to squeeze the fruit dry.

5. *We seem to view certain topics as important, possibly more important than the literary work.* Obviously, we do *not,* yet our actions often belie our beliefs. We emphasize the author's life, the milieu in which he wrote, the surface characteristics of the work. How many hours are spent in the scansion of poems with youngsters who have not yet succeeded in overcom-

ing their suspicions and resentment of poetry? Or how often do we try to discuss *point of view* in a short story with students who believe this is a matter of first person or third? To walk the "narrow ridge" is not easy, but this is what we must somehow learn to do.

These postures of the English teacher have surely been responsible in some measure for the change in our students' attitudes—from *wonder* to *what's the point?* Let us look now at what we might do to maintain our students' interest in literature.

Steps Toward Improvement

Basic to all other questions is the need for books. Obviously, in this American world of plenty we have not provided enough books. These figures were printed last spring in *Elementary English* (9):

> More than 40,700 schools in the United States have no school libraries, and 10,600,000 children attend these schools.
>
> Twenty-five million Americans have *no* public library service, and fifty million have only sub-standard service.
>
> Public schools with libraries have, on the average, only five books per pupil. Fewer than half of all college libraries have 50,000 volumes.

Our response, as English teachers, is typically: providing books is the taxpayer's responsibility. This means we overlook two facts: (1) *we* are taxpayers; (2) we should be a vocal element in our own communities in fighting for more books. Most teachers avoid the political arena, but here we have probably erred. As one of the chief guardians of the reading lives of our students, we *should* be a potent force with city and county officials or state legislatures. In a recent legislative session in Hawaii, the Hawaii Council of Teachers of English joined in a protest over a proposed cut in the library budget. Our voice was a small one, but a number of such small voices raised a loud cry, and the library budget passed the session untouched.

Since availability of books is, by all measures, the chief criterion of the amount of reading done, the providing of more books for our students is crucial.

A second demand made on us by our profession is to know books: (1) those that encompass our literary heritage; (2) those outstanding from the contemporary world of letters, books written for adults and those written expressly for the adolescent; and (3) the books our students are reading, because these books may not fall in either (1) or (2).

Goose Flesh and Glimpses of Glory   147

If we are to help our youngsters move from poor taste or pleasure with the mediocre to something better, we must know the kinds of things, specifically, which provide them with pleasure. To present only what seems to us the best is to perpetuate the decades-old error of English teachers everywhere: setting up standards for many who cannot understand such standards and see no relationship between the kind of book represented by the teacher's standard and the kind of reading which gives students satisfaction.

Knowing the kinds of books youngsters are reading is not to abandon standards nor to lower them. It does permit a realistic picture of how long the path to improved taste and judgment is and what that important first step for a student might be.

Further, for a teacher to understand an adolescent's world of books—those which Frank Jennings suggests are the under-the-desk or behind-the-textbook variety—is to build the confidence of the students in the knowledgeability of their teacher—about them *and* about books.

Another of our basic jobs is to know the adolescent and recognize the forces in his world today. Jennings has described this youngster:

> Here are young people, trembling on the threshold of adulthood. They want to know what it is like to hope and fail, to suffer, to die, to love wastefully. They want to have spelled out some of the awful consequences of going against society's grain. They want to dare greatly. They want to taste the fruits of values-in-action. The adolescent's world is fraught with change; its charms are "wound-up," its horizons are pulsing with expectancies and actualities. His most heartfelt cry is, as Sherwood Anderson warned us long ago, "I want to know why!" (6)

This adolescent lives in a day in which we view outer space as our frontier. A shot to the moon may take place almost momentarily.

Probably few people are fully aware of the implications of the stepped-up pace of today's world. Knowledge is accumulating in geometric progression, so fast that some companies find it cheaper to duplicate an experiment than to search for the results in print.

Competitors for the young person's time are more numerous and glamorous than ever before. In 1950 the U.S. Census reported fewer than 5,000,000 television sets in use. In 1960 the Census report was 65 million sets in 51 million households. How much do adolescents watch television? In a recent study of 2,000 junior and senior high school students in Texas (10), the investigators found that the junior high school student watched television, on the average, for more hours during a year than he spent in school. Although the high school student spent less time watching television, even he spent, on the average, 87% of the number of hours he spent in school in a year.

The adolescent of today is far different and lives in a different world from that of his counterpart of two decades ago. At the Secondary Section meeting last year, Dwight Burton condemned the boredom characteristic of many English classrooms today. One cause of such boredom, he said, is the teacher's failure to understand the modern high school student. The adolescent is a hardheaded materialist, well aware of the world in which he lives. Burton suggested that literature for such a reader "must be strong beer, not pink lemonade" (1).

The comments thus far have been about the most obvious necessities —providing books, knowing books, understanding adolescents—but these are not enough. Our greatest task, and the most difficult, is to help our students to become *involved* with the literature they read.

Necessity for Student Involvement

Unless the student himself deals with the ideas of the literary work and makes them a part of himself he has not really *read* that piece of literature. But how does a teacher help in the subtle process called, by Louise Rosenblatt, "a literary transaction." The teacher must be a guide but not a guard, one who stands in the wings rather than one who plays all the roles.

Essential to this involvement is the atmosphere created by the teacher in the classroom. The responsibility for interacting with a piece of literature is the student's, but the classroom must be pervaded by a spirit which permits a free expression of the *how* and *why* of this interaction. The adolescent reader must be free to comment upon, criticize, judge in whatever way he feels he must. This is not to suggest anarchy in the class but rather to underscore that youngsters to develop critical awareness must have the same freedoms we teachers want. If this freedom in the classroom is missing, the first wall has been built between the book and the young reader.

It is essential that the teacher help the young reader to find what Robert Heilman calls the *contemporariness* of literature. Heilman declares that the teacher of literature must be committed

> ... to a belief in the human constants which reappear, in whatever challenging diversity of dress, in all periods. The very diversity of dress may be of some advantage to us who are trying to ripen students, for the surface unfamiliarity may help reduce the exclusively emotional involvement that can make the literary experience only a state of heightened

excitement, make it all feeling and no knowledge. The more mature the work, the more it is, or is capable of being made, contemporary, and our job is to find the contemporariness, that is, the human constants that lie beneath all the different forms, styles, and idioms. And we have to believe that our students, as potential human beings, are capable of responding to the images of themselves and their kind—to their differences and their new depths—as they are refracted in multiple mirrors of literary artists (5).

Another essential for involvement is that students read works in which they can identify with the central characters or the theme. If they cannot do this—if the literature does not hit them deep down where they live (11), they will have not a literary experience, but the same kind of superficial reaction they may have to the headlines of any morning's newspaper.

All this suggests that a student must be involved in making judgments about the literary works in his curriculum. If a student believes a piece of literature is great because someone has told him it is great, he is not really reading; he is borrowing clichés and passing them off as his own.

In brief, it is our job as English teachers to help our students to develop a commitment to literature. Thornton Wilder's Emily says, "Oh, earth, you're too wonderful for anyone to realize you." She asks the Stage Manager: "Do any human beings ever realize life while they live it—every, every minute?" The Stage Manager answers, "No. . . . The saints and poets, maybe, they do some." It is the text of this paper that teachers of English must be among the chosen few if we are to realize one of our basic responsibilities.

The Teacher As Literary Man

Up to this point I have been concerned with problems and with some suggestions. Finally, we must focus on the key to whatever happens in the classroom—the teacher. To be a teacher of literature, one must be numbered among that company of literary men. We teachers of English must refresh ourselves continuously, with reading for our own pleasure and delight. Most teachers—even English teachers—read too little. Their reasons may be of the purest—they have too many themes to read, too many papers to correct. But the personal reading of the English teacher is as important to his students as the reading of another set of papers. Everyone's relationships with books must be nurtured. Besides we English teachers all need hyacinths for our souls. For each of us these hyacinths will be different. What, in the last month, have you read with great pleasure, possibly delight? To illustrate, my pleasures have been these: to discover Maurice Sendak's tiny four-volumed Nutshell Library, especially *Alligators All Around,* to explore again in Mencken's *The American Language,* to renew an old friendship with Paul Hazard's *Books, Children, and Men,* to see how Jean Lee Latham so successfully recreates another man of the sea—*John Ericsson of the Monitor*—to read with great pleasure Marcia Brown's *Once a Mouse,* to become absorbed in John Berryman's biography, *Stephen Crane,* to appreciate once again Thornton Wilder's *The Bridge of San Luis Rey.*

The need in teachers of English for a deep kinship with literature should mean something in the selection and preparation of teachers of English. Do literary men become high school teachers of English? Do we try to discover this characteristic, or more importantly, a lack of it? No, usually we count up credits in English, even if these are not synonymous with breadth of background, and may have very little to do with whether or not one is a literary man.

The English teacher who is not a literary man can be only a kind of carpenter in a classroom, never an artist. The high school student who maintains this wonder with books, who moves toward becoming a literary man, often does so in spite of, not as one inspired by such teachers. Students in the carpenter's classroom may learn certain facts, have certain experiences with literature, but literature for them, unless by accident, can bring no goose flesh, no glimpses of glory.

References

1. Burton, Dwight L. "Trailing Clouds of Boredom Do They Come." *English Journal* (April 1962):260-61.
2. Conant, James B. *Slums and Suburbs.* New York: McGraw-Hill Book Co., 1961, pp. 59-60.
3. Cotter, Janet M. *"The Old Man and the Sea:* An 'Open' Literary Experience." *English Journal* (October 1962):463.
4. Duff, Annis. *Longer Flight.* New York: The Viking Press, 1955, pp. 113-14.
5. Heilman, Robert B. "Literature and Growing Up." *English Journal* (September 1956): 310.
6. Jennings, Frank G. "Literature for Adolescents—Pap or Protein?" *English Journal* (December 1956):531.
7. Lawson, Robert, "The Caldecott Medal Acceptance." *The Horn Book* (July-August 1941):283-84.
8. Lewis, C. S. *An Experiment in Criticism.* Cambridge: Cambridge University Press, 1961, pp. 2-3.
9. "Some Notes on Libraries." *Elementary English* (May 1962):477.
10. SoRelle, Zell, and Walker, Jack. "What Is Television Doing to Our Children?" *Journal of Educational Research* (February 1962):236-7.
11. Ullman, James Ramsey. A paraphrase of a statement quoted in Carlsen, G. Robert. "Deep Down Beneath Where I Live." *English Journal* (May 1954):235.

CHAPTER SIX

In Search
of Social Realities

The complex and technological society of urban America is too diverse to rely upon primitive communications networks. As part of industrialization, mass media has become the expected way for the culture to find out about itself, to project its many images, to struggle to give favored values a place in the sun, to present alternative opinions for examination. Printed materials, because of their easy accessibility and relative permanence, have garnered a heavy share of this role.

A wide and diversified press presents a variety of values and attitudes for examination. The "free press" rubs shoulders with the "straight" daily newspaper and foreign language organs. Screen magazines vie for attention alongside horoscope information and intellectual fare. Fads and fashions compete for attention and set boundaries of socialization. In the press, the politically unsavory is pointed out as well as the risqué. Matinee idols are both declared and defamed as their behavior is alternately accepted and rejected. Screaming from headlines and billboards, the innermost urgings of American social patterns are made prominent, explored, and exaggerated.

The individual, the mythical man on the street, that is, that man who can and does read, responds to this massive bid for attention by making choices. It seems that he moves among the clamor selecting out those aspects which are nonthreatening or which reinforce the values he holds and rejecting or distorting those alien to him. He is not entirely impermeable to foreign values or tastes for they are sometimes couched in comfortable or desirable dress. Persuasive devices of the propagandist create a market for some otherwise obnoxious attitudes. Politically, he can be led to accept a war if it is said to protect the peace which he desires. He may develop a taste for cigaret smoking if he can be convinced it is the way that he will gain friends, maturity, or sophistication. As a part of this, the reader actively seeks, even if unconsciously, advice about the nature of the contemporary social milieu.

Nonreaders, those who *don't* as well as those who *can't* read, do not have this resource, this avenue of discovery of social reality. They are more acted upon than choice making as they respond to the salient features of everyday life. Their cultural deficit grows greater with every new twist of cultural consciousness.

T. W. Adorno

All mass media help define the nature of the culture in which they occur. Indeed, the choice of media as well as the content reflect and help define the very essence of the culture. In this article, written to analyze television, reading and other mass communications are examined in the perspective of the "mass culture."

How to Look at Television

The effect of television cannot be adequately expressed in terms of success or failure, likes or dislikes, approval or disapproval. Rather, an attempt should be made, with the aid of depth-psychological categories and previous knowledge of mass media, to crystallize a number of theoretical concepts by which the potential effect of television—its impact upon various layers of the spectator's personality—could be studied. It seems timely to investigate systematically socio-psychological stimuli typical of televised material both on a descriptive and psychodynamic level, to analyze their presuppositions as well as their total pattern, and to evaluate the effect they are likely to produce. This procedure may ultimately bring forth a number of recommendations on how to deal with these stimuli to produce the most desirable effect of television. By exposing the socio-psychological implications and mechanisms of television, which often operate under the guise of fake realism, not only may the shows be improved, but, more important possibly, the public at large may be sensitized to the nefarious effect of some of these mechanisms.

We are not concerned with the effectiveness of any particular show or program; but we are concerned with the nature of present-day television and its imagery. Yet, our approach is practical. The findings should be so close to the material, should rest on such a solid foundation of experience, that they can be translated into precise recommendations and be made convincingly clear to large audiences.

Copyright © 1954 by The Regents of the University of California. Reprinted from *Quarterly of Film, Radio and Television* (now *Film Quarterly*), Vol. VIII, No. 3, pp. 213-35, by permission of The Regents.

Improvement of television is not conceived primarily on an artistic, purely aesthetic level, extraneous to present customs. This does not mean that we naïvely take for granted the dichotomy between autonomous art and mass media. We all know that their relationship is highly complex. Today's rigid division between what is called "long-haired" and "short-haired" art is the product of a long historical development. It would be romanticizing to assume that formerly art was entirely pure, that the creative artist thought only in terms of the inner consistency of the artifact and not also of its effect upon the spectators. Theatrical art, in particular, cannot be separated from audience reaction. Conversely, vestiges of the aesthetic claim to be something autonomous, a world unto itself, remain even within the most trivial product of mass culture. In fact, the present rigid division of art into autonomous and commercial aspects is itself largely a function of commercialization. It was hardly accidental that the slogan *l'art pour l'art* was coined polemically in the Paris of the first half of the nineteenth century, when literature really became large-scale business for the first time. Many of the cultural products bearing the anticommercial trademark "art for art's sake" show traces of commercialism in their appeal to the sensational or in the conspicuous display of material wealth and sensuous stimuli at the expense of the meaningfulness of the work. This trend was pronounced in the neo-Romantic theater of the first decades of our century.

Older and Recent Popular Culture

In order to do justice to all such complexities, much closer scrutiny of the background and development of modern mass media is required than communications research, generally limited to present conditions, is aware of. One would have to establish what the output of contemporary cultural industry has in common with older "low" or popular forms of art as well as with autonomous art, and where the differences lie. Suffice it here to state that the archetypes of present popular culture were set comparatively early in the development of middle-class society—at about the turn of the seventeenth and the beginning of the eighteenth centuries in England. According to the studies of the English sociologist Ian Watt, the English novels of that period, particularly the works of Defoe and Richardson, marked the beginning of an approach to literary production that consciously created, served, and finally controlled a "market." Today the commercial production of cultural goods has become streamlined, and the impact of popular culture upon the individual has concomitantly increased. This process has not been confined to quantity, but has resulted in new qualities. While recent popular culture has absorbed all the elements and particularly all the "don'ts" of its predecessor, it differs decisively inasmuch as it has developed into a system. Thus, popular culture is no longer confined to certain forms such as novels or dance music, but has seized all media of artistic expression. The structure and meaning of these forms show an amazing parallelism, even when they appear to have little in common on the surface (such as jazz and the detective novel). Their output has increased to such an extent that it is almost impossible for anyone to dodge them; and even those formerly aloof from popular culture—the rural population on one hand and the highly educated on the other—are somehow affected. The more the system of "merchandising" culture is expanded, the more it tends also to assimilate the "serious" art of the past by adapting this art to the system's own requirements. The control is so extensive that any infraction of its rules is *a priori* stigmatized as "highbrow" and has but little chance to reach the population at large. The system's concerted effort results in what might be called the prevailing ideology of our time.

Certainly, there are many typical changes within today's pattern; e.g., men were formerly presented as erotically aggressive and women on the defensive, whereas this has been largely reversed in modern mass culture, as pointed out particularly by Wolfenstein and Leites. More important, however, is that the pattern itself, dimly perceptible in the early novels and basically preserved today, has by now become congealed and standardized. Above all, this rigid institutionalization transforms modern mass culture into a medium of undreamed of psychological control. The repetitiveness, the selfsameness, and the ubiquity of modern mass culture tend to make for automatized reactions and to weaken the forces of individual resistance.

When the journalist Defoe and the printer Richardson calculated the effect of their wares upon the audience, they had to speculate, to follow hunches; and therewith, a certain latitude to develop deviations remained. Such deviations have nowadays been reduced to a kind of multiple choice between very few alternatives. The following may serve as an illustration. The popular or semipopular novels of the first half of the nineteenth century, published in large quantities and serving mass consumption, were supposed to arouse tension in the reader. Although the victory of the good over the bad was generally provided for, the meandering and endless plots and subplots hardly allowed the readers of Sue and Dumas to be continuously aware of the moral. Readers could expect anything to happen. This no longer holds true. Every spectator of a television mystery knows with absolute certainty how it is going to end. Tension is but superficially maintained and is unlikely to have a serious effect any more. On the contrary, the spectator feels on safe ground all the time. This longing for "feeling on safe ground"—reflecting an infantile need for protection, rather than his desire for a thrill—is catered to. The element of excitement is preserved only with tongue in cheek. Such changes fall in line with the potential change from a freely competitive to a virtually "closed" society into which one wants to be admitted or from which one fears to be rejected. Everything somehow appears "predestined."

The increasing strength of modern mass culture is further enhanced by changes in the sociological structure of the audience. The old cultured elite does not exist any more; the modern intelligentsia only partially corresponds to it. At the same time, huge strata of the population formerly unacquainted with art have become cultural "consumers." Modern audiences, although probably less capable of the artistic sublimation bred by tradition, have become shrewder in their demands for perfection of technique and for reliability of information, as well as in their desire for "services"; and they have become more convinced of the consumers' potential power over the producer, no matter whether this power is actually wielded.

How changes within the audience have affected the meaning of popular culture may also be illustrated. The element of internalization played a decisive role in early Puritan popular novels of the Richardson type. This element no longer prevails, for it was based on the essential role of "inwardness" in both original Protestantism and earlier middle-class society. As the profound influence of the basic tenets of Protestantism has gradually receded, the cultural pattern has become more and more opposed to the "introvert." As Riesman puts it,

> ... the conformity of earlier generations of Americans of the type I term "inner-directed" was mainly assured by their internalization of adult authority. The middle-class urban American of today, the "other-directed," is, by contrast, in a characterological sense more the product of his peers—that is, in sociological terms, his "peer-groups," the other kids at school or in the block (1).

This is reflected by popular culture. The accents on inwardness, inner conflicts, and psychological ambivalence (which play so large a role in earlier popular novels and on which their originality rests) have given way to unproblematic, cliché-like characterization. Yet the code of decency that governed the inner conflicts of the Pamelas, Clarissas, and Lovelaces remains almost literally intact.* The middle-class "ontology" is preserved in

---

*The evolution of the ideology of the extrovert has probably also its long history, particularly in the lower types of popular literature during the nineteenth century when the code of decency became divorced from its religious roots and therewith attained more and more the character of an opaque taboo. It seems likely, however, that in this respect the triumph of the films marked the decisive step. Reading as an act of perception and apperception probably carries with itself a certain kind of internalization; the act of reading a novel fairly close to a *monologue interieur*. Visualization in modern mass media makes for externalization. The idea of inwardness, still maintained in older portrait painting through the expressiveness of the face, gives way to unmistakable optical signals that can be grasped at a glance. Even if a character in a movie or television show is not what he appears to be, his appearance is treated in such a way as to leave no doubt about his true nature. Thus a villain who is not presented as a brute must at least be "suave," and his repulsive slickness and mild manner unambiguously indicate what we are to think of him.

an almost fossilized way, but is severed from the mentality of the middle classes. By being superimposed on people with whose living conditions and mental make-up it is no longer in accord, this middle-class "ontology" assumes an increasingly authoritarian and at the same time hollow character.

The overt "naïveté" of older popular culture is avoided. Mass culture, if not sophisticated, must at least be up to date—that is to say, "realistic," or posing as realistic—in order to meet the expectations of a supposedly disillusioned, alert, and hard-boiled audience. Middle-class requirements bound up with internalization—such as concentration, intellectual effort, and erudition—have to be continuously lowered. This does not hold only for the United States, where historical memories are scarcer than in Europe; but it is universal, applying to England and Continental Europe as well.*

However, this apparent progress of enlightenment is more than counter-balanced by retrogressive traits. The earlier popular culture maintained a certain equilibrium between its social ideology and the actual social conditions under which its consumers lived. This probably helped to keep the border line between popular and serious art during the eighteenth century more fluid than it is today. Abbé Prévost was one of the founding fathers of French popular literature; but his *Manon Lescaut* is completely free from clichés, artistic vulgarisms, and calculated effects. Similarly, later in the eighteenth century, Mozart's *Zauberfloete* struck a balance between the "high" and the popular style which is almost unthinkable today.

The curse of modern mass culture seems to be its adherence to the almost unchanged ideology of early middle-class society, whereas the lives of its consumers are completely out of phase with this ideology. This is probably the reason for the gap between the overt and the hidden "message" of modern popular art. Although on an overt level the traditional values of English Puritan middle-class society are promulgated, the hidden message aims at a frame of mind which is no longer bound by these values. Rather, today's frame of mind transforms the traditional values into the norms of an increasingly hierarchical and authoritarian social structure. Even here it has to be admitted that authoritarian elements were also present in the older ideology which, of course, never fully expressed the truth. But the "message" of adjustment and unreflecting obedience seems to be dominant and all-pervasive today. Whether maintained values derived from religious ideas obtain a different meaning when severed from their root should be carefully examined. For example, the concept of the "purity" of women is one of the invariables of popular culture. In the earlier phase this concept

---

*It should be noted that the tendency against "erudition" was already present at the very beginning of popular culture, particularly in Defoe, who was consciously opposed to the learned literature of his day, and has become famous for having scorned every refinement of style and artistic construction in favor of an apparent faithfulness to "life."

is treated in terms of an inner conflict between concupiscence and the internalized Christian ideal of chastity, whereas in today's popular culture it is dogmatically posited as a value *per se*. Again, even the rudiments of this pattern are visible in productions such as *Pamela*. There, however, it seems a by-product; whereas in today's popular culture the idea that only the "nice girl" gets married and that she must get married at any price has come to be accepted before Richardson's conflicts even start.*

The more inarticulate and diffuse the audience of modern mass media seems to be, the more mass media tend to achieve their "integration." The ideals of conformity and conventionalism were inherent in popular novels from the very beginning. Now, however, these ideals have been translated into rather clear-cut prescriptions of what to do and what not to do. The outcome of conflicts is established, and all conflicts are mere sham. Society is always the winner, and the individual is only a puppet manipulated through social rules. True, conflicts of the nineteenth-century type—such as women running away from their husbands, the drabness of provincial life, and daily chores—occur frequently in today's magazine stories. However, with a regularity which challenges quantitative treatment, these conflicts are decided in favor of the very same conditions from which these women want to break away. The stories teach their readers that one has to be "realistic," that one has to give up romantic ideas, that one has to adjust oneself at any price, and that nothing more can be expected of any individual. The perennial middle-class conflict between individuality and society has been reduced to a dim memory, and the message is invariably that of identification with the *status quo*. This theme too is not new, but its unfailing universality invests it with an entirely different meaning. The constant plugging of conventional values seems to mean that these values have lost their substance, and that it is feared that people would really follow their instinctual urges and conscious insights unless continuously reassured from outside that they must not do so. The less the message is

---

* One of the significant differences seems to be that in the eighteenth century the concept of popular culture itself moving toward an emancipation from the absolutistic and semifeudal tradition had a progressive meaning, stressing autonomy of the individual as being capable of making his own decisions. This means, among other things, that the early popular literature left space for authors who violently diagreed with the pattern set by Richardson and, nevertheless, obtained popularity of their own. The most prominent case in question is that of Fielding, whose first novel started as a parody of Richardson. It would be interesting to compare the popularity of Richardson and Fielding at that time. Fielding hardly achieved the same success as Richardson. Yet it would be absurd to assume that today's popular culture would allow the equivalent of a *Tom Jones*. This may illustrate the contention of the "rigidity" of today's popular culture. A crucial experiment would be to make an attempt to base a movie on a novel such as Evelyn Waugh's *The Loved One*. It is almost certain that the script would be rewritten and edited so often that nothing remotely similar to the idea of the original would be left.

really believed and the less it is in harmony with the actual existence of the spectators, the more categorically it is maintained in modern culture. One may speculate whether its inevitable hypocrisy is concomitant with punitiveness and sadistic sternness.

Multilayered Structure

A depth-psychological approach to television has to be focused on its multilayered structure. Mass media are not simply the sum total of the actions they portray or of the messages that radiate from these actions. Mass media also consist of various layers of meanings superimposed on one another, all of which contribute to the effect. True, due to their calculative nature, these rationalized products seem to be more clear-cut in their meaning than authentic works of art, which can never be boiled down to some unmistakable "message." But the heritage of polymorphic meaning has been taken over by cultural industry inasmuch as what it conveys becomes itself organized in order to enthrall the spectators on various psychological levels simultaneously. As a matter of fact, the hidden message may be more important than the overt, since this hidden message will escape the controls of consciousness, will not be "looked through," will not be warded off by sales resistance, but it is likely to sink into the spectator's mind.

Probably all the various levels in mass media involve *all* the mechanisms of consciousness and unconsciousness stressed by psychoanalysis. The difference between the surface content, the overt message of televised material, and its hidden meaning is generally marked and rather clear-cut. The rigid superimposition of various layers probably is one of the features by which mass media are distinguishable from the integrated products of autonomous art, where the various layers are much more thoroughly fused. The full effect of the material on the spectator cannot be studied without consideration of the hidden meaning in conjunction with the overt one, and it is precisely this interplay of various layers which has hitherto been neglected and which will be our focus. This is in accordance with the assumption shared by numerous social scientists that certain political and social trends of our time, particularly those of a totalitarian nature, feed to a considerable extent on irrational and frequently unconscious motivations. Whether the conscious or the unconscious message of our material is more important is hard to predict and can be evaluated only after careful analysis. We do appreciate, however, that the overt message can be interpreted much more adequately in the light of psychodynamics—i.e., in its relation to instinctual urges as well as control—than by looking at the overt in a naïve way and by ignoring its implications and presuppositions.

The relation between overt and hidden message will prove highly complex in practice. Thus, the hidden message frequently aims at reinforcing conventionally rigid and "pseudo-realistic" attitudes similar to the accepted ideas more rationalistically propagated by the surface message. Conversely, a number of repressed gratifications which play a large role on the hidden level are somehow allowed to manifest themselves on the surface in jests, off-color remarks, suggestive situations, and similar devices. All this interaction of various levels, however, points in some definite direction: the tendency to channelize audience reaction. This falls in line with the suspicion widely shared, though hard to corroborate by exact data, that the majority of television shows today aim at producing, or at least reproducing, the very smugness, intellectual passivity, and gullibility that seem to fit in with totalitarian creeds even if the explicit surface message of the shows may be antitotalitarian.

With the means of modern psychology, we will try to determine the primary prerequisites of shows eliciting mature, adult, and responsible reactions—implying not only in content but in the very way things are being looked at, the idea of autonomous individuals in a free democratic society. We perfectly realize that any definition of such an individual will be hazardous; but we know quite well what a human being deserving of the appellation "autonomous individual" should *not* be, and this "not" is actually the focal point of our consideration.

When we speak of the multilayered structure of television shows, we are thinking of various superimposed layers of different degrees of manifestness or hiddenness that are utilized by mass culture as a technological means of "handling" the audience. This was expressed felicitously by Leo Lowenthal when he coined the term "psychoanalysis in reverse." The implication is that somehow the psychoanalytic concept of a multilayered personality has been taken up by cultural industry, and that the concept is used in order to ensnare the consumer as completely as possible and in order to engage him psychodynamically in the service of premeditated effects. A clear-cut division into allowed gratifications, forbidden gratifications, and recurrence of the forbidden gratifications in a somewhat modified and deflected form is carried through.

To illustrate the concept of the multilayered structure: the heroine of an extremely light comedy of pranks is a young schoolteacher who is not only underpaid but is incessantly fined by the caricature of a pompous and authoritarian school principal. Thus, she has no money for her meals and is actually starving. The supposedly funny situations consist mostly of her trying to hustle a meal from various acquaintances, but regularly without success. The mention of food and eating seems to induce laughter—an

observation that can frequently be made and invites a study of its own.*
Overtly, the play is just slight amusement mainly provided by the painful situations into which the heroine and her arch-opponent constantly run. The script does not try to "sell" any idea. The "hidden meaning" emerges simply by the way the story looks at human beings; thus the audience is invited to look at the characters in the same way without being made aware that indoctrination is present. The character of the underpaid, maltreated schoolteacher is an attempt to reach a compromise between prevailing scorn for the intellectual and the equally conventionalized respect for "culture." The heroine shows such an intellectual superiority and high-spiritedness that identification with her is invited, and compensation is offered for the inferiority of her position and that of her ilk in the social setup. Not only is the central character supposed to be very charming, but she wisecracks constantly. In terms of a set pattern of identification, the script implies: "If you are as humorous, good-natured, quick-witted, and charming as she is, do not worry about being paid a starvation wage. You can cope with your frustration in a humorous way; and your superior wit and cleverness put you not only above material privations, but also above the rest of mankind." In other words, the script is a shrewd method of promoting adjustment to humiliating conditions by presenting them as objectively comical and by giving a picture of a person who experiences even her own inadequate position as an object of fun apparently free of any resentment.

Of course, this latent message cannot be considered as unconscious in the strict psychological sense, but rather as "inobtrusive"; this message is hidden only by a style which does not pretend to touch anything serious and expects to be regarded as featherweight. Nevertheless, even such amusement tends to set patterns for the members of the audience without their being aware of it.

Another comedy of the same thesis is reminiscent of the funnies. A cranky old woman sets up the will of her cat (Mr. Casey) and makes as heirs some of the schoolteachers in the permanent cast. Later the actual inheritance is found to consist of the cat's valueless toys. The plot is so constructed that each heir, at the reading of the will, is tempted to act as if he had known this person (Mr. Casey). The ultimate point is that the cat's owner had placed a hundred-dollar bill inside each of the toys; and the heirs run to the incinerator in order to recover their inheritance. The audience

---

*The more rationality (the reality principle) is carried to extremes, the more its ultimate aim (actual gratification) tends, paradoxically, to appear as "immature" and ridiculous. Not only eating, but also uncontrolled manifestations of sexual impulses tend to provoke laughter in audiences—kisses in motion pictures have generally to be led up to, the stage has to be set for them, in order to avoid laughter. Yet mass culture never completely succeeds in wiping out potential laughter. Induced, of course, by the supposed infantilism of sensual pleasures, laughter can largely be accounted for by the mechanism of repression. Laughter is a defense against the forbidden fruit.

is given to understand: "Don't expect the impossible, don't day-dream, but be realistic." The denunciation of that archetypical daydream is enhanced by the association of the wish for unexpected and irrational blessings with dishonesty, hypocrisy, and a generally undignified attitude. The spectator is given to understand: "Those who dare daydream, who expect that money will fall to them from heaven, and who forget any caution about accepting an absurd will are at the same time those whom you might expect to be capable of cheating."

Here, an objection may be raised: Is such a sinister effect of the hidden message of television known to those who control, plan, write, and direct shows? Or it may even be asked: Are those traits possible projections of the unconscious of the decision-makers' own minds according to the widespread assumption that works of art can be properly understood in terms of psychological projections of their authors? As a matter of fact, it is this kind of reasoning that has led to the suggestion that a special sociopsychological study of decision-makers in the field of television be made. We do not think that such a study would lead us very far. Even in the sphere of autonomous art, the idea of projection has been largely overrated. Although the authors' motivations certainly enter the artifact, they are by no means so all-determining as is often assumed. As soon as an artist has set himself his problem, it obtains some kind of impact of its own; and, in most cases, he has to follow the objective requirements of his product much more than his own urges of expression when he translates his primary conception into artistic reality. To be sure, these objective requirements do not play a decisive role in mass media, which stress the effect on the spectator far beyond any artistic problem. However, the total setup here tends to limit the chances of the artists' projections utterly. Those who produce the material follow, often grumblingly, innumerable requirements, rules of thumb, set patterns, and mechanisms of controls which by necessity reduce to a minimum the range of any kind of artistic self-expression. The fact that most products of mass media are not produced by one individual but by collective collaboration—as happens to be true with most of the illustrations so far discussed—is only one contributing factor to this generally prevailing condition. To study television shows in terms of the psychology of the authors would almost be tantamount to studying Ford cars in terms of the psychoanalysis of the late Mr. Ford.

Presumptuousness

The typical psychological mechanisms utilized by television shows and the devices by which they are automatized function only within a small number of given frames of reference operative in television communication, and the socio-psychological effect largely depends on them. We are all familiar with the division of television content into various classes, such as light comedy, westerns, mysteries, so-called sophisticated plays, and others. These types have developed into formulas which, to a certain degree, preestablished the attitudinal pattern of the spectator before he is confronted with any specific content and which largely determine the way in which any specific content is being perceived.

In order to understand television, it is, therefore, not enough to bring out the implications of various shows and types of shows; but an examination must be made of the presuppositions within which the implications function before a single word is spoken. Most important is that the typing of shows has gone so far that the spectator approaches each one with a set pattern of expectations before he faces the show itself—just as the radio listener who catches the beginning of Tschaikowsky's Piano Concerto as a theme song, knows automatically, "Aha, serious music!" or, when he hears organ music, responds equally automatically, "Aha, religion!" These halo effects of previous experiences may be psychologically as important as the implications of the phenomena themselves for which they have set the stage; and these presuppositions should, therefore, be treated with equal care.

When a television show bears the title "Dante's Inferno," when the first shot is that of a night club by the same name, and when we find sitting at the bar a man with his hat on and at some distance from him a sad-looking, heavily made-up woman ordering another drink, we are almost certain that some murder will shortly be committed. The apparently individualized situation actually works only as a signal that moves our expectations into a definite direction. If we had never seen anything but "Dante's Inferno," we probably would not be sure about what was going to happen; but, as it is, we are actually given to understand by both subtle and not so subtle devices that this is a crime play, that we are entitled to expect some sinister and probably hideous and sadistic deeds of violence, that the hero will be saved from a situation from which he can hardly be expected to be saved, that the woman on the barstool is probably not the main criminal but is likely to lose her life as a gangster's moll, and so on. This conditioning to such universal patterns, however, scarcely stops at the television set.

The way the spectator is made to look at apparently everyday items, such as a night club, and to take as hints of possible crime common settings of his daily life, induces him to look at life itself as though it and its conflicts could generally be understood in such terms.* This, convincingly enough,

---

*This relationship again should not be oversimplified. No matter to what extent modern mass media tend to blur the difference between reality and the esthetic, our realistic spectators are still aware that all is "in fun." It cannot be assumed that the direct primary perception of reality takes place within the television frame of reference, although many movie-goers recall the alienation of familiar sights when leaving the theater: everything still has the appearance of being part of the movie plot. What is more important is the interpretation of reality in terms of psychological carry-overs, the preparedness to see ordinary objects as though some threatening mystery were hidden behind them. Such an attitude seems to be syntonic with mass delusions such as suspicion of omnipresent graft, corruption, and conspiracy.

may be the nucleus of truth in the old-fashioned arguments against all kinds of mass media for inciting criminality in the audience. The decisive thing is that this atmosphere of the normality of crime, its presentation in terms of an average expectation based on life situations, is never expressed in so many words but is established by the overwhelming wealth of material. It may affect certain spectator groups more deeply than the overt moral of crime and punishment regularly derived from such shows. What matters is not the importance of crime as a symbolic expression of otherwise controlled sexual or aggressive impulses, but the confusion of this symbolism with a pedantically maintained realism in all matters of direct sense perception. Thus, empirical life becomes infused with a kind of meaning that virtually excludes adequate experience no matter how obstinately the veneer of such "realism" is built up. This affects the social and psychological function of drama.

It is hard to establish whether the spectators of Greek tragedy really experienced the catharsis Aristotle described—in fact this theory, evolved after the age of tragedy was over, seems to have been a rationalization itself, an attempt to state the purpose of tragedy in pragmatic, quasi-scientific terms. Whatever the case, it seems pretty certain that those who saw the *Oresteia* of Aeschylus or Sophocles' *Oedipus* were not likely to translate these tragedies (the subject matter of which was known to everyone, and the interest in which was centered in artistic treatment) directly into everyday terms. This audience did not expect that on the next corner of Athens similar things would go on. Actually, pseudo-realism allows for the direct and extremely primitive identification achieved by popular culture; and it presents a facade of trivial buildings, rooms, dresses, and faces as though they were the promise of something thrilling and exciting taking place at any moment.

In order to establish this socio-psychological frame of reference, one would have to follow up systematically categories—such as the normality of crime or pseudo-realism and many others—to determine their structural unity and to interpret the specific devices, symbols, and stereotypes in relation to this frame of reference. We hypothesize at this phase that the frames of reference and the individual devices will tend in the same direction.

Only against psychological backdrops such as pseudo-realism and against implicit assumptions such as the normality of crime can the specific stereotypes of television plays be interpreted. The very standardization indicated by set frames of reference automatically produces a number of stereotypes. Also, the technology of television production makes stereotypy almost inevitable. The short time available for the preparation of scripts and the vast material continuously to be produced call for certain formulas. Moreover, in plays lasting only a quarter to half an hour each, it appears inevitable that the kind of person the audience faces each time should be indicated drastically through red and green lights. We are not dealing with the problem of the existence of stereotypes as such. Since stereotypes are an indispensable element of the organization and anticipation of experience, preventing us from falling into mental disorganization and chaos, no art can entirely dispense with them. Again, the functional change is what concerns us. The more stereotypes become reified and rigid in the present setup of cultural industry, the less people are likely to change their preconceived ideas with the progress of their experience. The more opaque and complicated modern life becomes, the more people are tempted to cling desperately to clichés which seem to bring some order into the otherwise ununderstandable. Thus, people may not only lose true insight into reality, but ultimately their very capacity for life experience may be dulled by the constant wearing of blue and pink spectacles.

Stereotyping

In coping with this danger, we may not do full justice to the meaning of some of the stereotypes which are to be dealt with. We should never forget that there are two sides to every psychodynamic phenomenon, the unconscious or id element and the rationalization. Although the latter is psychologically defined as a defense mechanism, it may very well contain some nonpsychological, objective truth which cannot simply be pushed aside on account of the psychological function of the rationalization. Thus some of the stereotypical messages, directed toward particularly weak spots in the mentality of large sectors of the population, may prove to be quite legitimate. However, it may be said with fairness that the questionable blessings of morals, such as "one should not chase after rainbows," are largely overshadowed by the threat of inducing people to mechanical simplifications by ways of distorting the world in such a way that it seems to fit into pre-established pigeonholes.

The example here selected, however, should indicate rather drastically the danger of stereotypy. A television play concerning a fascist dictator, a kind of hybrid between Mussolini and Peron, shows the dictator in a moment of crisis; and the content of the play is his inner and outer collapse. Whether the cause of his collapse is a popular upheaval or a military revolt is never made clear. But neither this issue nor any other of a social or political nature enters the plot itself. The course of events takes place exclusively on a private level. The dictator is just a heel who treats sadistically both his secretary and his "lovely and warmhearted" wife. His antagonist, a general, was formerly in love with the wife; and they both still love each other, although the wife sticks loyally to her husband. Forced by her husband's brutality, she attempts flight, and is intercepted by the general, who wants to save her. The turning point occurs when the guards surround the palace to defend the dictator's popular wife. As soon as they learn that she has departed, the guards quit; and the dictator, whose "inflated ego" explodes at the same time, gives up. The dictator is nothing but a bad, pompous, and cowardly man. He seems to act with extreme stupidity; nothing of the objective dynamics of dictatorship comes out. The impression is created that totalitarianism grows out of character disorders of ambitious politicians, and is overthrown by the honesty, courage, and warmth of those figures with whom the audience is supposed to identify. The standard device employed is that of the spurious personalization of objective issues. The representatives of ideas under attack, as in the case of the fascists here, are presented as villains in a ludicrous cloak-and-dagger fashion, whereas those who fight for the "right cause" are personally idealized. This not only distracts from any real social issues but also enforces the psychologically extremely dangerous division of the world into black (the outgroup) and white (we, the ingroup). Certainly, no artistic production can deal with ideas or political creeds *in abstracto* but has to present them in terms of their concrete impact upon human beings; yet it would be utterly futile to present individuals as mere specimens of an abstraction, as puppets expressive of an idea. In order to deal with the concrete impact of totalitarian systems, it would be more commendable to show how the life of ordinary people is affected by terror and impotence than to cope with the phony psychology of the big-shots, whose heroic role is silently endorsed by such a treatment even if they are pictured as villains. There seems to be hardly any question of the importance of an analysis of pseudo-personalization and its effect, by no means limited to television.

Although pseudo-personalization denotes the stereotyped way of "looking at things" in television, we should also point out certain stereotypes in the narrower sense. Many television plays could be characterized by the sobriquet "a pretty girl can do no wrong." The heroine of a light comedy is, to use George Legman's term, "a bitch heroine." She behaves toward her father in an incredibly inhuman and cruel manner only slightly rationalized as "merry pranks." But she is punished very slightly, if at all. True, in real life bad deeds are rarely punished at all, but this cannot be applied to television. Here, those who have developed the production code for the movies seem right: what matters in mass media is not what happens in real life, but rather the positive and negative "messages," prescriptions, and taboos that the spectator absorbs by means of identification with the material he is looking at. The punishment given to the pretty heroine only nominally fulfills the conventional requirements of the conscience for a second. But the spectator is given to understand that the pretty heroine really gets away with everything just because she is pretty.

The attitude in question seems to be indicative of a universal penchant. In another sketch that belongs to a series dealing with the confidence racket, the attractive girl who is an active participant in the racket not only is paroled after having been sentenced to a long term, but also seems to have a good chance of marrying her victim. Her sex morality, of course, is unimpeachable. The spectator is supposed to like her at first sight as a modest and self-effacing character, and he must not be disappointed. Although it is discovered that she is a crook, the original identification must be restored, or rather maintained. The stereotype of the nice girl is so strong that not even the proof of her delinquency can destroy it; and, by hook or by crook, she must be what she appears to be. It goes without saying that such psychological models tend to confirm exploitative, demanding, and aggressive attitudes on the part of young girls—a character structure which has come to be known in psychoanalysis under the name of oral aggressiveness.

Sometimes such stereotypes are disguised as national American traits, a part of the American scene where the image of the haughty, egoistic, yet irresistible girl who plays havoc with poor dad has come to be a public institution. This way of reasoning is an insult to the American spirit. High-pressure publicity and continuous plugging to institutionalize some obnoxious type does not make the type a sacred symbol of folklore. Many considerations of an apparently anthropological nature today tend only to veil objectionable trends, as though they were of an ethnological, quasi-natural character. Incidentally, it is amazing to what degree television material even on superficial examination brings to mind psychoanalytic concepts with the qualification of being a psychoanalysis in reverse. Psychoanalysis has described the oral syndrome combining the antagonistic trends of aggressive and dependent traits. This character syndrome is closely indicated by the pretty girl who can do no wrong, who, while being aggressive against her father exploits him at the same time, depending on him as much as, on the surface level, she is set against him. The difference between the sketch and psychoanalysis is simply that the sketch exalts the very same syndrome which is treated by psychoanalysis as a reversion to infantile developmental phases and which the psychoanalyst tries to dissolve. It remains to be seen whether something similar applies as well to some types of male heroes, particularly the super-he-man. It may well be that he too can do no wrong.

Finally, we should deal with a rather widespread stereotype which, inasmuch as it is taken for granted by television, is further enhanced. At the same time, the example may serve to show that certain psychoanalytic interpretations of cultural stereotypes are not really too far-fetched; the latent ideas that psychoanalysis attributes to certain stereotypes come to the surface. There is the extremely popular idea that the artist is not only maladjusted, introverted, and *a priori* somewhat funny; but that he is really an "aesthete," a weakling, and a "sissy." In other words, modern synthetic folklore tends to identify the artist with the homosexual and to respect only the "man of action" as a real, strong man. This idea is expressed in a surprisingly direct manner in one of the comedy scripts at our disposal. It portrays a young man who is not only the "dope" who appears so often on television but is also a shy, retiring, and accordingly untalented poet, whose moronic poems are ridiculed.* He is in love with a girl but is too weak and insecure to indulge in the necking practices she rather crudely suggests; the girl, on her part, is caricatured as a boy-chaser. As happens frequently in mass culture, the roles of the sexes are reversed—the girl is utterly aggressive, the boy, utterly afraid of her, describes himself as "woman-handled" when she manages to kiss him. There are vulgar innuendos of homosexuality of which one may be quoted: the heroine tells her boy friend that another boy is in love with someone, and the boy friend asks, "What's he in love with?" She answers, "A girl, of course," and her boy friend replies, "Why, of course? Once before it was a neighbor's turtle, and what's more its name was Sam." This interpretation of the artist as innately incompetent and a social outcast (by the innuendo of sexual inversion) is worthy of examination.

We do not pretend that the individual illustrations and examples, or the theories by which they are interpreted, are basically new. But in view of the cultural and pedagogical problem presented by television, we do not think that the novelty of the specific findings should be a primary concern. We know from psychoanalysis that the reasoning, "But we know all this!" is often a defense. This defense is made in order to dismiss insights as irrelevant because they are actually uncomfortable and make life more difficult for us than it already is by shaking our conscience when we are supposed to enjoy the "simple pleasure of life." The investigation of the television problems we have here indicated and illustrated by a few examples selected at random demands, most of all, taking seriously notions dimly

---

* It could be argued that this very ridicule expresses that this boy is not meant to represent the artist but just the "dope." But this is probably too rationalistic. Again, as in the case of the schoolteacher, official respect for culture prevents caricaturing the artist as such. However, by characterizing the boy, among other things by his writing poetry, it is indirectly achieved that the artistic activities and silliness are associated with each other. In many respects mass culture is organized much more by way of such associations than in strictly logical terms. It may be added that quite frequently attacks on any social type seek protection by apparently presenting the object of the attack as an exception, while it is understood by innuendo that he is considered as a specimen of the whole concept.

familiar to most of us by putting them into their proper context and perspective and by checking them by pertinent material. We propose to concentrate on issues of which we are vaguely but uncomfortably aware, even at the expense of our discomfort's mounting, the further and the more systematically our studies proceed. The effort here required is of a moral nature itself: knowingly to face psychological mechanisms operating on various levels in order not to become blind and passive victims. We can change this medium of far-reaching potentialities only if we look at it in the same spirit which we hope will one day be expressed by its imagery.

References

1. Riesman, David. *The Lonely Crowd.* New Haven: Yale University Press, 1950, p. 5.

R. Phillip Carter, Jr.

The person who does not read as well as the person who cannot read is disenfranchised, disconnected from enhancing social communication. Those who read are more socially mature than those who do not. Here, a study in education explores some of the dimensions of the social perception of retarded readers.

The Adult Social Adjustment of Retarded and Non-Retarded Readers

Sociologists attest that contemporary society is more complex than ever before. The velocity with which changes are taking place on the local, state, national, and international levels makes the intricacies of living more demanding of each individual. Shifts in the labor force call for increased education, while more and more vocations insist upon a high school diploma as a minimum job requirement. With increased autonomy, the decision-making process often rests solely with the individual. Therefore, if an individual is to make critical evaluations and rational decisions, he must be well informed. He must be cognizant of his environment and integrated with it. Research has indicated that the possession of effective reading skills facilitates this integration process as well as enhancing personal and social adjustment. That is to say, adequate mastery of the various reading skills promotes the self-assurance which enables a person to participate in social communication. This then leads to social acceptance, which in turn provides a sense of security.

Research has indicated that failure to learn to read often results in personal and social maladjustment in and out of school with prevalent symptoms of nervous tension, bold front, retreat reactions, counter-attack, withdrawn reactions, extreme self-consciousness, submission, timidity, and indifferent and recalcitrant reactions. Aggressive behavior and marked fears are also noted within groups of reading failures (1,3,4,8,10). In *Reading Difficulty and Personality Organization,* Gann reports that in comparison to other groups, poor readers are "emotionally less well-adjusted and less stable, insecure and fearful in relation to emotionally challenging situations, and socially less adaptable in relation to the group" (2).

Reprinted with permission of R. Phillip Carter and the International Reading Association.

Further studies indicate that superior and above-average readers engage in significantly more extra-curricular activities than do poor readers and that they also participate in social events to a great extent (7,9). In terms of verbal communication, the poor reader has difficulty in communicating his feelings and ideas to others, which may account for his lack of participation in social functions.

Through a case-study approach, Preston (5) studied reading failures as they functioned in their home situation, in their social world, and in their school world. One hundred children were chosen from the reading failures in Grades 2 through 10 in the San Francisco and Oakland schools. These children possessed average English vocabularies, normal intelligence (I.Q. 90-140), and exhibited no physical defects which might have led to maladjustment. A control group of 67 children with similar qualifications was formed. Through the use of the personal interview with child and parent, a mass of data was gathered relative to the aforementioned areas. In contrasting the reading failures with the controls, a significant difference was found regarding social adjustment. The results indicated that 50 percent of the reading failures experienced serious difficulty in getting along with their classmates. In summarizing the data, she reports that three times as many of the controls adapted well socially while four times as many of the reading failures became social failures also (5). Careful study of the results indicated that the difficulties which were associated with reading failure interfered with the normal development of the child and served as a detriment to future social adjustment.

Throughout these reports it is significant to note that in each case the subjects involved were of normal intelligence and presented no physical defects which might have precipitated maladjustment. The fact that emotional and social problems were frequently concomitant with reading retardation, however, is a principal concern of this investigation.

Since the vast majority of research has studied the retarded reader as he functioned in the school setting or in his home setting during the years in school, these questions arise: What happens to these individuals after leaving the formal educational situation? Can we assume that the emotional and social problems which accompanied reading retardation in high school dissipate once the separation occurs? Do persons identified as poor readers but of normal intellectual capacity adjust successfully to various demands of adult living?

Methodology

To answer these questions, information concerning the social adjustment that disabled readers have made as adults was considered relevant and important. To implement this investigation an instrument was developed which would assess the degree to which a person was cognizant of, integrated with, and participated in his environment. Eleven items were constructed of a general and specific nature and were based upon the same rationale which was used to construct the California Test of Personality and the Vineland Social Maturity Scale. For the purposes of this investigation a person was considered socially adjusted if he indicated adjustive responses to eight of the eleven items.

It must be understood that when we speak of social adjustment we are implying a dynamic process and not an act or occurrence which takes place at a specific point in time. This means that there is a continual and reciprocal influence between an individual and his social environment. The term further indicates that a person does his adjusting within the context of a society and more specifically within his interactions with other people. It is not enough for a person merely to profess values that are congruent with those of society; he must also demonstrate these in this interactive process.

It should also be understood that the final evaluation represents a judgment regarding a class of responses and not types of persons. It in no way attempts to classify an entire individual, for it is commonly agreed that within an organism both adjustive and non-adjustive elements may be present. Rather, the evaluation represents a state of adjustment and not an individual's process of adjusting.

As this investigation was concerned with adult adjustment, the initial consideration regarding the selection of subjects was that of age. The second consideration involved the aspect of reading retardation. Subjects were therefore selected from the files of a Reading Clinic which served the needs of an entire school system in a large midwestern metropolitan area. Meeting the various selection criteria were 61 white males, 19 years of age or older, who had been out of high school one or more years. The final researched population included 35 persons who were living in the metropolitan area and were available for a personal interview. Based upon the results of standardized achievement tests administered in the seventh and eighth grades, 23 persons were reading one or more years below grade level upon entering high school. These persons constituted the retarded reader group and will be referred to as Group I. The remaining 12 persons, who were reading at or above grade level upon entering high school, constitute the non-retarded reader group and will be referred to as Group II. Both groups are described in Table I regarding chronological age and intellectual status.

Results

To determine whether there was a significant difference between the retarded reader group and the non-retarded reader group regarding adult social adjustment, the Chi Square statistic was utilized. This analysis in-

TABLE I

The Chronological Age Range, Mean, and Standard Deviation, and the Intelligence Quotient Range, Mean, and Standard Deviation of the Persons in Group I and Group II

	Group I N = 23	Group II N = 12
C.A. Range	19.6–25.1	19.6–24.9
C.A. $\bar{X}$	22.1	21.3
C.A. S.D.	1.91	2.88
I.Q. Range	89–128	90–135
I.Q. $\bar{X}$	104.1	105.1
I.Q. S.D.	8.43	13.96

dicated that the difference was significant beyond the .001 level of confidence ($x^2 = 12.230$). The application of the Yates correction for continuity formula (for small samples) did not alter the significance level. Therefore, according to the data, there exists a close relationship between reading retardation and social maladjustment. The analysis further supports the notion that the personal and social maladjustments which were prevalent in school as concomitants of reading retardation persist into adult life. This conclusion substantially confirms the inferences of Preston (5), Zolkos (11), and Sandefur (6). Even though the environmental characteristics of the adult may be different, the retarded reader still lacks the most needed of all human feelings, the feeling of being able to participate in social communications. As a result he becomes socially withdrawn and is soon divorced from social activities. He is no longer integrated with his environment nor cognizant of it.

Important to the guidance function are the personal and social maladjustments which often accompany reading retardation during the school years. In light of this, perhaps the most significant finding of this study is the fact that these maladjustments persisted into the adult life of these retarded readers. This would indicate that school personnel must not only consider the reading deficiency itself, but they should also attend to the accrued emotional and social problems that this deficiency has created. This implies creating an environment within which a student can meet success (this is especially important for males) and develop into an emotionally and socially stable individual. He should be made to feel that he is an integral part of the school environment and he should be assisted in acquiring communication skills necessary for effective participation in his school and adult social life. Such skills could well be part of a high school reading program geared to the needs of all students, and especially to those who will not continue their formal schooling beyond high school.

References

1. Bouise, L. M. "Emotional and Personality Problems of a Group of Retarded Readers." *Elementary English* 32 (December 1955):544-548.
2. Gann, Edith. *Reading Difficulty and Personality Organization.* New York: Kings Crown Press, 1945.
3. Gates, Arthur I., and Bond, Guy L. "Failure in Reading and Social Maladjustment." *Journal of the National Education Association* 25 (October 1936):205-206.
4. Lantz, Beatrice, and Liebes, Genevieve B. "A Follow-Up Study of Non-Readers." *Journal of Educational Research* 36 (April 1943):604-626.
5. Preston, Mary I. "Reading Failure and the Child's Security." *American Journal of Orthopsychiatry* 10 (1940):239-252.
6. Sandefur, Joseph T. "A Study of the Scholastic and Social Implications of Remedial Reading Classes in Selected Senior High Schools." Ph.D. dissertation, Indiana University, Bloomington, 1958, 121 pp.
7. Sheldon, William D., and Cutts, Warren C. "Relation of Parents, Home, and Certain Developmental Characteristics to Children's Reading Ability." *Elementary School Journal* 53 (May 1953):517-521.
8. Sutter, Betty. "I Hate Reading." *Elementary English* 24 (March 1947):163-170.
9. Tabarlet, B. E. "Poor Readers and Mental Health." *Elementary English* 35 (December 1958):522-525.
10. Witty, Paul A. "Reading Success and Emotional Adjustment." *Elementary English* 27 (May 1950):281-296.
11. Zolkos, Helena H. "What Research Says About Emotional Factors in Retardation in Reading." *The Elementary English Journal* 51 (May 1951):512-518.

CHAPTER SEVEN

In Search of Ethnic Identity

Children most frequently want to know who they are Just as they learn other facts about themselves, they want to know how they are linked to the community of man and how they are different. They question their connections with history as well as their ties to contemporary action. As they go about their daily lives choosing behaviors they believe to be effective, they want to belong to something. Invariably they will seek information about their ethnic, religious, and other affiliations.

The maturing individual's search for ethnic identity should lead to rich discoveries in reading. Reading offers a resource to answers for such questions. The search for identity with all the power of the drive for developing a positive self-concept should lead to school reading of relevant materials. As the healthy adolescent probes into many corners for resolutions to his problems, there is no doubt that he will meet directly biased materials as well as more objective pieces. The American public school is a natural place to examine such materials from many sources.

But, unfortunately, this has not been so. It is probably fair to say that denial of ethnic materials in school has helped to create the lack of interest in reading among the minorities of America. The lack of relevant books or stories, the poverty of positive models with whom they could identify, the shallow or even false statements in textbooks must all tend to turn students from school and from reading. Woefully, the progress in this regard has been slow and is not yet complete. As part of a self-fulfilling prophecy, the bigoted and mean can point accusingly to illiterate minorities, taunting that *those people* cannot learn to read.

Still, on the positive side of the ledger, changes are being made. Some educators suggest our society is shifting from a goal-oriented one to a society that emphasizes the *role* of individuals. American concern for civil rights, particularly in school, has made popular the core-taught reading-ethnic studies courses in big city high schools. Where textbooks are not meeting these newly expressed needs, the use of ephemeral materials, pirated articles, pamphlets, posters, teacher-made devices have filled in. All of this is intended to capitalize upon the needs of students for ethnic identity.

Michael Harris

The maltreatment of the American Chinese and the American Indian are rarely public knowledge. Abstractions of our complex daily lives seem to obscure injustices to individuals. In this book review, Michael Harris examines the possibility of fair treatment for these two minorities.

Distorted Accounts of Indians and Chinese

"There is not one Indian in the whole country who does not cringe in anguish and frustration because of textbooks," Rupert Costo, president of the American Indian Historical Society, told the late Senator Robert F. Kennedy in a testimony here two and a half years ago.

There is not one Indian child who has not come home in shame and tears after one of those sessions in which he is taught that his people were dirty, animal-like, something less than a human being. . . .

Costo and Miss Henry have provided a meticulous listing of examples from American school textbooks that distort the role of American Indians. Perhaps the most notorious is "Land of the Oaks," published by the Oakland Unified School District and used in that community's public schools from 1953 until it was withdrawn in 1967. The book contained such observations as, "It might be that the Indians were so untidy that germs were afraid of them. They seemed to keep healthy in spite of the lives they led."

Some statements in the Oakland book are patently false. Everybody knows that Indians understand medicinal herbs and plants, but according to "Land of the Oaks," "If an Indian got sick, he was almost sure to die, since little was known about the proper treatment of illness and injury."

In all, 168 books are criticized. Some books used in Bureau of Indian Affairs' schools on reservations contain descriptions of Indians as "sav-

---

From the *San Francisco Sunday Examiner and Chronicle, This World*, August 30, 1970. "Distorted Accounts of Indians and Chinese" by Michael Harris. The reviewed books are *Textbooks and the American Indians* by Jeanette Henry; Rupert Costo, editor, and *The Unwelcome Immigrant: The American Image of the Chinese, 1785–1882* by Stuart C. Miller.

ages." Some texts contain grave distortions of facts and treat Indians as interlopers on lands their tribes had occupied for tens of centuries. In others, there are serious omissions. And sometimes authors who think they are being benevolent treat American Indians with cloying condescension.

Stuart Miller, associate professor of social science at San Francisco State College, has made a similar and equally thorough study of American portrayals of Chinese immigrants. Over and over again American writers solemnly reported the main trouble with the Chinese was that they were "imbeciles" incapable of receiving an education.

The most startling acts of mistreatment were defended. John Quincy Adams said the Opium War to force the Chinese government to permit the importation of that drug was England's way to promote trade and "extend her liberating arm to the farthest bound of Asia."

Chinese were accused of trying to spread unspeakable diseases in the United States by passing out Chinese-made cigars to innocent victims. They were described as promoters of cholera, bizarre tortures and white slave dens.

The New York Herald offered its readers six columns of frightening reading under the multiple headlines: "Heathen Chinese . . . The Coolie Merchants and Their Victims . . . Who is Responsible for the Asian Inundation . . . The Traffic in Human Flesh." The New York World published an article headed, "Two Mongolian Minotaurs—Shocking Debauchery of Innocents," after a mob of whites demolished a Chinese laundry in Milwaukee.

These two books offer similar, frightening examples of the effects of prejudice. The observations in Miller's book seem preposterous because the Chinese of today are unrecognizable from the caricatures created by ignorant or malicious writers in the 19th century. But at least those libels are no longer being perpetrated. The accounts offered school children about American Indians are just as outrageous, but unfortunately the Indian victims are still being made to suffer.

Nick C. Vaca

In the past decade the phenomenal growth of YA or Young Adult novels with their refreshing candor about social problems has created a rash of fictionalized accounts of the travail of ethnic minorities. Frank Bonham has been a leader among such authors. Here, the editor of prominent Mexican American work protests the anglicization of Viva Chicano.

The Chicano in Fiction

It is a pity that at a time when serious literature on the Chicano is so wanting that Frank Bonham should choose to title his latest book for young readers "Viva Chicano." For there is really very little about it that is Chicano.

This remains true in spite of the fact that the protagonist, Joaquin "Keeny" Duran, along with numerous other characters, have Chicano names; that the book contains a sprinkling of Spanish words and phrases with "bato loco" being decidedly overused; that it is set in a barrio (Dogtown) in Los Angeles, and that Emiliano Zapata appears as a latter day Charlie McCarthy to Joaquin's rational alter-ego.

What Viva Chicano really is, is an impassionate plea for youth, that has probably been engendered by Bonham's welfare interest for wayward youths of any race. If Joaquin were substituted by a protagonist of any other color or race the essential quality of the book would not have been altered.

It is writing such as this that leads many Chicanos to speculate whether in fact an Anglo can accurately portray the Chicano existence. Instead of feeling infused with the symbolic qualities of Chicanoism or of being exposed to those sometimes imperceptible clues that are distinctively Chicano, the reader comes away with a feeling of having been entertained by a simplistic and naive narrative of what caused Joaquin to go wrong and what eventually caused him to go right.

To the more aware Chicano reader, Bonham's account of what caused Joaquin to run afoul of the law will infuriate him. For Bonham neatly divides Joaquin's existence into two worlds—the good and the evil. And as

---

From the *San Francisco Sunday Examiner and Chronicle, This World,* September 6, 1970. "The Chicano in Fiction" by Nick C. Vaca. A review of *Viva Chicano* by Frank Bonham.

luck would have it and Bonham writes it, all evil resides within the geographical boundaries of Dogtown and the psychological boundaries of Joaquin's family. Thus all evil resides with the Chicanos.

Along the Road

From the beginning of the book we are told that were it not for Joaquin's promiscuous mother with her incessant screaming that has driven Joaquin to leave home more than once, all would be cool. The same is to be said of Joaquin's club. The Aztecs (a pubescent social club that pretends at being a fighting gang) whose constant dropping of "reds" and drinking of wine (Ripple or Red Mountain no doubt) does nothing to help steer Joaquin along the yellow brick road to becoming a good citizen. However, on the side of "goodness" we have the Anglos.

There is Joaquin's (Bonham insists on calling him Keeny) parole officer, Mr. Baker, whose paternal understanding is a constant source of hope for Joaquin. We also have Rosie and Peggy, two Anglo women who run homes for wayward youths and whose compassion and understanding sustain Joaquin through various parts of his ordeal to straighten himself out with the police. Lastly we have the stolen cardboard image of Emiliano Zapata, an image that we soon discover is capable of speaking; well, not really speaking, for Zapata's mysticism is later clarified by Mr. Baker who explains that Zapata's voice is actually Joaquin's alter-ego expressing itself. But for a while at least, Joaquin really believes that Zapata speaks and that this revolutionary of years gone by is really reincarnated in that stolen cardboard image.

However, the advice that comes from the mouth of Zapata is more reminiscent of a Father Flanagan than of a Mexican revolutionary.

What will infuriate not only the aware Chicano but other aware readers is that Bonham never once writes of those factors that are external to Dogtown and Joaquin's family as being causes for the condition in which not only Joaquin finds himself, but all of Dogtown. For this reason there is no mention of unfair police practice toward Chicano youths, institutional prejudice against Chicanos, and the economic factors that would lead a Joaquin to a world of delinquency.

We are thus left to believe that if Joaquin left his mother and Dogtown (thereby rejecting his whole existence as a Chicano) to live in Peggy's home for wayward youths, then he would be all right.

It is such superficial works as this one that acidly point to the absolute necessity for literature on Chicanos by Chicanos.

Meyer Weinberg

Real change in the relevance of school materials must come through the front, not the back, door. Materials smuggled in by teachers, contraband imported by children cannot change the school codes quickly enough to affect the millions we need to reach. In an exciting publication, Integrated Education, *Meyer Weinberg proposes a strategy to bring about change.*

A TVA For Textbooks

Changes in textbook practices will come when (1) the textbook industry sees the business necessity of change, (2) the civil rights movement takes on a major part of the responsibility for initiating change, and (3) the schoolmen modify their reluctance to depart significantly from established practices.

1. *The textbook industry.* The greatest obstacle to change is the high prosperity that has afflicted the industry. Nothing so conduces to conservatism as the obvious fact that the established ways are profitable. Businessmen do not rock the boat when the vessel is full. Even the distinguished publisher of Lincoln Steffens and T. S. Eliot is discovered worshiping at the double-image of "northern" and "southern" editions of the same schoolbook. Exhortation to change, however, will get us nowhere, as can be demonstrated by the case of the television industry. The publishers will produce textbooks for an integrated society whenever they find it profitable. All proposals for change must reckon with this fact.

2. *The civil rights movement.* The civil rights movement has performed an essential democratic assignment—it has insisted upon translating the promise of mass education into a reality. Much to its credit, it has given major impetus to a re-evaluation of the history of the Negro American. Thus far, the re-examination is little more than rudimentary. And the accomplishment in terms of actual textbook content is hardly more than token. Inclusion in textbooks of photographs of dark-appearing persons and

---

Meyer Weinberg, "A TVA for Textbooks," *Integrated Education,* Vol. 3, No. 3, June–July 1965.

preparation of supplements to textbooks fairly summarizes the achievement. Substantial progress will have been achieved when publishers produce a number of *integrated* American histories.

Significant change, however, will either come from the civil rights movement or it will not come at all. The prospect is, in my opinion, fairly good that it will. The movement can initiate a kind of TVA for textbooks. You will recall the plight of farmers in the Tennessee Valley during the first three decades of this century. Electrification passed them by primarily because the private power companies asserted the unprofitability of serving a limited demand. TVA demonstrated that electric power could be generated and distributed economically and profitably; it thus served as a yardstick against which to measure the performance of private firms. Government became a long-term factor in the electric power industry and at the same time private firms adjusted to the new reality of lower rates and expanded demand.

An invaluable asset the civil rights movement possesses is the goodwill of a large section of the academic world. Scholars are eager to apply their intelligence and knowledge to socially-relevant research and writing. The time is ripe for a response to this eagerness. The civil rights movement could well organize a national commission on, let us say, research into the history of the Negro American. Research groups could be organized on a regional basis, perhaps grouped around selected universities; these groups could specialize on topics of their own choice, as informed by discussion with the national commission. Financial support for such research and writing could be provided in amounts comparable with those provided by commercial publishers. (These latter are erroneously thought by non-writers to be enormous. In fact, however, they are not. In addition, most books—including textbooks—are written without benefit of any advance royalty whatever.)

Once a manuscript were completed, it could be marketed in either of two ways. First, it could be printed and distributed on contract or, by a university press, with the proceeds going to the authors after the advanced sums are repaid. Second, a completed manuscript could be offered to a commercial publisher with provision for repaying sums advanced. In the latter case, the author's bargaining advantage would be greatly strengthened. School boards are themselves a likely source of funds.

A basic financial reason for the present "regional" editions is that southern states often band together and confront publishers with a large potential sale: "Either revise or lose the combined order." Publishers have jumped at the command. Northern buyers of school books, traditionally unconcerned with the issue of integration, have not thrown *their* economic weight around. The reason is simple: Social studies textbooks written in a bland style are highly acceptable "up North." But with the advent of the civil rights movement it becomes politically possible to have large cities and states band together and assert their bargaining ability.

Indeed, it is not inconceivable that the boycott weapon be used against those publishers who switch photos and paragraphs in accordance with segregative preconceptions. This, after all, is an almost exact analogue to the conditions giving rise to the current boycott by the Southern Christian Leadership Conference.

3. *The schoolmen.* Well-documented surveys have shown the deep and continuing intellectual violence accomplished by many present-day school textbooks. Through omission and commission, racial myths are perpetuated, racial stereotypes strengthened, and the human dignity of minorities demeaned. But the greatest victim of this treatment is truth itself. To write a history of the United States without mentioning the role of the Negro during the period 1877–1954 is simply bad history. To deal with the Constitution only as an ideal construct, without examining the voluminous primary sources on deprivation of voting rights, is poor political science. To mention the 1954 Supreme Court desegregation decision but fail to describe the tokenistic character of desegregation is not even good reporting.

If traditional avenues of textbook publication are inadequate to the challenge of our times, the civil rights movement will seek more effective avenues.

CHAPTER EIGHT

Reading for Utility

Reading is also important for utilitarian reasons. This is particularly so in a technological and capitalist culture. The machinery, social as well as industrial, of this computerized era demands a high degree of reading ability of all who would take advantage of its products. Nearly every aspect of both work and leisure are tempered by reading ability. Many employment possibilities simply are not open to the functionally illiterate. And, once on the job, promotion is not possible for those of poor reading skills.

The poor reader is disadvantaged whether it be as direct prey to unscrupulous merchants or simply the inability to attend to his problems with the many agencies of welfare and recreation. As the amount of information available to know has grown, the ability to read and deal with information sources has been more and more a correlate of the "haves" of the society. Industrialization over the past century has tended to eliminate great numbers of manual laborers while the world of new industries such as space and medical technology, computer and audio-visual sciences demand highly specialized literacies. Trade unions demand minimal reading and math skills of all apprentices. Productive employment and the world of work are denied those who cannot read.

Everyday life is hampered and distorted by illiteracy, too. In the department store and supermarket, the facts due consumers, those of weight and size, quality and kind, are doled out in print. Sales contracts and conditions are written as are bargains and efficiencies. Operating instructions, difficult for the literate, are impossible for the poor reader. Hand in hand with the hardships imposed by illiteracy go the fear and suspicion of defective materials, mercenary dealers, the *laissez-faire* marketplace.

Reading for Utility

In leisure simple skills of reading become important. Many of the road signs of "the good life" depend upon written communication. From initial contact to reinforcement, the advantages of cultural aspects depend upon the literate use of media. Participation and enjoyment of the opportunities of the community rely upon adequate response to the media dealing with such events. It does not seem to be merely a matter of great use of one media to the exclusion of others, either. The nonreader is not a more avid movie fan nor articulate televiewer; rather, the evidence seems to indicate that some central feature distinguishes the literate as persons who use all media to a greater extent. People who have been educated to enjoy media use more of them all, including reading, than do those who have not.

Bernard Asbell

It has been demonstrated in great cities all over the country that the maps of poverty, illiteracy, and minority group status are one. Hunger and illiteracy go hand in hand. This poignant report describes some of the aspects of this problem in Chicago, Illinois.

Illiteracy: The Key to Poverty

There is a man in Chicago who dares think he has discovered the biggest cause of American poverty and how his city can begin to get rid of it. In fact, how any city can begin to get rid of it. His method—and this is not a flippancy—is as simple as teaching the ABC's.

Raymond M. Hilliard, the ruddy-faced, compassionate Director of Public Aid for Cook County, Illinois, recently was surprised to learn, after a long career of studying poverty, that most people who are extremely poor have in common a single, secret, crippling trait: They are virtually illiterate. He soon made other surprising discoveries. Impoverished illiterates and near-illiterates, no matter what their age, can be taught to read and write at insignificant cost ($5.50 a month), often in a few months, and many can be made employable and even employed. Perhaps most important, their education often leads to lifting the school interest and grades of their children. "This," says Hilliard, "is the most hopeful thing I've ever had hold of."

To appreciate the seeming hopelessness against which Hilliard pits his hope, one must realize how many Americans are poor and how poor they are. Not the $1.25-an-hour miniminum-wage poor, but the empty-pocket poor. In addition to the tens of millions of miserably rewarded sharecroppers and scavengers, mop slingers and laundry sorters, and the job seekers and their wives and youngsters who make do on unemployment-compensation checks, there are still 7 1/2 million souls who are even less well off. More than the combined populations of Los Angeles, Chicago, Pittsburgh, and Boston! Those are the Americans who live by the grace of public welfare. Their parents were poor, and unless something extraordinary is

---

Bernard Asbell, "Illiteracy: The Key to Poverty," *McCalls,* February 1964.

done rapidly, most of their children will be poor. For the modern variety of "hard core" poverty has something in common with the elegance and security of established wealth. It is inherited.

Within months, one man rose from hopelessness to hope: Sam Frost, a fifty-four-year-old ex-laborer with mighty shoulders and a stony, solemn, awesomely proud jaw. Frost (I have changed his name, but not his story) has fourteen children, the oldest still in school. In 1959, after a thirty-four-year history of steady employment, he was out of a job and could not for the life of him find a new one. Uneasiness turned to fear, then to terrible feelings of uselessness. Backaches and abdominal pains stabbed at him. These are the occupational diseases of the unemployed; they seem to vanish only under the miracle drug of opportunity. Soon Frost reached the end of his downhill path: He and his large family landed on relief.

Two years ago, Frost, like thousands of Chicagoans on relief, was given a test in the three R's. Like many others, he failed to show the formal learning of even a fifth-grade child. Soon he was "requested" to go to school two nights a week and do considerable homework in between (anyone refusing would forfeit his relief checks, but almost everyone went gladly). In a year and a half, Frost, an eager student, progressed from a near-illiterate to a possessor of an eighth-grade certificate—and more. His teacher, who volunteered to coach Frost after classes, feels Sam is almost ready to take an achievement exam for a high school diploma.

That still is not the most remarkable of Frost's accomplishments. Shell Oil Company admitted him to training as a gas-station attendant and taught him how to fill out a shift foreman's report, an intricate procedure for balancing all merchandise sold against money taken in. Frost mastered this better than some experienced foremen. Soon, several station owners jointly hired Frost to circulate from station to station, combining the figures from shifts into daily round-the-clock reports and finally into monthly reports. Also, he coaches station managers in better methods of record keeping. After more than five decades of ignorance, all this happened in less than two years.

Now Milwaukee, Baltimore, Newark, and other cities are also starting to send relief recipients to school. Like Chicago, they are teaching illiterates to read and write, others to qualify for grammar school and high school diplomas. These cities don't expect to find a Sam Frost behind every relief check; but they are convinced that only the thin walls of elementary schooling separate many good, useful men from productive employment of their native intelligence.

The intelligence exists, ready to be tapped, even though anyone able to read these words will find it hard—almost impossible—to appreciate the native cleverness an illiterate must possess to make his way through a wordy world. Just as a blind man "sees" with his ears and fingers, or a deaf man "hears" by staring at lips, the illiterate must "read" his way around.

Andrew Timmons has that special cleverness. Standing near the entrance of the public-housing project in Chicago where he lives with his wife and seven children, I pointed to a small wooden sign stuck in the dirt. It said, "Help us keep our lawn beautiful." I asked, "What does that sign say?" He replied confidently, "It says, 'Stay off the grass.'" I asked how he knew that. He said, "That's what those signs always say."

At thirty-seven, Timmons (that is not his real name) distinguishes one street from another by its houses, not its street signs. When he once had a job downtown as a car washer—the only job he could get in the past nine years—he was able to find his way home on the Cottage Grove bus because he knows it is number four ("I can read numbers"). When his wife sends him out for a can of tomato soup (which has only words on the label), he never brings home vegetable soup by mistake. He shops in the kind of grocery store where you ask for things, not where the customer selects from the shelf. Food is more costly there, but what can he do? Also, he has learned the ceremonial lies of the illiterate. Every culture has its ceremonial lies. Much as the educated suburbanite serves the best Scotch, so his guests won't know he's broke, Timmons sometimes tucks a newspaper under his arm, so his neighbors won't suspect he can't read. When people give him papers to fill out (sometimes job applications), he says, "I just got my hands dirty. Could you put this in your typewriter, and I'll tell you the answers?"

Timmons cannot, however, decipher a warning that says "Poison," a movie marquee, a big newspaper headline—or the tiny letters on newspapers' back pages that say "Help Wanted." He would be unable to compete for a job if he knew where to find one. Timmons, his wife, and his seven children are on relief, all of them supported by his fellow citizens who *do* know how to read and write.

Why didn't Timmons— and the rest of the ignorant poor—learn when they had the chance? The fact is that while other children were going to school, Timmons, a native citizen of the land of free education and equal opportunity, was not given the chance to go.

"Where I was raised," he told me (he had grown up in Jasper County, Mississippi), "hardly none of the kids ever went to school a day. Nobody from the school made you go. My grandfather—he raised me 'cause my mother died when I was seven—figured going to school wouldn't help me pick cotton any better, so why go? I hardly ever thought a thing about it till I was about fourteen and saw some kids in a store looking at magazines and things, and I wished I could do some of that. But it was too late."

Some did have the exceptional strength to defy such disadvantages; but even then, defeat was almost inevitable. One of Timmons' housing-project neighbors—also on relief—is a spunky woman in her fifties. I'll call her Maybelle Masters. Growing up in Shelburne, Mississippi, she became determined not to mature into an ignorant, helpless adult. At fifteen, she enrolled in the first grade.

"Walking four miles in the mud was the only way to get to school," she told me. "Lots of kids didn't go, because they didn't have boots. On rainy days, the school would be closed, because the rain would come down through the roof."

At the age of twenty—a fifth-grader—Maybelle got married and quit school. The United States Census calls her literate because she reported attending school for five years, the minimum standard for "functional literacy." Yet she cannot read and write. "When they ask me how long I went," says Mrs. Masters, "I say five years, but the truth is I didn't go even eighteen months. School was only open from January to April. Sometimes the cotton wasn't all picked in January, so you couldn't start school till the work was done. In April, the planting started. You stopped going to school when the work started in the fields. So maybe I went two months a year, maybe three."

Five "years" of schooling left her virtually as uneducated as Andrew Timmons, who had had none.

Every large city is loaded with Andrew Timmonses, with burdened, bewildered women and their ragged children, the inheritors of what Hilliard calls "infectious ignorance." Chicago is typical, with 270,000 on relief. Some are Southern Appalachian mountaineers (sometimes said to be the only white Anglo-Saxon Protestants who, as a class, are victims of discrimination and deprivation). Some are Puerto Ricans, Mexicans, American Indians. But overwhelmingly they are Negroes who came from the Deep South or whose parents did.

Much as America enjoys regarding itself as a nation of universal education, the 1960 census tells us that 8 million adults over twenty-five—one out of every dozen—attended school less than five years and are therefore labeled "functionally illiterate." The statistic is far smaller than the truth. Selective Service officials, for example, reject 22 percent of draft registrants for failing a simple mental test; in southern states, the percentage of failures varies from 35 up to 56. These men aren't deliberate flunkers; the test is mined with devices for trapping malingerers. Testing officers say that the young men fail mainly because they can't read the questions.

In Oklahoma City, a meat-packer and two unions agreed jointly to retrain 170 workers displaced by new machines. They found 110—or 65 percent—too uneducated "to show promise of benefiting from training." More bluntly, the workers couldn't read and do simple figuring. In Michigan, a group of 761 unemployed were tested for retraining; 515—or 68 percent—failed. In Chicago, 4,500 on relief were tested; 1,900 were unable to read well enough to pass.

Hardly any jobs remain for such ignorant laborers. The road-gang worker has been replaced by the bulldozer and grading machine, operated by men of training. Even the janitor is no longer a mindless floor sweeper. He must operate cleaning machines, study a manual for making repairs, read instructions for careful mixing of cleaning agents. In the modern restaurant, a short-order cook must read scribbled orders from waitresses.

Illiteracy, therefore, is no longer an unfortunate statistic. It has become a serious national threat.

Hilliard, the Chicago welfare chief, started to be aware of this fact in January 1959. He was disturbed by a chart on his desk and called in his energetic research director, Deton J. Brooks, Jr. A recession had just ended. Employment was picking up. According to past experience, relief rolls should be declining. But they kept rising. Why was this happening?

Hilliard and Brooks decided on an intensive study of a large, crowded, poverty-stricken neighborhood called Woodlawn, where 25 percent of all households were on relief. One of their findings seemed to tower in significance above all others. According to the census, 6.6 percent of relief recipients had five years of schooling or less. But standard tests in the three R's revealed that 51 percent of the able-bodied adults were unable to read and write at a fifth-grade level. The remainder, who tested higher, were so little above functional illiteracy that the difference hardly mattered. Nearly all were too uneducated for the simplest jobs in the modern labor market.

"Here, then," said Hilliard, reporting his findings to a convention of welfare officials, "is the major cause of today's poverty. Here is the reason for the high cost of relief. Punishing these people for their poverty won't help. Badgering them with investigations, violating their small rights of privacy, condemning them for alleged immorality, putting them in jail, calling them loafers and idlers and cheats and frauds, which few of them are, will avail nothing. . . . These only divert attention from real solutions."

As a real solution, Hilliard set about to teach fifty thousand relief recipients to read and write better. By last December, the eight thousand most urgently needing education were going to school, but money was lacking for the rest. The Chicago Board of Education has been footing the entire cost, providing classrooms and paying regular schoolteachers $4.50 an hour for the two evening sessions per week that classes are held. To carry these costs, the Board of Education siphoned off money earmarked for Americanizing the foreign-born; later, Hilliard obtained Federal and state funds to finance the classes.

The biggest initial problem was trying to arrange baby-sitters to free mothers for school. If women's organizations were prepared to offer such help, Hilliard believes, they would make a unique contribution to helping families rid themselves of poverty. Lacking such help, welfare caseworkers undertook the huge job of arranging mutual baby-sitting among the student mothers. Last summer, when classes were changed to daytime to save custodial costs in school buildings, the baby-sitting problem became so difficult that many of the sessions had to be canceled.

Considering how many schemes for teaching literacy to adults have sprung up, one would think the techniques were down to a science. In Yakima, Washington, the LARK (Literacy for Adults and Related Knowledge) Foundation has organized classes as far east as Michigan. In St. Louis, the Adult Education Council has aggressively sought to educate illiterates. Indiana Central College started a course for teaching teachers of illiterates. Daily TV instruction programs—one series produced in Philadelphia, another in Memphis—have been lent to other cities, in the hope that illiterates will tune in. But everywhere, teachers are groping for effective teaching methods.

This came as a shock to Robert L. Dixon, a junior high school teacher supervising some Chicago welfare classes. He recalls the first orientation meeting of several hundred teachers. "Before you ask what textbooks you are to use," the speaker said, "let me tell you that we have none. We know that the Little Red Hen won't do for adults, but we don't know what *will* do. Your students are not like immigrants who want to learn to speak English. For most of your students, English is the only language they know. This challenge is new. We will have to find our way by experimenting."

Dixon faced his first class, composed entirely of Negroes like himself, with uneasiness. His chief tools were a piece of chalk and a blackboard. His twenty students sat with pencils poised over notebooks. There were two women for each man. Young people far outnumbered the elderly.

> First, I wondered how much they know about the world [Dixon told me]. Next, I wondered how much they know that I don't know. I had to keep reminding myself that they had rich experiences I know nothing about. One had been a paint mixer, one a drill-press operator, a few housewives and mothers, each with full lives, some longer than mine. I had to remind myself not to lump them together with a simple label like "illiterate."
>
> Then I began to wonder how much they think I know, what they imagined book learning really is. This made me wonder—and this was the most troubling of all—how much they expected of me.

His students came with uneasiness, too.

"I wondered," said Eddie O'Brien, a father of twelve, "how much education a man needed so he could get himself a job, and how long it would take. I was forty-two already and didn't have much time."

O'Brien took it as no joke when Dixon distributed play money and set up a shelf full of commodities for "sale." As pupils "bought" things, the teacher spun a line of talk, meanwhile shortchanging each of his customers. They were first embarrassed, then stunned as Mr. Dixon revealed the simple ways in which salesmen can fleece the uneducated.

These ways had cost O'Brien his last job. For seven years, he had worked for a baking company, stacking baked goods as they came down automatic conveyors and sweeping crumbs from the floor. He took home $84 a week.

"I wanted to be like the rest of the people," O'Brien told me. "I bought a used car, some furniture we needed, a TV set, clothes for the kids. Those salesmen, they always kept telling me it wasn't hard, just a dollar down, a dollar a week. Before I knew it, I was caught in the trick bag."

The "trick bag" had many hidden pockets. If educated people are often swindled for overlooking fine print, how easy to skin someone unable to read even big print. One day, a lawyer informed O'Brien he could be saved from his creditors only by claiming personal bankruptcy. The lawyer would gladly arrange this for $300. Payments would be easy: $100 down, $40 a month. When the fourth payment for the lawyer fell due, O'Brien was unable to pay. Thus he forfeited the $220 he had already paid, and the lawyer abandoned the case. O'Brien's creditors descended on the baking company to claim slices of his wages, and he was fired for "excessive wage assignments," a phrase well known in slum districts. Soon his family was on relief.

Students like Eddie O'Brien come eager to learn. After the first embarrassment at being exposed to friends as uneducated, many are seized with a desire to spell their children's names. They recite the names to the teacher and become absorbed in the magical process of copying down the letters—sometimes the first meaningful syllables they have ever written. One woman, after three months of tutelage, brought her teacher an elaborate chocolate cake. She carried it proudly and announced, "I got a book all about cooking and *read* how to make it."

Eddie O'Brien describes his sense of achievement differently: "I feel like a caged bird that all at once got out." His escape has indeed been dramatic, for he escaped into the exhilarating world of self-dependence and self-respect. O'Brien is now averaging $450 a month driving a taxi. He is one of the most successful of almost five hundred drivers lifted from the literacy classes and relief rolls and trained for jobs by the Yellow Cab Company. Once they had demonstrated that they could read street signs, they were taught Chicago's house-numbering system, the location of the city's seventy-eight most important buildings, and how to fill out trip reports. Also, they were given special training in meeting the public—and how to buy sensibly on the installment plan. Now, Yellow Cab expects to train a thousand relief recipients, possibly more.

The Chicago Urban League brought the Yellow Cab story to the Shell Oil Company because major oil companies have been troubled by a shortage of high-grade gas-station attendants. Sales are lost by employees who don't seem to care, and the man who meets the customer can make or break the reputation of his company.

With trepidation, Shell undertook to train a group of men from the literacy classes. Strange things happened. In tests for spelling, for example, men continued to have trouble with words like "which," but racked up high scores in technical words like "detergency" and "differential." Company officials accepted this as a surprising sign that the men were burning late lamps. It helped destroy company fears that "reliefers" were natural loafers. Still, the company was skeptical. Yet two months after the men went to work, seven out of thirty-five had already been promoted to shift foremen, taking charge of men who had been on the job a year or more. Station owners reported that the new men were among their best employees. The training program is now permanent.

While the star trainee at Shell, Sam Frost, who became the roving bookkeeper, was working furiously to learn, his eighteen-year-old son, a recent high school dropout, began talking about going back to school, and his grammar school children headed for their homework whenever Daddy did.

Commissioner Hilliard is convinced that educating mothers is equally important. Half the homes in Negro slum neighborhoods are headed by women, most of them abandoned early in marriage. Hilliard's research director, Deton Brooks, explains:

> In a matriarchal structure, women transmit the culture. If the woman is illiterate, she transmits the values, the images of an illiterate's world. This is extremely dangerous, for the future of these children and the society that may soon have to support them as illiterate adults.

Extending this reasoning, Hilliard is convinced that literacy classes strike at the roots of broken homes. He concludes:

> You can see a straight line operating from illiteracy to illegitimacy. The American culture teaches all men—even Negro men segregated from the main culture—that a father's job is to be a provider. The man who had been abandoned by his father and in turn abandons his children is convinced he can never succeed as a good American father. Where's his

chance to provide? From the day he takes his vows, he knows he can't fulfill his function, that his manhood has been taken away, that his marriage is doomed, and that the insecurity of his woman has begun.

Instead of heaping more contempt on this man, let's look for ways that will let him stay at home. Let's give him at least the meagerest education, to help him find a decent job at a decent wage, and give him some assurance that he won't be the first one fired because of his color. Then you'll start to see a downslide in the illegitimacy rate. That's how far you can extend the possible results of something as simple as teaching the ABC's.

David Dempsey

The "Right to Read" assumes all the complex dynamics of social class in America. Often seeming to be one of the underlying causes of deprivation, illiteracy is probably an interactive agent, an effect as well as a cause of poverty. This author also reports some successes in efforts to encourage reading.

The Right to Read

"Millions of Americans read so poorly that they can barely read at all." This statement by the National Reading Council—set up last year by President Nixon—underscores one of the country's greatest social problems. An estimated three million adults are totally illiterate. Another twenty-five million job holders have "reading deficiencies . . . serious enough to deny them advancement." Five million young people are unable to read well enough to qualify for most types of employment. Eight million school children suffer from reading disorders requiring special remedies. The council speaks of a "reading disease" of epidemic proportions, an opinion buttressed by one authority, Dr. Samuel Sava, who argues "that a figure of 25 percent for functional illiteracy for the male population at large would not be far off the mark."

The startling thing about these figures is that not only do more Americans go to school than ever before but on the average they stay in school longer. Paradoxically, as the educational level of the country has risen, so has the rate of functional illiteracy. For this, one logically blames the schools; yet, the problem is not so simple. As American industry makes increasingly sophisticated demands upon even its lowest paid workers, standards of "literacy" rise, too. Today, only about 15 percent of the jobs in the United States are "unskilled" (compared to 30 percent in 1945). By the end of the decade, it is predicted that this figure will drop to 5 percent. Under these conditions, literacy takes on a new meaning, and this year's

---

David Dempsey, "The Right to Read," *Saturday Review*, April 17, 1971. Copyright © 1971 Saturday Review, Inc.

The Right to Read

slogan for National Library Week—"You've got a right to read"—assumes a special urgency. The right to be able to read is, today, a condition of economic, to say nothing of cultural, survival.

When the National Reading Council was organized, under the chairmanship of AT&T Vice President Walter W. Straley, no single government body had ever attempted to coordinate an attack on the "reading disease" in the sense that the National Institute of Health researches and seeks cures for physical ailments. One of the council's first acts was to commission Louis Harris & Associates to measure the "survival" literacy rate in the United States—that is, the percentage of Americans lacking the practical reading skills necessary to "survive" in this country.

The test used in the survey was the ability of the respondent to fill out application forms such as those used for Social Security, public assistance, Medicaid, and a driver's license. The findings were not too surprising. Functional illiteracy is highest for big-city dwellers and for rural inhabitants, with the latter group slightly worse off than the former in the ranges measured. Fewer people who live in small towns and cities had difficulty reading the forms. Suburban residents showed up best. Geographically, the South had the highest range of illiteracy, and people in the West showed the fewest reading problems.

Practical illiteracy decreases in direct proportion to income. Five percent of those who earn less than $5,000 a year missed more than 30 percent of the answers, but only 1 percent of those with an income of $15,000 or higher did that poorly. Illiteracy among white respondents is about half that of blacks. Even among members of the low-income group, the range for non-whites is much higher than that for whites. The youngest age group proved to be the most literate; the oldest (fifty and over) the most deficient. Between the sexes, women surpass men slightly in reading ability, although no one is quite sure why.

Until a few years ago, it was widely assumed that the reading difficulties of many children were caused by dyslexia, a disorder supposedly the result of MBD (minimal brain damage); but this theory could hardly explain why dyslexia should be more prevalent among poor children than among their more fortunate peers. Recently, a committee of medical and reading experts appointed by the Secretary of Health, Education and Welfare concluded that MBD is a small factor in the total problem, and that not more than 2 to 5 percent of the school-age population suffers from physiological disorders that make learning how to read difficult.

The explanation, rather, lies in the cultural disorder underlying the family background of the student, the poor nutrition (a child may lack the energy level to concentrate, although he may be inherently bright), the absence of physical and social amenities. Studies indicate that the best readers come from homes that have lots of appliances and lots of rooms, but not necessarily lots of books.

From this the logical, but erroneous, conclusion might be drawn that if we should simply fill up the homes of non-readers with dish washers and turn on the hot water, the children would necessarily be turned on to print. This might help, but it would not solve the problem. Middle-class culture is as much a symptom of achievement as a reason for it. One appliance, however, that is specifically useful is television. Today, the right to read implies the right to watch TV. As Dr. Sava points out, television stimulates reading and "supplies conceptual background or comprehension and extends interests." But this gives rise to paradox. Although television may improve reading skills, it conditions the child to an electronic mode of communication so that the immediate benefit to books may prove to be a long-term loss.

Moreover, as the poverty child grows older, his limited access to books may choke off an interest in reading. Ghetto libraries are not always geared to ghetto needs: (To the poor, a library can be just another forbidding, middle-class institution.) The very act of teaching "literacy" can discourage a desire to read. Professor Philip Ennis, of Wesleyan University, points out that "The pressure to read for practical purposes can be so heavy and ... onerous due to the training of 'how to read a page' in school that the use of print for other motives can be endangered."

It was with this in mind that the National Book Committee, the Ford Foundation, and the National Endowment for the Humanities combined forces to set up a Books Exposure project in Fall River, Massachusetts, three years ago. Carried out in five "culturally disadvantaged" elementary schools, this experiment in motivation emphasized reading at home as well as at school, and for pleasure rather than achievement.

Fall River proved to be a good choice; as a decaying textile city, it exhibited in microcosm most of the educational problems that attend the economic and social ills of the large metropolis. The school drop-out rate was high (33 percent in high school, an even higher percentage in junior high) and 25 percent of the school population was foreign-born, chiefly Portuguese. By and large, the children came from non-reading backgrounds. Previous efforts to improve their reading skills had been "costly and generally ineffective."

The research design in this project consisted of fifteen experimental and fifteen control classrooms, at grade levels one through five. Some fifty-seven volunteers were recruited, most of them local adults. In the experimental groups, reading sessions were held once a week, during school hours. Children were allowed to take books home, and they were given four books a year, of their own choice, as gifts. They also wrote their own poems, book reports, and stories. Emphasis was on "surrounding children with stimulating adults who encourage them to read, . . . share their excitement about books, and give them books of their own to keep."

The control groups, by comparison, were supplied with books, which the students were allowed to borrow, but there were no volunteers, no reading sessions, no writing projects, and no gift books. The results, when measured against the experimental units, were dramatically lower in the development of "reading attitudes," although both groups showed improvement over previous performance. In sum, continued exposure to books created a desire to read for pleasure, and when this was reinforced by group reading, adult stimulation, and book ownership, the children for the first time tended to prefer reading to many other forms of activity, and to "become increasingly careful in their choices."

Books Exposure is now moving on for tryouts in Boston and Minneapolis. Among older children, similar success in turning non-readers into readers has been achieved in "crash programs" such as that carried out in the nearly all-black Marshall High School on Chicago's South Side. A few years ago, Principal Henry Springs set up educational (he doesn't call it remedial) reading classes for students who wanted to catch up. "We keep these reading labs open from eight o'clock in the morning until ten at night, and the students come in," Springs told a conference organized by the National Book Committee. "The students run the bookshop, and they sell the books [primarily black-oriented] as fast as we can purchase them. . . . Some of the youngsters can't read these books, but they carry them around all the time." It is not just a matter of chance that more than 50 percent of Marshall graduates now go on to college.

The National Reading Council hopes to enlist ten million volunteer tutors by 1976 to work with children who need help. A network of training centers will be set up across the country, model tutorial programs are to be conducted in various cities, and a public relations campaign will recruit volunteers and sell the idea to local communities, with the necessary funding to come from the Office of Education and other federal agencies.

"Tutoring breaks down the unproductive teacher-class relationship and, by definition, sets up a high productive arrangement of one-to-one where concern is paramount," the council declares. In tests to date, the most effective tutors have proved to be older children. "It has been shown that such programs upgrade the reading skills of not only the pupil but the tutor as well," the council adds.

Well and good, but where do we go from here? Fortunately, public libraries are beginning to take up the challenge of the ghetto in "outreach" programs directed at non-borrowers and (in many cases) non-readers. This is sometimes done by setting up neighborhood, or storefront, centers manned by community personnel. The Brooklyn Public Library's "3 Bs" project places small collections of paperbound books in bars, beauty salons, and barber shops. A few cities run free bus service for children in the district to get them into the library. The New Haven center ties in books with handicraft, art, music, and language clubs for young people. In some libraries, phonograph records provide background music for reading sessions, as well as enticement for the rock-happy young.

All of these programs have two things in common: They direct their primary efforts at poverty areas, and, hopefully, they extend the idea of literacy beyond the merely functional. Ultimately, for the millions of marginally literate in this country, reading must become its own reward. The right to read means more than knowing how to fill out a form.

PART THREE

Promising Programs

CHAPTER NINE

Personalized Reading Programs for the Guidance of Emotional Growth

Much human need is motivated by the desire for self-actualization, realization of potential. The mere capacity to act in certain ways seems to create the necessity to do so. Because this need is so strong, teachers who would create permanent reading habits should consider programs that contribute to the emotional lives of their students. The child must need to learn to read. To initiate that need, we must help him discover the connection between the needs he has and their satisfaction in reading. The professional reading teacher can help students find very personal emotional experiences in reading.

We have come to recognize the legitimacy of satisfying needs through reading. It has been many years since the development and introduction of the first edition of *Reading Ladders for Human Relations* (2). The work of Caroline Shrodes (1) and others is eloquent testimony to the notion that reading can affect people in predictable ways. Those authors (3) support a planned strategy for the presentation of literature which will take the reader through a three-step emotional process of identification, catharsis, and insight. The deliberate preparation of reading experiences for their emotional value need not be polarized to appear to be the evil function of a brain-washing demon but, rather, may simply be the cautious concern for the impact of reading materials. Whether we prepare for it or not, however, students will be affected by reading matter.

Personalized reading programs pivot about concepts of developing interests in reading and reading interests. On one hand, teachers have aspirations that students will grow in certain ways. At the same time, they want to "begin where the student is." The personalized program hopes to develop student reading interests while simultaneously, through repeated satisfactions, developing an interest in reading as a way of problem solving. Proponents of these strategies believe emotional growth and positive mental health to be the most valid foundations upon which to build school programs.

References

1. Russell, David H., and Shrodes, Caroline. "Contributions of Research in Bibliotherapy to the Language Arts Program." *The School Review* (September 1950).
2. Taba, Hilda *et al. Reading Ladders for Human Relations.* Washington, D.C.: The American Council on Education, 1947.
3. Zaccharias, and Moses. *Facilitating Human Development.* Urbana, Illinois: Stipes Publishing Co., 1969.

**David H. Russell
and Caroline Shrodes**

Here, perhaps the two most well-known theorists connected with bibliotherapy team up for its defense. In this two-part series, Professors David Russell and Caroline Shrodes spell out the background, nature, and implications of bibliotherapy—the use of reading for emotional growth.

Contributions of Research in Bibliotherapy to the Language-Arts Program. I*

New ideas and procedures continually spring into action in an enterprise as vital as the school. The creative teacher and the interested group of children or adolescents compose a dynamic situation in which new practices either evolve or erupt. A fresh approach to the study of the community, an original story or play, novel insights in history or science, and other creative developments are always appearing in a good school.

Among the newer interests of some such schools today is the process of bibliotherapy. Teachers and children are increasingly using books, not simply to practice reading skills, but to influence total development. The influence of reading upon personalities is a current concern of an increasing number of librarians and language-arts teachers.

A Theory of Bibliotherapy

Bibliotherapy may be defined as a process of dynamic interaction between the personality of the reader and literature—interaction which may be utilized for personality assessment, adjustment, and growth. This definition suggests that bibliotherapy is not a strange, esoteric activity but one that lies within the province of every teacher of literature in working with every child in a group. It does not assume that the teacher must be a skilled

---

*References for Part I and Part II will be found following Part II.

David H. Russell and Caroline Shrodes, "Contributions of Research in Bibliotherapy to the Language Arts Program. I," *School Review,* Vol. 58, No. 7, October 1950, University of Chicago Press. Copyright © 1950 by The University of Chicago. All rights reserved. Printed in U.S.A. Reprinted with permission.

therapist, nor the child a seriously maladjusted individual needing clinical treatment. Rather, it conveys the idea that all teachers must be aware of the effects of reading upon children and must realize that, through literature, most children can be helped to solve the developmental problems of adjustment which they face.

Lest, by this definition, bibliotherapy be made to seem too commonplace, it may be well to point out that the process is not involved every time a child or adolescent has a book in his hand. Many literature periods are still of the sort Henry Seidel Canby calls "cross-word-puzzle scholarship," with emphasis upon literary details rather than upon enjoyment and emotional response to a work of art. Even in the latter approach to literature, thoughtful teachers of the language arts are no longer sure that a particular selection or poem is a "good" one for all members of a class. They are realizing that the piece of literature which may have a profound effect on one child leaves another utterly unmoved. They are becoming aware that every story, poem, or selection is read by a specific individual who brings to it his own complex perceptions and reactions, based on his particular needs. The book that illustrates courage to one child may give hints on home decoration to another; the story that suddenly gives an adolescent insight into his own family situation may be utterly boring to his neighbor in the class. Interaction between the work of literature and the individual may or may not take place.

If there is a genuine therapeutic effect from reading, it may be explained theoretically in terms of *identification, catharsis,* and *insight,* terms originating in psychoanalytic literature but now more widely accepted by psychologists. In such terms, bibliotherapy becomes a process of identifying with another character or group so that feelings are released and the individual develops a greater awareness of his own motivations and rationalizations for his behavior.

Identification is the real or imagined affiliation of one's self (or sometimes a parent or a friend) with a character or group in the story read. It may be facilitated by various conditions (54). It may augment self-esteem if the character is admired or increase feelings of belonging by reducing the sense of difference from others. It may increase understanding of the parent or friend, be productive of a more realistic attitude toward his limitations or strengths, and even reduce a sense of guilt which was a product of earlier difficulties with that parent or friend.

Thus, identification usually involves *catharsis.* The fact that the reader feels he is the character read about means that he shares the character's motivations and conflicts and experiences vicariously the character's emotions. As the reader puts himself in the place of others, he comes to understand the needs and aspirations of these others—and of himself. Reading may therefore provide a release of tension through symbolic gratification of socially unacceptable urges or substitute gratification of socially approved motives.

Finally, when the self-recognition in identification is borne out in reality, the identification represents *insight*—seeing one's self in the behavior of the character and thereby achieving an awareness of one's own motivations and needs. If his adjustments to life-situations are maladaptive, the individual's recognition of himself in the character may help in breaking certain habits. On the other hand, if the character appears to work out a satisfactory solution to his problem, opportunity is provided for the reader to incorporate some of the character's behavior in his own methods of adjustment to a similar problem.

Identification does not always lead to insight, for it may consist simply in imputing one's own motives to others, in reading one's own interpretation into the behavior of the fictional character. One form of such identification is to seek a scapegoat and vent upon the chosen character a strong emotion felt in an earlier affective experience. In general, however, the close interrelationships and interaction of identification, catharsis, and insight are apparent. Implicit in this discussion are other mechanisms of behavior such as projection, rationalization, repression, autism (46), and compensation—all of which influence the degree and nature of any therapeutic process which may occur.

This summary of a theory of bibliotherapy is put largely in psychoanalytic terms. Although research in psychology and medicine has not yet identified all their implications, they are terms which have been incorporated into the work of many clinics and the writing of many psychologists (60). At present they seem to give the best theoretical explanation of the process of bibliotherapy. As Shrodes (62) has pointed out, dynamic psychology, field theory, and the newer emphasis upon autism in perception and cognition, as well as psychoanalytic theory, may be shown to have congruent points of view in explaining the diagnostic and the adjustment values of bibliotherapy. The eclectic nature of the theory is further illustrated in some of the possible values of bibliotherapy stated in the literature on the subject.

Values of Bibliotherapy

Divergent attitudes toward the values of reading include Plato's injunction that myths are not good for the morals of the young, Francis Bacon's assertion that "reading maketh a full man," and Adler's conviction that reading improves thinking (1). In addition to the recreational and informational values usually attributed to reading, a number of therapeutic values have been stated. As might be expected, some of the first of these statements were medical. In his book *Fear,* Oliver says, "The right kind of book may be applied to a mental illness just as a definite drug is applied to some bodily need"(47:291). Menninger states:

> The whole matter of bibliotherapy, of the relief of suffering by the psychological processes induced by reading, is a field in which we have little scientific knowledge. But our intuition and our experience tell us that books may indeed "minister to a mind diseased" and come to the aid of the doctor and even precede him [43:ix].

Other writers have mentioned more specific values of bibliotherapy. Although often stated from the clinical point of view, many of these have implications for the school's language-arts program. Appel (5) believes bibliotherapy can help the individual in six ways. It can help him 1. to acquire information and knowledge about the psychology and physiology of human behavior; 2. to live up to the injunction, "Know thyself"; 3. to become more extroverted and find interest in something outside himself; 4. to effect a controlled release of unconscious difficulties; 5. to use the opportunity for identification and compensation; and 6. to clarify difficulties and to acquire insight into his own behavior.

Bryan (11) believes that bibliotherapy can help develop maturity and nourish and sustain mental health. She states such specific values as giving the person the feeling that he is not the first to encounter the problem he is facing; permitting the reader to see that there is more than one solution to his problem or more than one choice to be made; helping the reader to see the basic motivation of people involved in situations such as his own; helping the reader to see values in experience in human, rather than material, terms; providing facts needed in solving a problem; and encouraging the reader to plan and execute a constructive course of action.

In addition to some of the points made above, Gottschalk (26) believes that reading may have therapeutic values by stimulating the patient to discuss problems which he ordinarily avoids because of fear, shame, or guilt; by helping the patient to analyze and synthesize further his attitudes and behavior patterns; by providing vicarious life-experiences without exposing the person to the real dangers of actual experience; by reinforcing, through precept and example, acceptable social behavior and inhibiting infantile patterns of behavior; by stimulating the imagination; and by enlarging the individual's sphere of interests.

Smith and Twyeffort (66) regard the development of insight as the crucial factor in bibliotherapy. In addition to points made above, they believe reading may be a valuable adjunct to treatment in helping the patient achieve insight, defined as an emotional as well as an intellectual appreciation of the causes of his difficulties; may assist toward a better understanding of the manifold function of personality, especially the role of the emotions and the nature of complexes; may aid the patient in verbalizing and externalizing his problems; may help dispel a sense of isolation; may show how persons with the same personal liabilities tackled apparent failure with some success; may facilitate frank stock-taking of personal assets and liabilities; and may begin deeper changes in a person who is inclined to respond at a superficial level.

In an earlier book (51) and a recent chapter (50) Rosenblatt analyzes the contributions of imaginative literature less in medical terms and more in relation to the work of the teacher. She believes that prolonged contact with personalities in books may have such social effects as 1. leading to increased social sensitivity, enabling the reader to put himself in another's place; 2. developing the habit of interpreting the interactions of temperament upon temperament; 3. enabling one to feel the needs, sufferings, and aspirations of other people; 4. helping an individual to assimilate the cultural pattern by acquainting him with the attitudes and expectancies of his group; and 5. releasing the adolescent from provincialism by extending awareness beyond his own family, community, and national background. In addition, Rosenblatt gives a number of personal values in bibliotherapy, such as those stated by other authors. She further recognizes the preventive values of literature. She believes that literature may prevent the growth of neurotic tendencies through vicarious participation in other lives and that the guilt-possessed or rebellious adolescent may understand himself better even if his conduct is not prized in his environment. She states: "Frequently literature is the only means by which he can discover that his own inner life reflects a common experience of others in his society"(51:243).

These possible values of bibliotherapy help to extend the concept of the process. They indicate some of the newer possible uses of literature in the clinic or classroom with a group or an individual. Most of the writers quoted agree that bibliotherapy provides opportunity for catharsis and greater insight into one's own motivation and the behavior of others. They agree that in bibliotherapy some sort of integration of intellectual perception and emotional drive takes place.

An analysis of the formal research which illustrates in specific situations the theoretical values of bibliotherapy given in this article and a discussion of bibliotherapy in the schools will be presented in an article to follow.

David H. Russell
and Caroline Shrodes

Contributions of Research in Bibliotherapy to the Language-Arts Program. II

A theory of bibliotherapy and its possible values and a bibliography of writings on the subject were presented in the first part of this article, which appeared in last month's issue [October 1950] of the *School Review*. Part II presents a digest of the research on bibliotherapy and suggests implications for practice and further research.

Research and Professional Literature on Bibliotherapy

The scanty literature available on bibliotherapy gives theories of the process and leads for further research, but it contains few definitive answers for teachers, librarians, psychologists, and psychiatrists. Many of the articles have been written for and by librarians and others working with patients in general and mental hospitals, and these efforts are largely descriptive rather than experimental. In educational literature, studies of the relationships between reading difficulties and personality maladjustments have been summarized by Gates (24), by Wilking (73), and by Russell (52). Russell points out that evidence of the positive effects of reading is largely lacking. Most of the writing summarized below deals with hypotheses about the process of bibliotherapy. A few illustrations of the use of

---

David H. Russell and Caroline Shrodes, "Contributions of Research in Bibliotherapy to the Language Arts Program. II," *School Review*, Vol. 58, No. 8, November 1950, University of Chicago Press. Copyright © 1950 by The University of Chicago. All rights reserved. Printed in U.S.A. Reprinted with permission.

bibliotherapy in case-study approaches to research in medical institutions, in libraries, and in schools can be given.

General summaries of research in bibliotherapy. These studies are limited in scope and content. In a pioneer volume in 1923 Jones (30) discussed uses of books in hospital libraries and gave classified reading lists. Bryan later wrote a series of three articles (10,11,12) which developed a theory of bibliotherapy and gave steps needed to make it a more exact science. While most writers use the term with reference to mental-hygiene literature and to books of a didactic nature concerned with adjustment, personality, child-rearing, and similar topics, Bryan includes the whole range of literature— novels, plays, poetry, religion, art, and scientific books—in the materials to be used in bibliotherapy. Schneck (58) gave one of the most complete lists of bibliographies for use in bibliotherapy, but he confined his account largely to materials for use in general hospitals and with neuropsychiatric patients. Other lists have been developed by Appel (5), the Elliotts (21), and Levine (34). Tyson (69) reviewed some of the recent writing on bibliotherapy before analyzing the content of mental-hygiene textbooks, popular books, and a popular journal on personal adjustment. Shrodes (62) listed 113 items in her study developing a theory of bibliotherapy and applying it in case studies of college students.

General descriptions. A number of studies related more or less closely to the field of bibliotherapy are also available. A pioneer investigation by Downey (18) attempted to divide readers into three main categories: persons who are detached, impersonal *spectators* as they read; persons who are *participants* as they read, becoming deeply involved in the emotions and situations of the story; and persons who become emotionally involved but are *philosophers* about the story because their projections are not egocentric so much as mature reactions to the story.

In a summary of the first years of development of projective methods of studying personality, Sargent (56) includes some references on drama, story-telling, and language in relation to personality which have implications for bibliotherapy. Although not strictly research, Rosenblatt's exploratory work (51) contains many ideas fundamental to a theory of bibliotherapy. Waples and Others (71) have also studied the influences of reading upon people from a somewhat different point of view from the one expressed in the first part of this discussion. Gray (27) has summarized thirty studies dealing with the effects of reading on information and beliefs, attitudes and morale, public opinion, voting, crime, and antisocial behavior. Carlsen (14), in a study of the influence of reading upon attitudes, found that white adolescents at the eleventh-grade level vary in their reactions to stories about Negroes in terms of their previous attitudes to Negroes. In a study somewhat more closely related to the present theme, Loban (36) reviews some of the previous work in bibliotherapy as background for his comparison of the responses to ten literary selections made by two groups of adolescents who were rated as extremely high and low in their capacity for sympathy. His study emphasizes the need of adolescents for a teacher's help in discussing the significant causes underlying behavior and events in a story.

Medical uses. Medical explorations (rather than experiments) in bibliotherapy seem to be the most numerous group described in the literature. Schneck (57) has described the bibliotherapy project which has been operating at the Menninger Foundation in Topeka, Kansas, for several years. Earlier, Menninger (43) described briefly a few examples of bibliotherapy, and Schneck (59) has reported on two other cases from this clinic. Some early reports (16) on the use of bibliotherapy in United States Veterans Hospitals are available, and more information should be forthcoming from this source. Bradley and Bosquet (9) advised physicians on the use of books for children, suggested four therapeutic uses of literature, and attached a short bibliography of useful stories and books.

As a result of experience in using mental-hygiene literature, rather than imaginative literature, Gottschalk (26) believes that patients with mild psychoneurotic disturbances are more likely to be helped by supervised reading than are severely disturbed or psychotic patients. Gagnon (23) disagrees with Gottschalk and emphasizes the danger in furnishing early and mild cases of schizophrenia with books which might facilitate their flights from reality. However, he states that reading may have sedative effects on persons in moderate manic or excitable states. Smith and Twyeffort (66) believe that many maladjustments are due to ignorance or inaccurate knowledge and, therefore, recommend books with mental-hygiene content. Moore (45) describes work with adolescents. After giving early examples of bibliotherapy in hospitals and in the Delaware Human Relations classes, he describes two cases in which "the data ... presented give us a glimpse of a technique of great therapeutic importance"(45:232).

A number of the reports cited are of interest to librarians. These include the writings of Jones (30), of Bryan (10,11,12) and of Schneck (57,59), mentioned above, and another article in which Quint (49) points out the values of reading in a total program of maintaining contact with reality. Although not research, librarians may be interested in anthologies, such as those of Shrodes, Van Gundy, and Husband (63) and of Strode (68), which are collected for the purpose of giving psychological and sociological insights through literature. A few studies of the use of the library to influence specific attitudes are available, such as Jackson's investigation (29) of the attitudes of white children in Atlanta, Georgia, toward Negro children before and after reading material dealing with Negro children.

Educational applications. Studies dealing with the positive use of literature in school situations for therapy are likewise meager, although a beginning in experimentation is evident. In addition to Loban's work (36), an early study by Lind (35) gives reports obtained through interview and written document of what thirty adults thought the four main values of reading were to them as children. Russell's more recent study (54) of 680 teachers' memories of books read as children found a variety of remembered effects, including identification with characters, enjoyment of humor and fantasy, enrichment of everyday experiences, imitation of activities as in dramatic play, and added knowledge of facts.

Articles by Sister Mary Agnes (40,41) and the investigation by Sister Lorang (37) developed some hypotheses which require further investigation. Sister Mary Agnes found some improvement in the adjustments of four out of five children in the upper elementary grades after the reading of four or five books, although only one of the five children saw any connection between his own problems and those of the characters in the books. Sister Lorang used a questionnaire to get the opinions of 2,308 high-school students, in eight schools, about specific books and magazines that they had read and the effects of this reading on them. Fifty-three percent of the group said they had tried to act like a character in a book and 21 percent like a character in a magazine.

A publication by Kircher (32), influenced by the work of Moore (45), emphasizes the dynamic character of the reading process and its help in emotional adjustment. Unlike some other writers, Kircher believes literature may produce a delayed response, that solutions contained in it may be utilized a considerable time after the reading. She also gives an annotated bibliography of children's stories and adds the principles or solutions which they may contain for children reading them.

Smith (67) reviewed some of the research on the personal and social influences of reading and reported a study in which teachers asked 502 children in Grades IV through VIII if they remembered any book, story, or poem which had changed their thinking in any way. About 60 percent of the group reported changes in attitude, but only 9 percent changes in behavior as a result of reading; 30 percent told of changes in thinking as a result of new or enlarged concepts obtained through reading.

Another study of a different sort, based on the hypothesis that reading has direct influence on attitudes and adjustments of children, is that of Child and Others (15) who analyzed a group of third-grade textbooks in reading for the social ideas and stereotypes contained in them. The study offers no proof that children are affected by reading such textbooks, but it is useful in pointing out the middle-class backgrounds of the books and in listing some of the ideas implied which teachers often take for granted without examining them critically. Using a somewhat similar method, Wenzel (72) applied the ideas of Rosenblatt (51) and of Sample (55) in analyzing certain children's stories. The illustrations are useful examples of how a teacher, a librarian, or small groups may analyze fictional materials to find ideas implicit in them which may be more or less unconsciously absorbed into children's attitudes.

The values of literature in inducting the child into his culture have been investigated by the Shaftels (61), who made an exploratory study of the use of problem stories based upon the developmental tasks of middle childhood. After reading and discussing the stories, the children were given opportunity to act out their solutions. Other references to psychodrama are given in the summary by Sargent (56). The use of reading in conjunction with psychodrama and sociodrama to arrive at the solution of children's problems would seem to be a fruitful lead for further research and practice.

Although not conducted in the school situation, procedures used by Panken (48) seemed to show the usefulness of bibliotherapy with a group of juvenile delinquents for whom psychotherapy was unavailable. In children's letters to the judge—letters answered by him personally—there was some evidence that carefully selected books may stimulate healthy identifications, alter antisocial attitudes, and ameliorate the effects of a bad environment.

Not all the writing on bibliotherapy is as positive about its benefits as are the studies mentioned above. For example, Goldsmith (25) found that children are not usually able to draw inferences from fables. Therefore, the belief that fables are concrete examples of abstract truths, useful in character education, may be seriously questioned. Russell (53) suggests that literature can be expected to influence adjustments only if the children are able to read easily and well, if wide varieties of suitable materials are available, if a permissive reading environment exists, and if school and community experiences reinforce the reading. The importance of a permissive environment and of an opportunity to manipulate the elements of a reading situation toward several possible interpretations or reconstructions is suggested by Husband (28). He also states:

> In the degree that a reading situation exerts a compulsion toward preciseness in interpretation, it tends to create a negative response, which diminishes with the progressive development of reading maturity or sophistication (28:266).

In a study of the effects of reading a novel on a tenth-grade group, Meckel (42) is cautious of expecting positive effects automatically to follow reading. He states that his findings do not justify concluding that a pupil having tensions and anxieties may be given a novel which deals with the same tensions and anxieties and expecting therapeutic results to follow automatically. On the contrary, the data suggest that these anxieties, if they are serious, may tend to repress and to block the desired response to the very situations and ideas having potential therapeutic value.

Auerbach makes somewhat the same point in connection with mental-hygiene literature:

> Each book is read ... by a specific individual who brings to the book he is reading his own complex reactions and biases, based on his particular needs. ...
> The more mature the reader is, the more he will pick what he needs or distort what he reads to fit his emotional needs (7:40,54).

The literature on bibliotherapy contains both research evidence and opinion which should act as a brake on undue claims for the process. Apparently, there is no guaranty that a particular piece of literature will influence a certain child or adolescent or that an influence, if it exists, will operate in the direction desired.

Implications for Research and Practice

Need for validation. The positive values claimed for bibliotherapy in certain studies and the reservations about it raised in others point clearly to the necessity of validating the procedure experimentally. From at least the days of the Greeks, great teachers have always used literature in attempts to influence their pupils' attitudes and ideals. Nearly all the studies cited above claim some influence on the adjustments of the persons who have read prescribed books or stories, but these claims have not always been validated by study of the later behavior of the patient or pupil. One attempt to validate the process has been made by Tyson (69) who sought the opinions of authors, analysts, and college undergraduates regarding the value of bibliotherapy. Six of the eight psychoanalysts favored it as an adjunct to individual treatment. There was a general consensus that reading has value as a source of information and as reassurance for persons with mild personality disorders. Obviously, much more work in the validation of the process of bibliotherapy is needed.

Extension into schools. Besides lack of validation, another limitation evident in the literature is the paucity of work with the average or the mildly disturbed person outside the clinic or hospital. Several writers suggest that bibliotherapy is more likely to be successful with younger people; several, that it is most applicable in cases of only mild disturbance. The implications for schools and colleges, with their facilities for recommending books and discussing them in group-guidance situations, would seem to be fairly clear.

In this practice, limitations, such as reading ability of pupils and home and community influences, must also be recognized. But work so far done in the field indicates the possibility that literature can be used most effectively not in institutions for the mentally ill but in schools where it is possible to influence the adjustment of the so-called "normal" child or youth.

Types of reading. A third implication for research and practice concerns the values of imaginative versus didactic and factual literature. A number of analysts cited above prescribe factual books for their patients and, in truth, believe that these are best for the individual who needs more contact with reality. On the other hand, psychiatrists and psychologists admit that great artists are penetrating interpreters of the human personality. Since the great writer has the power to understand, describe, and project to the reader some phase of personality, he should be enlisted as an ally in diagnosis and therapy. These are some suggestions that admonitory, prescriptive reading is largely an intellectual exercise whereas the identification, projection, and other mechanisms involved in reading imaginative literature may incorporate into the reading situation the emotional behavior associated with most maladjustment. A further possibility is that *both* factual and fictional materials are useful, depending upon the particular needs of the individual, and, therefore, that the teacher's or librarians's task is to find some balance between these types of material.

Use of literature in appraising personality. A fourth implication for research concerns the values of literature in assessment of personality or diagnosis of personality difficulties. Some skilful language-arts teachers study a pupil's reading interests. If they find that these deviate widely from the norm of the group in which the child or adolescent is found, they gain information about that pupil. The current interest in projective techniques suggests that research might go much further in using reactions to pieces of literature as one means of studying personality. If individual perception of ink blots or vague pictures can give such clues, reactions to selections from literature would seem to be a fruitful source of study of personality.

Bibliotherapy in clinical treatment. A fifth implication for research concerns the use of bibliotherapy in clinical situations. There is some evidence that bibliotherapy makes for economy of time and effort in that an individual may be reading and thinking about his problems when he is away from the clinic or therapist. In view of present shortages of skilled clinical workers and the very recent establishment of such services by some school systems, research on bibliotherapy as a facilitation of treatment should be undertaken.

Relations between reading materials and the reader. A final implication for research is of especial concern to school people. Bibliotherapy may be regarded as only one phase of a larger-scale study of relationships between reading materials and the reader. In the past, literature has been studied in terms of its own structure and in terms of the person producing it. The time is long overdue for comprehensive studies of the *effects* of literature upon the reader. In such studies, bibliotherapy will have an important place because certain characteristics and effects may be observed more easily in the somewhat extreme cases involved in bibliotherapy. Research on bibliotherapy should, therefore, prove fruitful of hypotheses to be tested with children and adolescents in ordinary classroom situations.

Suggestions for Librarians and Teachers

In addition to the six implications for research, a number of suggestions arising out of the literature concern more directly the work of librarians and language-arts teachers.

Matching reading with the difficulty. One problem is: What kind of story for what kind of difficulty? Should the adolescent with parent-child problems be advised to read a story of family conflict, or must he be approached more indirectly? Will the quiet, recessive boy profit by reading about a person like himself or an extroverted, popular adolescent? In one clinic Menninger (43) finds it impractical to prescribe books on the basis of one diagnostic category, of etiological factors, or of type of personality. Rather, the individual's present psychological status, his emotional state, the amount of his withdrawal from reality, and his ability to profit from reading are taken into account.

The answer for teachers or librarians, then, is not clear cut. The recommendation of pleasant, cheerful books instead of stories dealing with emotionally disturbed characters, morbid themes, or unhappy endings may seem to be a good beginning for a child or youth who is himself unhappy and disturbed, but at some later time, perhaps, he will need to read stories which deal more directly with his problem. Perhaps the child or adolescent who has already built fairly satisfactory psychological defenses should not be forced to tear these down because of a more direct discussion of his problems in literature. The teacher or librarian can, at best, work on an experimental basis, trying different sorts of stories and giving opportunities for discussing and restructuring these in the group situation, with perhaps deeper analysis in individual interviews.

Involvement of entire language-arts program. This suggestion merges into the one given by Husband (28), the Shaftels (61), and others that children and youth need opportunities to discuss a character, to disagree with a solution, to dramatize or act out their own solutions. Thus, not only the literature period but the whole language-arts program is involved. The modern teacher uses the child's or adolescent's problems as one source of motivation for writing a personal letter or history for the teacher, not something shared with the whole group. Through this personal writing, the teacher's and pupil's insight into a problem may be increased. The teacher may become less concerned with split infinitives and more concerned with split personality; unity and coherence in the paragraph may become subordinated to unity and coherence of the self.

The teaching of reading. There are also implications from bibliotherapy for the teaching of reading. A child or adolescent must be able to read rather easily the material presented to him if identification and positive emotional response are to develop, but the teaching of reading cannot stop at accurate word recognition or even at comprehension. Particularly in the upper-elementary and the secondary-school grades, the dynamic nature of the reading of literature must be considered by the teacher. The selective nature of perception and cognition, the fact that even young children may discover in reading what they want to discover needs further emphasis in the whole program of reading instruction. Crossen (17), for example, has shown that a group of ninth- and tenth-grade pupils unfavorable to the Negro make lower scores on a critical reading test based on materials about Negroes than a similar group with indifferent (neither favorable nor unfavorable) attitudes toward the Negro.

The teaching of reading, at least beyond the initial learning stages, must be directed not only toward accuracy and objectivity but also toward positive emotional values. Children and adolescents need many opportunities to use their reading in creative ways for enrichment of their experience and better understanding of themselves and others.

Cautions for teachers. A few writers and speakers have suggested recently that the language-arts teacher should not attempt bibliotherapy, that it is too difficult and dangerous a process to be tried out by untrained persons. The writers of this article have some sympathy for this point of view. They are aware that few teachers are trained therapists. They are equally aware, however, that most psychologists and psychotherapists have no final answers to problems of influencing human adjustment, that experimentation is needed in attempting to meet personal needs of children and adolescents as well as adults. It seems that bibliotherapy offers one such experimental approach, particularly when correlated with other procedures attempting to improve insight and adjustment. These two articles have emphasized, furthermore, the planned use of literature with the so-called "normal" child, the individual whose problems and tensions are the usual developmental ones rather than deep-seated conflicts. In such cases the dangers of using emotionally charged literature should be less.

Contributions of Research to the Language-Arts Program. II 219

But even to attempt bibliotherapy on this level, the teacher must have certain resources. In addition to those mentioned in previous statements, he must know a wide range of books—books which illustrate the ideas to be presented to the child or adolescent. Wide reading of stories for youth should be supplemented by knowledge of books about juvenile literature, such as Eaton's *Reading with Children* (20), Duff's *Bequest of Wings* (19), Arbuthnot's *Children and Books* (6), Smith's chapter on "Guiding Individual Reading" (64), and even Lenrow's *Reader's Guide to Prose Fiction* (33). Teachers in both elementary and secondary schools will find particularly helpful the publications *Literature for Human Understanding* (3) and *Reading Ladders for Human Relations* (4). A group of teachers may build similar lists to fit the needs and problems of youth in a particular community.

In addition to knowing books, the teacher must know the child or adolescent. He must be aware of the usual characteristics of children of the age level with which he is working and recognize any deviations from the usual shown by an individual or group. He will profit by knowing something of the individual's abilities and interests; by knowing the pattern of the child's reading interests in relation to the rest of his group; by having some personal reports from the pupil about his family, his activities, and his ambitions; by observing his behavior in classroom, in informal groups, or on the playground. As time and energy permit, the teacher must have informal interviews with the pupil, both before and after bibliotherapy is begun. In beginning the process, he will know enough about the child or adolescent to suggest a story in which identification is often pleasant and easy.

This knowledge of books, plus knowledge of children or adolescents, puts such a burden on the teacher that once again the process of bibliotherapy seems impossibly difficult. But what language-arts teacher can teach without knowing something about books and about children? The knowledge and understanding are there for any good teacher; it is simply a case of directing them along a channel leading to therapy through literature. Furthermore, in most schools the sole responsibility does not rest upon the teacher. The best approach to bibliotherapy is often a co-operative approach involving the teacher, the librarian, the school counselor or psychologist, and others who know the child well. An occasional case conference of such persons to discuss the individual and suggest reading and other therapeutic measures is desirable.

Finally, bibliotherapy may be conceived as an attempt to unite practices in education, in clinical work, and in mental hygiene. Teachers of the language arts and of psychology may use bibliotherapy to illustrate ideas common to both fields. Clinical workers may use it with economy for diagnosis, prognosis, and therapy. Mental-hygiene experts may include it in an expanding program of positive mental health and prevention of mental disorders. Research and practice are urgently needed in schools and other institutions if this new technique for human welfare is to become generally available.

References

1. Adler, Mortimer. *How To Read a Book.* New York: Simon & Schuster, 1940.
2. Alexander, Franz, and French, Thomas M. *Psychoanalytic Therapy.* New York: Ronald Press, 1946.
3. American Council on Education, Committee on Intergroup Education. *Literature for Human Understanding.* Washington: American Council on Education, 1948.
4. American Council on Education, Committee on Intergroup Education. *Reading Ladders for Human Relations.* Washington: American Council on Education, 1949 (revised).
5. Appel, Kenneth E. "Psychiatric Therapy." *Personality and the Behavior Disorders,* Vol. II. Edited by J. McV. Hunt. New York: Ronald Press, 1944, pp. 1107-63.
6. Arbuthnot, May Hill. *Children and Books.* Chicago: Scott, Foresman & Co., 1947.
7. Auerbach, Aline B. "Can Mental Hygiene Books Improve Mental Health?" *Child Study* 26 (Spring 1949):39-40.
8. Blanchard, Phyllis. "Adolescent Experience in Relation to Personality and Behavior." *Personality and the Behavior Disorders,* Vol. II. Edited by J. McV. Hunt. New York: Ronald Press, 1944, pp. 691-713.
9. Bradley, Charles, and Bosquet, E. S. "Uses of Books for Psychotherapy with Children." *American Journal of Orthopsychiatry* 6 (January 1936):23-31.
10. Bryan, Alice I. "The Psychology of the Reader." *Library Journal* 64 (January 1939): 7-12.
11. Bryan, Alice I. "Personality Adjustment through Reading." *Library Journal* 64 (August 1939):573-76.
12. Bryan, Alice I. "Can There Be a Science of Bibliotherapy?" *Library Journal* 64 (October, 1939):773-76.
13. Burton, Dwight. "Books To Meet Students' Personal Needs." *English Journal* 36 (November 1947):469-73.
14. Carlsen, George R. "A Study of the Effect of Reading Literature about the Negro on the Racial Attitudes of a Group of Eleventh-Grade Students in Northern Schools." Ph.D. dissertation, University of Minnesota, 1948.
15. Child, Irvin L.; Potter, Elmer H.; and Levine, Estelle M. *Children's Textbooks and Personality Development: An Exploration in the Social Psychology of Education.* Psychological Monographs, 60, no. 3. Evanston, Illinois: American Psychological Association (Northwestern University), 1946.
16. Creglow, Elizabeth. "Therapeutic Value of Properly Selected Reading Matter." *U.S. Veterans Administration Medical Bulletin* 7 (November 1931):1086-89.
17. Crossen, Helen J. "Effects of the Attitudes of the Reader upon Critical Reading Ability." *Journal of Educational Research* 42 (December 1948):289-98.
18. Downey, June E. "Literary Self-projection." *Psychological Review* 19 (July 1912): 299-311.
19. Duff, Annis. *"Bequests of Wings."* New York: Viking Press, 1944.
20. Eaton, Anne Thaxter. *Reading with Children.* New York: Viking Press, 1940.
21. Elliott, H. S., and Elliott, G. L. *Solving Personal Problems.* New York: Henry Holt & Co., 1936.
22. Frank, Lawrence K. *Projective Methods.* Springfield, Illinois: Charles C. Thomas, 1948.
23. Gagnon, Salomon. "Is Reading Therapy?" *Diseases of the Nervous System* 3 (July 1942):206-12.

24. Gates, Arthur I. "The Role of Personality Maladjustment in Reading Disability." *Pedagogical Seminary and Journal of Genetic Psychology* 59 (September 1941):77-83.
25. Goldsmith, Sadie. "The Fable as a Medium for Character Education." *Elementary English Review* 16 (October 1939):223-25, 228.
26. Gottschalk, Louis A. "Bibliotherapy as an Adjuvant in Psychotherapy." *American Journal of Psychiatry* 104 (April 1948):632-37.
27. Gray, William S. "The Social Effects of Reading." *School Review* 55 (May 1947): 269-77.
28. Husband, John D. "A Technique for the Evaluation of Growth in Certain Affective Phases of Reading among High School Pupils." *Journal of Educational Research* 39 (December 1945):265-71.
29. Jackson, Evalene P. "Effects of Reading upon Attitudes toward the Negro Race." *Library Quarterly* 14 (January 1944):47-54.
30. Jones, E. Kathleen, ed. *The Hospital Library.* Chicago: American Library Association, 1923.
31. Kaufman, F. W., and Taylor, W. S. "Literature as Adjustment." *Journal of Abnormal and Social Psychology* 31 (July 1936):229-34.
32. Kircher, Clara J. *Character Formation through Books: A Bibliography.* Washington: Catholic University of America Press, 1945.
33. Lenrow, Elbert, for the Commission on Secondary School Curriculum, Progressive Education Association. *Reader's Guide to Prose Fiction.* New York: D. Appleton—Century Co., 1940.
34. Levine, Maurice. *Psychotherapy in Medical Practice.* New York: Macmillan Co., 1942.
35. Lind, Katherine Niles. "The Social Psychology of Children's Reading." *American Journal of Sociology* 41 (January 1936):454-69.
36. Loban, Walter. "Adolescents of Varying Sensitivity and Their Responses to Literature Intended to Evoke Sympathy." Ph.D. dissertation, University of Minnesota, 1949.
37. Lorang, Sister Mary Corde. *The Effect of Reading upon Moral Conduct and Emotional Experience.* Studies in Psychology and Psychiatry, 6, no. 5. Washington: Catholic University of America Press, 1945.
38. McCaul, Robert L. "The Effect of Attitudes on Reading Interpretation." *Journal of Educational Research* 37 (February 1944):451-57.
39. MacKinnon, Donald W. "Psychodiagnosis in Clinical Practice and Personality Theory." *Journal of Abnormal and Social Psychology* 44 (January 1949):7-13.
40. Mary Agnes, Sister. "Social Values in Children's Poetry." *Elementary English Review* 22 (April 1945):133-38.
41. Mary Agnes, Sister. "Bibliotherapy for Socially Maladjusted Children," *Catholic Education Review* 44 (January, 1946):8-16.
42. Meckel, Henry C. "An Exploratory Study of Responses of Adolescent Pupils to Situations in a Novel." Ph.D. dissertation, University of Chicago, 1946.
43. Menninger, Karl A. *Human Mind.* New York: Alfred A. Knopf, Inc., 1937.
44. Moore, Thomas V. "Bibliotherapy in Psychiatric Practice." *Current Therapies of Personality Disorders.* Edited by Bernard Glueck. New York: Grune & Stratton, 1946, pp. 132-53.
45. Moore, Thomas V. *The Nature and Treatment of Mental Disorders.* New York: Grune & Stratton, 1943.
46. Murphy, Gardner. *Personality.* New York: Harper & Bros., 1947.
47. Oliver, John R. *Fear.* New York: Macmillan Co., 1928.
48. Panken, Jacob. "Psychotherapeutic Value of Books in the Treatment and Prevention of Juvenile Delinquency." *American Journal of Psychotherapy* 1 (January 1947):71-86.
49. Quint, Mary D. "The Mental-Hospital Library." *Mental Hygiene* 28 (April 1944): 263-72.
50. Rosenblatt, Louise M. "The Enriching Values of Reading." *Reading in an Age of Mass Communication.* Edited by William S. Gray. New York: Appleton-Century-Crofts, 1949, pp. 19-38.
51. Rosenblatt, Louise M. *Literature as Exploration.* New York: D. Appleton—Century Co., 1938.

52. Russell, David H. "Reading Disabilities and Mental Health: A Review of Research." *Understanding the Child* 16 (January 1947):24-32.
53. Russell, David H. "Reading Success and Personality Development." *Elementary English* 25 (February 1948):73-82.
54. Russell, David H. "Identification through Literature." *Childhood Education* 25 (May 1949):397-401.
55. Sample, Hazel. *Pitfalls for Readers of Fiction.* Chicago: National Council of Teachers of English, 1940.
56. Sargent, Helen. "Projective Methods: Their Origins, Theory and Application in Personality Research." *Psychological Bulletin* 42 (May 1945):257-93.
57. Schneck, Jerome M. "Studies in Bibliotherapy in a Neuropsychiatric Hospital." *Occupational Therapy and Rehabilitation* 23 (December 1944):316-23.
58. Schneck, Jerome M. "Bibliotherapy and Hospital Library Activities for Neuropsychiatric Patients." *Psychiatry* 8 (February 1945):207-28.
59. Schneck, Jerome M. "Bibliotherapy for Neuropsychiatric Patients: Report on Two Cases." *Bulletin of the Menninger Clinic* 10 (January 1946):18-25.
60. Sears, Robert R. *Survey of Objective Studies of Psychoanalytic Concepts.* Social Science Research Council Bulletin, no. 51. New York: Social Science Research Council, 1943.
61. Shaftel, George, and Shaftel, Fannie R. "Report on the Use of a 'Practice Action Level' in the Stanford University Project for American Ideals." *Sociatry* 1 (December 1947): 57-245; 2 (March, 1948):65-253.
62. Shrodes, Caroline. "Bibliotherapy: A Theoretical and Clinical-Experimental Study." Ph.D. dissertation, University of California, Berkeley, 1949.
63. Shrodes, Caroline; Van Gundy, Justine; and Husband, R. W. *Psychology through Literature: An Anthology.* New York: Oxford University Press, 1943.
64. Smith, Dora V. "Guiding Individual Reading." *Reading in the High School and College.* Forty-seventh Yearbook of the National Society for the Study of Education, Part II. Chicago: Distributed by the University of Chicago Press, 1948, pp. 180-205.
65. Smith, Dora V. "Nature of the Reading Program to Meet Personal and Social Needs." *Promoting Personal and Social Development through Reading.* Edited by William S. Gray. Supplementary Educational Monographs, no. 64. Chicago: University of Chicago Press, 1947, pp. 11-16.
66. Smith, Lauren H., and Twyeffort, Louis H. "Psychoneuroses: Their Origin and Treatment." *The Cyclopedia of Medicine, Surgery and Specialties.* Vol. XII. Edited by G. M. Piersol and E. L. Bortz. Philadelphia: F. A. Davis Co., 1945, pp. 858-83.
67. Smith, Nila Banton. "Personal and Social Values of Reading." *Elementary English* 25 (December 1948):490-500.
68. Strode, Josephine. *Social Insight through Short Stories.* New York: Harper & Bros., 1946.
69. Tyson, Robert. "The Validation of Mental Hygiene Literature." *Journal of Clinical Psychology* 4 (July 1948):304-6.
70. Tyson, Robert. "Content of Mental Hygiene Literature." *Journal of Clinical Psychology* 5 (April 1949):109-14.
71. Waples, Douglas; Berelson, B. R.; and Bradshaw, F. R. *What Reading Does to People.* Chicago: University of Chicago Press, 1940.
72. Wenzel, Evelyn. "Children's Literature and Personality Development." *Elementary English* 25 (January 1948):12-31.
73. Wilking, S. Vincent. "Personality Maladjustment as a Causative Factor in Reading Disability." *Elementary School Journal* 42 (December 1941):268-79.

Eunice S. Newton

One of the more popular reading-core instructional teams in high school is the remedial reading/ethnic studies combination. This author recommends the use of ethnic studies materials for the development of self-concepts. The implications of this practice to relevance and involvement are evident.

Bibliotherapy in the Development of Minority Group Self-Concept

Within the past few years special projects and services have proliferated which are designed to increase the academic attainment of students who progress ineffectively in conventional American educational programs. Despite differences in the materials and activities of these innovative programs, and in spite of the fact that the target populations range from pre-school to the college years, almost without exception their proponents subscribe to belief in the vital role that a positive concept of self plays in the development of a fully-functioning personality (5). A positive concept of self, it is argued, is essential to the learner's personal, social, and intellectual growth and development. Bibliotherapy is frequently utilized in these compensatory programs as one of the vehicles through which personal and ethnic identification may be effected as a means of enhancing concepts of self.

An examination of the educational activities of some of the current programs for inadequately-functioning students will reveal that while bibliotherapy is presented as a standard feature to be utilized in the development of self-concept, rarely if ever is there given the rationale of its use or specific suggestions for practical classroom application of bibliotherapeutic procedures. In this paper, therefore, an attempt will be made to (1) review significant psychological theory relevant to the development of self-concept through identification, (2) present a rationale for the use of bibliotherapy in this process, and (3) suggest some possible bibliotherapeutic procedures to be utilized specifically by teachers of so-called minority groups—Negro,

---

Eunice S. Newton, "Bibliotherapy in the Development of Minority Group Self-Concept," *Journal of Negro Education,* Vol. 38, No. 3, Summer 1969.

Puerto Rican, Appalachian white, American Indian, Mexican and, most recently, Cuban.

Theories on the Acquisition of Self-Concept

The composite portrait of the child who does not benefit from conventional educational programs has been drawn within recent years with increasing accuracy by Clark, Goldberg, Davis, Deutsch, and others (9). The relevant literature attests to the fact that the so-called minority-group child learns of his assigned inferior status at an early age and, as a result, experiences deep feelings of humiliation and rejection. Consequently, even prior to his ability to verbalize his feelings, the minority-group child may become confused about his personal worth because of the lack of social support for positive self-esteem. Under certain conditions usually found in depressed areas in our country today—physical and economic deterioration, family transiency and instability—the child may develop conflicts with regard to his feelings about himself and about the group with which he is identified. The end product of these conflicts, doubts, and confusions frequently is self-hatred, a defeatist attitude, and a lowering of personal ambition.

Personality theorists (8,10) emphasize that from early childhood the individual's concept of self is an important factor in guiding both his immediate behavior and the later development of his personality. The child acts consistently in terms of the kind of person he believes himself to be—bright or stupid, attractive or unattractive, capable or inadequate in meeting the challenges of life. The concept of self is thus his personality viewed from within, and into it are integrated the sum total of the child's experiences.

The development of a concept of self appears to evolve through a sequence of experiences similar in nature to those in the development of attitudes—emotional interaction of the learner with an adult or peer model. The learning of attitudes and the development of concept of self, therefore, may be explained by the same general process which we believe functions in other types of learning. It is generally accepted today that the learner confronts a situation, identifies goals, makes a provisional try, and finds his expectations confirmed or denied. In his choice of beliefs (whether about himself or others), he is guided to certain provisional tries, beliefs, by the example of other people—that is, the learner imitates certain models. He "tries on" roles successively and adopts those with which he feels "comfortable"—roles which meet his needs and already developed attitudes.

The child's first identification is normally with his parents (or parent substitutes) within the immediate family circle. The parents are termed the "primary identifying figures" and the child's initial interaction is believed to establish with them his basic style in subsequent coping behavior with others. Whether the child's personality will be basically *adient, abient,* or *ambient* may be a result of his early emotional interaction with his primary identifying figures (3).

Adults outside of the home may be identifying figures, too. Teachers, recreation leaders, and close relatives with whom the child frequently intermingles, as well as his intimate and constant playmates all may be categorized as "secondary identifying figures." In a hierarchy of prepotency, these secondary identifying figures influence the development of the child's concept of self almost as much as the primary figures. In fact, as the early and middle childhood years wane, the role of the secondary identifying figures customarily increases in importance, and for many children quickly exceeds that of the primary ones.

As reading, television, and community contacts broaden his knowledge of people, usually by the time the child is eight years old his choices of identifying figures increase markedly. It is possible for him to establish strong identification with fictional characters, historical personages, or famous athletes. In some instances, these "tertiary identifying figures" exert critical control of and make vital contribution to the molding of the child's self-concept at this stage of his development.

Identification is a complex way of perceiving another person—partly rational and partly emotional. At this time, psychological theory cannot adequately identify the totality of the process whereby a child selects his chief models. Sometimes the child himself does not know whose example he follows. It is believed that in some instances a veritable human *pasticcio* has been constructed by the child from which he emulates salient traits. It is vitally important that the teacher of minority group children understand the development of self-concept, for the self-concept in the fully-functioning personality dictates the outcome of the teaching-learning interplay.

The Role of Bibliotherapy in Developing Concept of Self

Bibliotherapy is based on the belief that a person is affected by what he reads. This belief is as old as literate society and has been remarked upon in some of the literature of antiquity (2). While bibliotherapy is formally defined as "the use of selected reading materials as therapeutic adjuvants in medicine and psychiatry," for teachers and other educators bibliotherapy is simply the directed reading of books to aid in modifying the attitudes and behavior of children and youth. The effect of reading upon the young has been studied widely and has been, also, the subject of provocative speculation and heated debate.

While direct personal influence of the child's primary and secondary identifying figures is paramount in the formation of self-concept, it has been long appreciated that models in literature may make a positive contribution. The fact that a literary figure may arouse such close empathy that significant influences upon the reader result is of ancient acceptance. In classical times, the library was often called "the healing place of the soul"(7), and the curriculum of both past and present educational institutions has included the study of literature as a valuable source of vicarious interaction in the human experience. The possibility of the learner following examples of successful living and avoiding the errors others have made is widely endorsed by educators as reasonable expectations of directed reading.

It is accepted by theorists in the field of bibliotherapy that books may be the sources of significant models only to the extent that the learner's psycho-social needs are being met (1). It has been suggested that "wish fulfillment" may be the determining module in identifying with a literary character or notable personage. The child's wishes, dreams, or desires may be gratified through "putting himself in the model's shoes" where he may find the role satisfying and fulfilling to his needs. Stated another way, in the evolvement of literary identifying figures, there is an inextricably interdependent relationship between the nature of the reader and the nature of the reading material. For the educator, in its highest level of conception, bibliotherapy is guided reading which takes the learner beyond literal comprehension to discovery through identification of new and personal values. At this level of reading comprehension the learner approaches Roger's (11) conceptualization of "pervasive learning"—learning that affects the individual's present and future behavior, his attitudes, and his personality. This is the kind of learning in which there is a change in self in the direction of self-enhancement.

Bibliotherapeutic Methods for Teachers of Minority Group Learners

Teachers of minority group children and youth may introduce them to the "world of books" in the expectation that a sense of self-discovery may result from discovering the common elements in human experience. A dual role is required of these teachers: they must be cartographers of the map of the "world of books" as well as skillful guides able to lead their students through the peaks, valley, plains, and rivers of the accumulated record of the culture of man.

In earlier sections of this paper, the theoretical bases were established for the processes whereby concepts of self are developed and for the role

Bibliotherapy in the Development of Minority Group Self Concept 227

of bibliotherapy in self-identification. At this point, guidelines for teachers of minority-group children and youth will be presented which may be used in guided reading for the development of self-concept. While the principal materials, presented in the ensuing part of the paper, will be limited specifically to the Afro-American minority, the guidelines have broad applicability to Puerto Rican, American Indian, Mexican, Appalachian White, and Cuban groups.

Directed Reading of Afro-American Content

Within recent years as an adjunct to the Afro-American's new, vigorous thrusts for comprehensive inclusion in the American way of life, there has been published a body of biographical and autobiographical literature about distinguished personalities of African antecedents who have made signal contributions to America. In addition to the foregoing, several historical works and historical fiction have appeared which purport to present the story of the Afro-American in America, both past and present. These literary efforts which have appeared in hitherto unprecedented volume are of a wide range in format, age appeal, and standards; but for the most part, they represent sincere efforts to fill in a long neglected area in American history.

Unlike the teacher of a few decades ago, the teacher of Afro-American children today finds no dearth of works of fiction and nonfiction which abound in easily identifiable racial and ethnic characters, plots, settings, and themes. The volume and diversity of this recent literature, however, poses a critical problem concerning its most profitable use in today's schools. In addition to the customary problems of book selection with works of varying literary standards, there is a new problem complicating book selection caused by ambiguous and paradoxical educational objectives currently besetting the Afro-American community. The teacher of Afro-American children is called upon today to decide *which* models in literature possessing *which* societal values shall the students be encouraged to emulate in the realization of *which* educational goals for living in *which* "world"—integrated or separated.

Within the framework of his school's objectives, the teacher of Afro-American children must plan and execute his bibliotherapy program through 1. selecting and utilizing appropriate guidelines for matching children and books, 2. establishing criteria for book selection, and 3. developing guided reading activities which insure maximum literary identification.

1. *Guidelines for Matching Learners and Books.* From research in human growth and development, learning theory, and children's interests, the teacher of minority group children and youth may secure significant infor-

mation about the characteristics and needs of the young at different ages and stages of development. It should be noted that the findings of these researches transcend racial and ethnic vagaries and as such have broad applicability. A few generalizations with pertinent bibliotherapeutic implications from these fields of study will be presented at this point. Through understandings such as the following the teacher may secure increased competence in bringing together the right book and the right child.

(a) From child development theory is garnered the pivotal premise concerning the uniqueness of the individual. Inherent in this principle is the fact that since one's biological heritage cannot be replicated, each person's life has its own story, and its own particular themes and continuity. Thus, one's experiences and aspirations help mold the individuality of one's present and future behavior. Closely allied with this primary concept are theories of the dynamic unity of the human organism, the sequential unfolding and development of phylogenetic characteristics from conception to maturity, the universality of human needs, and the important role of the environment in shaping the quality and quantity of intellectual development. Theories of the multi-dimensional and multi-determined nature of behavior, also, have special merit for the teacher of minority group children. *It may be implied from the foregoing that the literary needs of children would be infinitely diverse and highly specialized, and that the environmental opportunities and the child's needs at different ages and stages of development should be continually considered in guided reading activities.*

(b) From learning theory the teacher of minority groups may find the following generalizations helpful. Learning may be conceived of as problem solving behavior resulting from goal seeking motives. The degree of relevance of the learning activity to the student's life style, and the magnitude of the personal involvement and interaction with the environment will all contribute to the success of the learning. Approval, recognition, and reward —especially from an identifying figure whom the learner holds in high regard—will similarly enhance learning. *It may be implied from the foregoing that guided reading should be an integral part of the in-school and out-of-school life of the child, and that book selection should utilize the student's goals, preferences and interests as primary motivational and orientational forces.*

(c) Finally, from researches of children's interests, the teacher of minority group children may find the following guides of help in matching books and children: Interests are determined by a multiplicity of factors—physiological structure and needs, culture-based sex roles, experiences, and level of psycho-socio development. Interests are learned and are needs satisfying. To a great extent, interests depend upon the child's environmental opportunities for experiencing and learning. The child who feels adequate for the task at hand because of cumulative success is able to explore new areas of living—whether through real or vicarious activities. *It may be implied from the foregoing that directed reading which satisfies psycho-socio needs should be capitalized upon and used to extend the child's interests.*

2. *Criteria for Book Selection.* For the teacher who wishes to assist students in the selection of books which are expected to supply Afro-American identifying figures and situations, a thorough knowledge of this field of literature is required. Knowing the individual needs, interests, and abilities of children and knowing the world of books are the two sides of the coin of effective book selection. Since there is no shortage of tools to assist in the selection of books, the possibility of eliminating unwise choices can today be minimized.

The criteria in general acceptance today for evaluating books transcend racial and ethnic themes and characterization (6). The essentials of effective writing upon which books are judged include the nature of (a) the plot, (b) the quality of content, (c) the theme, (d) the characterization, and (e) the style. While surveying the book or a qualified resumé, the teacher should read with the following questions in mind: Does the book tell a good story, or in the case of non-fiction, are the factual sources reliable? Is the content worth the presentation? Is there meaning or significance behind the story? Are the characters credible, viable, consistent in their portrayal? Is the style appropriate to the plot, subject, theme, and characters? In addition to the preceding criteria, the format of the book should be evaluated; for it has been found that illustrations, typography, and even the quality of the paper as well as the jacket design can all attract or repel a potential reader.

Without the help which the teacher may secure from specialized book selection aids, it would be almost impossible for him to cover the current field of Afro-American literature. The catalogs, book lists, and periodicals that follow are a few of the distinguished publications in this field.

Adventuring With Books, National Council of Teachers of English. Champaign, Illinois, 1968. (This is a carefully selected list of old favorites and books of recent publication which are classified and annotated.)

Books About Negro Life for Children, Augusta Baker, New York: New York Public Library, 1967. (Selected titles which are submitted to stringent criteria as to themes, language, and format. The entries are briefly annotated and classified as to age groupings.)

Children's Catalog, Marion L. McConnel and Dorothy H. West. New York: H. W. Wilson Company, 11th ed., 1966. (Classified list giving titles, author, publisher, date, price, approximate grade level, and brief synopsis.)

Council on Interracial Books for Children, Inc. #9 E. 40th Street, New York 10016. (A list of "recommended" books of fiction and non-fiction that present fairly and constructively the pluralistic society in America—as to color, economic level, religion, urban and nonurban.)

The Horn Book. The Horn Book, Inc. Boston: Published six times yearly. (It includes current reviews of books for children and youth classified by subject and age level. Reproductions of many illustrations from newest books are incorporated as well as articles about authors and illustrators.)

The International Library of Negro Life and History, New York: Publishers Company under the auspices of the Association for the Study of Negro Life and History, 1967. (Five comprehensive volumes which treat the history of the Negro in medicine, music and art, the theatre, the Civil War, and historical biography.)

The Negro in Schoolroom Literature, Minnie W. Koblitz, ed., New York: Center for Urban Education, 33 W. 42nd Street, 1967. (A comprehensive bibliography of over 350 books about the Negro American heritage. Listings include full bibliographic information, grade levels, critical annotations for kindergarten through sixth grade.)

We Build Together, 3rd Rev., Charlemae Rollings, ed., Champaign, Illinois: National Council of Teachers of English, 1967. (A reader's guide to Negro life and literature for elementary and high school use. This new edition contains perceptive and complete annotations of books about the Negro in various avenues and levels of life in America.)

3. *An Approach for Directed Reading Activities.* At its highest level of conception, the reading process is a virtual dialogue between the reader and the author which involves subtle interaction with the mood, tone, and plot of the story. In order for children and youth to secure the most from literature, it has been long-established that they must learn the skills of interpreting what is read even as they must master the learning-to-read skills. It has been assumed, and research has substantiated it, that the greater the degree of reader comprehension, the greater are the chances for meaningful identification.

For a number of years teachers have used a variety of activities in an attempt to get students personally and deeply involved in comprehending literature. Book reports, book reviews, teacher directed discussions, and book fairs and displays have been used most frequently to stimulate interest in and understanding of recreatory and therapeutic reading. To a lesser extent have been used the graphic arts, music, the dance, and informal drama. It is the position of this paper that in this age of profuse auditory and simultaneous visual-auditory communication, it would be wise to incorporate these modes of expression as the dominant part of literary interpretation.

The image of the minority group child portrays him as generally favoring concrete, stimulus-bound learning situations and possessing perceptual styles uncomplementary to isolated, abstract, visual stimuli. In addition, this child is reported as responding most effectively to learning situations in which the goals are easily recognizable and readily attainable (4). For these reasons it would seem profitable to have the directed reading activities for the minority group child utilize such promising instructional innovations as:

(1) *Peer directed reading discussions.* Encourage students to "do their own thing" when communicating their feelings, views, and understanding of the author's theme, mood, perspective. Let the students select the classmate whose "style" would probably be best for interpreting or sharing a particular book.

(2) *Relating popular music and dances to literary works.* Why not allow students to find popular "soul" records for classroom presentation which reflect their views of a character's traits, predicament, or role? Why not encourage the creation of or display of current dances which in the student's view are expressive of critical moments of a story?

(3) *Open-ended book reviewing.* Students should not necessarily have to agree with an established view as to the motives of a character. As long as a student can present a rationale for his view which is defensible from some aspect of reality, the class should be able to accept it.

(4) *Informal dramatics and role playing.* Singly or in small groups students may participate in charades, pantomimes, or a form of the TV game "Password" in order to get their classmates to guess the names of characters in stories read by the entire group. Students may review a story up to the climax and then act out the most exciting part. The tape-recorder may be used by individual students or small groups to record unstructured reactions to stories for sharing with classmates or other classes.

(5) *Graphic arts to interpret literary reactions.* In the spirit of the current vogue of free expression in tempera, oils, clay, wood, *et al.,* there is no reason why students should not be encouraged to use these media for literary interpretation. The author's mood, theme, or central plot could all be expressed as well as specific characters' dominant traits in non-realistic reactions. Unhampered oral explanations of the choice of certain colors to express one's view of a literary episode or tone should prove a fertile source of catharsis-like therapy.

A Final Word

In American today, with a sense of urgency perhaps never before witnessed in any literate society, we are striving to ensure the maximum development of all the children of all of the people. We are consciously attempting to bring into fruitful participation in our culture the able-bodied and able-minded from all segments of our society. Functional literacy is essential for even marginal participation in our way of life, and the higher level skills of comprehending beyond literal meanings are now required of the citizen who aspires to a place in our world in the upper socio-economic strata.

It is the thesis of this paper that despite the philosophy of Marshall McLuhan, understanding the printed word will be pivotal to full participation in our culture during the lifetime of those alive today. Especially for the minority group child is it important that literacy be developed commensurate with his potential. It is submitted herein that bibliotherapy may be an effective medium through which the dual goals of the development of a positive self-concept and increased literary involvement and interpretation are realized.

References

1. American Council on Education. *Reading Ladders for Human Relations.* 4th ed. Washington, D.C.: The Council, 1963.
2. Beatty, William K. "An Historical Review of Bibliotherapy." *Library Trends* 11 (October 1962):107-17.
3. Cronbach, Lee J. *Educational Psychology.* 2nd ed. New York: Harcourt, Brace, and World, Inc., 1963.
4. Deutsch, Martin. "The Disadvantaged Child and the Learning Process." *Education in Depressed Areas.* New York: Bureau of Publications, T.C., Columbia University, 1963.
5. Gordon, Edmund W., and Wilkerson, Doxey A. *Compensatory Education for the Disadvantaged, Programs and Practices: Pre-School Through College.* New York: College Entrance Examination Board, 1966.
6. Huck, Charlotte S., and Kuhn, Doris Y. *Children's Literature in the Elementary School.* 2nd ed. Holt, Rinehart, and Winston, Inc., 1968.
7. International Reading Association Bibliography # 16. *Bibliotherapy: An Annotated Bibliography.* Newark, Delaware: IRA, 1968.
8. Kvaraceus, William C., et al. *Negro Self-concept: Implications for School and Citizenship.* New York: McGraw-Hill Book Co., 1965.
9. Passow, A. Harry, ed. *Education in Depressed Areas.* New York: Bureau of Publications, T.C., Columbia University, 1963.
10. "Psychological Aspects of Education in Depressed Areas." *Part II, Education in Depressed Areas.* New York: Bureau of Publications, T.C., Columbia University, 1963.
11. Rogers, Carl. *Client-Centered Therapy.* Boston: Houghton-Mifflin Co., 1951.

CHAPTER TEN

Individualized Reading Programs for Self-Selection of Materials

From the vast complexity of American life, each of the students we meet brings a network of needs and values that is uniquely his own. By the time youngsters reach high school age, their interests are so varied, their needs so diversified, few general reading tasks seem sensible. Individualized reading programs appear to many to serve the various needs of the youth that schools have brought together.

Individualization of instruction has been a popular educational slogan for half a century. For many reasons it has particular appeal to the high school teacher of reading. First, no one who has ever taught a "homogeneous" reading group has ever found the members of the group to be truly similar. Second, student motivation is often a problem in high school courses which poor readers take. Finally, a major goal of reading courses must be to develop reader independence. Thus, for reasons under one or another of these headings, individualized reading programs have attracted many proponents.

In individualized programs, the student selects his own reading fare from available trade books and ephemeral materials. The self-selection of materials overcomes the problem of motivation and "relevance." In the selection process itself, students commit themselves to the reading materials. They are far more likely to enjoy a book they have chosen than one chosen for them.

The bug-a-boo of readability and how to choose books your students *can* read is eliminated, for, with guidance, *they* make the decision. Questions of readability are particularly vexing for high school teachers who see even their poorest readers tackle difficult materials of high interest. These same readers are apparently unable to deal with the simplest of materials with lesser motivation. The skills program is worked out with each student as the need arises rather than based upon some preorganized program. In a series of interviews, the teacher acts as diagnostician who helps students plan their own learning.

Independence in reading can be more easily prompted by an individualized program that involves students in discovering their own reading interests and tastes, commits them to seeking satisfactions through reading, and causes learning to be the result of a partnership of student and teacher. The teacher's role in such a program is that of director of learning and resource rather than dispenser of knowledge and corrector of workbooks. For both students and teachers, this is a positive if radical departure from the typical classroom.

**Bruce C. Appleby
and John W. Conner**

Bruce Appleby and John Conner's excellent account of their reading program demonstrates the way in which teachers can help readers of various abilities in the same classroom. Perhaps most important of the implications here is that the teacher must be an avid reader. In addition to classic titles, he must be resourceful and alert to the "now" literature which students will read. This is particularly true for teachers of remedial readers.

Well, What Did You Think of It?

Yesterday, Dave walked into our English office, pushed aside a pile of books and papers, sat down and remarked, "Well, I finished reading the book. What did you think of it?" The lavender dust jacket of a current novel by a local writer's workshop instructor came into focus, and we began to trade impressions of the book, exchanging critical assumptions, finally trading titles of books we have enjoyed which our conversation about this book brought to our minds. Fifteen minutes later, Dave stood up, smiled wistfully, and said, "I wish I were taking 'Individualized Reading' again this semester. I've only read about five books so far this semester and last semester, by this time, I had read over thirty." Next week, or the week after next, Dave will be back to exchange impressions about a book or books we have suggested, and to ask us what we thought of a book he had suggested to us. Dave has the individualized reading bug. He has been bitten, infected, and constantly reinfects himself by his informal visits with us. We hope he never recovers from his current illness!

Dave is a product of a one-semester course in individualized reading which is offered on an elective basis to junior and senior students at University High School. Dave's wistful wish to re-enroll in "Individualized Reading" is typical of a growing number of our students who are so pleased with their progress that they automatically re-enroll for a second semester. It is gratifying to report that, although four semesters of English are required for all junior and senior students at University High School, five and even

---

Bruce C. Appleby and John Conner, "Well, What Did you Think of It?" *English Journal.* Copyright © 1965 by the National Council of Teachers of English. Reprinted by permission of the publishers and Bruce Appleby and John Conner.

six semesters are becoming the average. And "Individualized Reading" is a prime reason for this growth in student interest.

How do you teach individualized reading? Jeannette Veatch (*Individualizing Your Reading program,* New York: G. P. Putman's, 1959) and Dwight L. Burton (*Literature Study in the High School,* New York: Holt, Rinehart and Winston, 1964) provide excellent sources for tailoring a variety of programs. Our own program is based upon the ideas in such sources as these and the planning of the English department head at University High School, G. Robert Carlsen.

Our students are introduced to individualized reading through a curricular strand of units which begin in Grade 7 and extend through Grade 10. With this background of specific individualized reading experiences, they are ready at the eleventh and twelfth grades for the fuller experience of an entire semester devoted to personal reading development.

Practice and Procedure

On the first day of class, we explain to the students that the nature of the course is found in its title, "Individualized Reading." Each student starts a reading profile sheet by answering two questions: "Where have you been in your reading?" (What titles have you read for enjoyment the last few years? What type of book do you enjoy reading?) and "Where are you going in your reading?" (Do you have a particular plan in mind? Are there authors or themes you are interested in or curious about?) Students are told to sign for individual conferences on the schedule sheet, where they indicate their names and the titles and authors of books. During a classroom period, the students sit and read. If a student finishes what he is reading during the period, we give him a library pass so he may find another book. Conferences are held in the back of the room or in the hall, in order that nothing interferes with the students' reading. Allowing approximately ten minutes per conference, we find we can talk to four students each day. If two students have read the same book, conferences are arranged for both at one time.

The first task for the teacher is to develop a list of suggested titles for each student by perusing his reading profile sheet, determining his areas of interest and the type of book he is curious about. This list can be developed from many sources, the most important being the teacher's personal reading background. Of the many good reading lists and sources available, we have found the following most helpful: *Books for You* (NCTE, 1964), *Patterns in Reading* (Jean Carolyn Roos, ALA, 1961), *Good Reading* (The Committee on College Reading, New American Library, Mentor, 1964) and

Reading Ladders for Human Relations (American Council on Education, 1963). By guiding the student throughout the semester, we encourage him to deepen, then widen his reading interest, noting the direction and growth of his reading maturity.

Patterns of Reading

We have noticed that there are group and individual patterns of reading which develop within any given class. The group pattern occurs when one student tells another who tells another about a book which he has discovered. For example, Joyce started reading *Green Mansions*. Within a week and a half, seven students who sat around Joyce were reading and had signed up for conferences on *Green Mansions*.

Local showing of a movie based on a novel, such as Golding's *Lord of the Flies*, will prompt several students to read it. Scripts of new plays will arouse interest.* Titles suggested by the teacher to an individual will pass around the class with astounding rapidity, as has been observed with Daphne du Maurier's *Rebecca*, Heller's *Catch-22*, Steinbeck's *The Winter of Our Discontent*, or Carson McCuller's *The Heart Is a Lonely Hunter*.

The individual patterns which develop fall into three categories, according to the student's ability.

Students above average start out reading popular adult novels about which they have heard, but have not had the time to read. They then tend to read more esoteric books, often by controversial writers. An outgrowth of this phase is to read as much as possible of what has been written by one author; the student is trying to form a personal critical opinion of that author even though he may not like all of that author's writings. Rather than interest in a particular author, sometimes the student will turn to a theme, such as social criticism in the 1930's or the Negro in contemporary American fiction. Often, the above-average student will become more definitely part of the group pattern after this point. He will notice what others in the class are reading and become curious as to why.

Typical of the above-average student's reading pattern, Al started by reading *Fail-Safe* (Burdick and Lederer), *Seven Days in May* (Knebel and Bailey), *The American Way of Death* (Mitford), *Franny and Zooey* (Salinger), and *Clock Without Hands* (McCullers). *The Plague* (Camus), *Les Jeus Sont Fait* (Sartre) which he was also reading for third year French, *The Doctor in Spite of Himself* (Molière), *After the Fall* (Miller), and *An American Tragedy* (Dreiser) were next. Curiosity led Al to Faulkner, who fascinated and aggravated him. *The Sound and the Fury; Sartoris; The Ham-*

---

*For example, the February 1, 1964, *Saturday Evening Post's* publication of Arthur Miller's controversial play, *After the Fall*.

let; As I Lay Dying; Light in August; The Unvanquished; Absalom, Absalom; Go Down, Moses; A Fable; and some short story collections seemed to satisfy Al's curiosity. Several books by Carson McCullers, some more Salinger, and *Shadow on the Rock, Song of the Lark, Lost Lady,* and *O Pioneers* by Willa Cather rounded out the semester. Al is obviously not an average student, having read a total of 35 books. The pattern of his reading, however, is typical of the academically able in a course of this nature.

Students of average ability often start out reading popular adult novels which are currently being widely discussed. Generally, the average student will then fall into a pattern of reading based on his favorite type of book, such as war stories, historical romance, or adventure stories. Here, the teacher has an excellent opportunity to help the student develop this interest and to lead him gently to new areas and ideas within it. Often the average student indiscriminately samples books following his investigation into a favorite type. Generally, we encourage this in order to help him widen his reading interests and knowledge.

Typical of the average student's reading pattern, Ben started by reading *West Side Story* (Shulman), *On the Beach* (Shute), and *Black Like Me* (Griffin). *Catcher in the Rye* (Salinger) followed, as Ben wanted to know why it was so popular. *PT-109* (Donovan), *Kon Tiki* (Heyerdahl), *Mutiny on the Bounty* (Nordhoff and Hall), and *Call of the Wild* (London) were next read, as Ben investigated his "favorite" of war and adventure stories. A few more of these were followed by *A Connecticut Yankee in King Arthur's Court* (Mark Twain). Ben enjoyed this novel as a good adventure story, but was also able to see some of its satirical implications. Depending on the student's ambition and personal motivation, the number of books read during the course of the semester by the average student will vary from around eight to 16.

Below-average students offer what is perhaps the greatest challenge and the greatest reward. Generally, the pattern of the below average student centers around his particular preference in reading to the exclusion of other types of books, *i.e.*, war stories, romance, true adventure, hot-rodding, or mysteries. The teacher can do a great deal with and for this student by suggesting a variety of titles within his interest and by helping him to see the wealth of materials available. In working with the below-average student, even in the upper grades, a knowledge of literature for the adolescent can prove most valuable.

Typical of the below-average student, Bob indicated on his reading profile sheet that he liked "war stories. Nothing else—war stories." A preliminary conference revealed "I've read all the war stories that have been written." Bob was asked if he had read *The Strong Men* (Brick). Since he hadn't, Bob started with it. *Rifles for Watie* (Keith), *April Morning* (Fast), and *Behind Enemy Lines* (Sanderson) followed. As a tangent to his interest, Bob struggled through *One Day in the Life of Ivan Denisovitch* (Solzhenitsyn). Bob tackled *Battle Cry* (Uris) next. The length of the novel and the number of characters proved difficult for Bob, but he did enjoy the book. At the teacher's suggestion, Bob read *All Quiet on the Western Front* (Remarque). A new world of literature was opened to Bob, based on his interest, yet completely different from the type of story he had previously read.

Another and even more dramatic example of what this approach to literature can accomplish is seen in the case of Barb, a junior with an I. Q. of 89. On her reading profile sheet, Barb indicated she liked romances, yet insisted, despite other suggestions made by the teacher, on reading *To Kill a Mockingbird* (Lee). Barb's reading was not controlled by her interests, but by what her peers were reading. Observe a student like Barb trying to read something beyond her ability, struggling to complete two pages a class period, and you will see how we reacted. Finding a book for this high interest-low ability student proved a problem. Many excellent adolescent novels were rejected, because they didn't seem right for Barb's ability or personality. Finally, Vivian Breck's excellent novel *Maggie* was suggested to Barb, with the idea that the teacher was curious to have Barb's opinion. The day Barb finished this book, she sat in class and cried. Why? She understood it. She enjoyed it. The book was able to meet and combine her interests, ability, and rate of reading and yet hold her curiosity. Most importantly, "It's the first book I ever finished all on my own."

Conferences

For the teacher, the most heartening aspect of this entire program is found in the conferences. To be able to sit and talk with our students about what they are reading, how they react to what they are reading, and what they are getting out of the books they have chosen is stimulating, delightful, and enlightening. Student-teacher rapport runs very high and, because the teacher is reading what the students are reading, the students feel and know the teacher is genuinely interested in their reading and their progress. When we began this course, we feared that discipline might be a problem, particularly with those students we considered bad risks. Because of the rapport, there has been no problem.

During the conference, the student and teacher discuss the book on a number of levels. We try to ascertain how much the student has enjoyed the book by asking questions which will reveal such things as: (1) How many different levels of meaning has he employed in approaching the book? (2) How does he associate the book with his previous reading? (3) What relations to his experiences were implied in the book? (4) How has he progressed in his reading as a result of having read this particular book? (5) How does this book fit into his general reading program and plan?

Each conference results in a student's answering a question about or indicating an opinion of a particular aspect of the book on a 4 x 6" card. These cards are *not* book reports; instead the student discusses a particular aspect of the book such as characterization, handling of theme, fidelity, comparison to a similar book, etc.

Since the student will have finished a book before the conference, we often end it with a question on what he is now reading and what he plans to read next. Here the teacher can guide the student into a wider and deeper approach to reading based on his interests and abilities.

Reading Project

The reading project is an outgrowth of the students' interests and patterns in that each one chooses an author, theme, or genre in which he is particularly interested. He reads a minimum of four books which center in his chosen topic. The project then consists of the student's writing an analysis of his chosen topic. We want students to make up their own minds about the material read, not to parrot the opinion of others, so usually we limit the students to the books they have read. We do sometimes encourage the better students to use outside references. (An alternative we offer the students on the reading project is to do an oral report, although relatively few students choose this option.)

Approximately three weeks before the end of the semester, our students are to have finished their reading projects. They are told about the project at the beginning of the semester, but are not encouraged to begin active work until the beginning of the second quarter.

A widely divergent and rather amazing range of topics results from the reading project. In one semester, a far above average senior did his reading project on "An Interpretive Study of Twentieth Century Man as Seen in the Plays of Arthur Miller"; an average student investigated "Realistic Language in Four War Novels"; a below-average student was concerned with the fidelity of "Hot Rod Terms in H. G. Felsen's Novels."

Grading

An inevitable question is "How do you grade students?" We have found that the best answer is to let the students decide how they will be graded. Five years ago, when our present English curriculum was initiated, the students enrolled in Individualized Reading decided there should be three criteria for grading: (1) number of books read, (2) quality of conferences and cards, and (3) the level of each book. Each class has been offered an opportunity to modify the grading system. Our present system, which follows, reflects these modifications.

1. Number of books read. This measure *alone* is unreliable in that books vary so greatly in length and difficulty. Nevertheless, the students have always felt that quantity of reading is important.

2. Number of books is multiplied by an estimate of the student's perceptiveness into what he has read. The student is graded on the conference and card on a cumulative 1 to 4 scale: 1—no understanding beyond plot; 2—some application to his own life; 3—some implications for larger human ideas; 4—understanding of levels of meaning, esthetic values, and relationships with other reading.

3. The product of criteria one and two is multiplied by an estimate of the level of the book. Each book is given a numerical rating on the following scale:

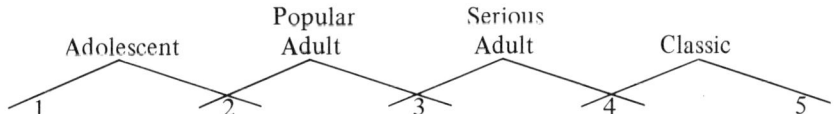

By multiplication of the three factors, a student reading adolescent materials which he understands completely may achieve as high a grade as one who reads serious adult materials which he does not completely understand. To be sure, the grading is based on subjective evaluations by the teacher, but it does standardize procedures and provides a quantitative score.

It is very important, in using this grading system, to modify it to the grade level and ability of each group. The scale must be applied in a sense of being completely movable. What would be judged and placed on the serious adult level in the seventh grade might be placed on the popular adult level for eleventh grade. For example, *Hawaii* (Michener) is serious adult level reading to the seventh grader, but popular adult to the eleventh grader. Making the scale movable allows for differences in reading ability in any particular grade.

Teacher Preparation

What special preparation does an individualized reading program require of the teacher? Essentially, this program requires (1) a knowledge of the developmental tasks of adolescents (see Robert J. Havighurst, *Human Development and Education,* New York: McKay, 1953), (2) a knowledge of the reading interests of young people (see Geneva Hanna and Mariana McAllister, *Books, Young People, and Reading Guidance,* New York: Harper, 1960, or George W. Norvell, *The Reading Interests of Young People,* Boston: D. C. Heath, 1950, and *What Boys and Girls Like to Read,*

Morristown, N. J.: Silver Burdett, 1958), and (3) a wide acquaintance with good books. A good book is here defined as any book which is right for one of your students at this time in his life. Generally, the right book for most seventh through tenth graders will be found in that large body of literature labeled literature for the adolescent, and the right book for a tenth through twelfth grader is more likely to be found in adult literature. We have suggested some sources for learning about good books. However, there is no substitute for personal reading and evaluation. A file including book cards for each book you have read is an invaluable aid in assisting students with further reading suggestions.

Code of Procedures

We believe that the success of our program is directly related to the following code of procedures:

1. The teacher has read or skimmed most of the books that the students read.
2. The teacher must resist the temptation to recommend a "better quality" book than the one the student has just finished reading simply for the sake of "quality." The next book read must be read because it is of interest to the student, not because it is of interest to the teacher.
3. The teacher must resist the temptation to present any planned classroom activity which prevents individual reading and book conferences.
4. There is no specific level where reading must begin. The individual reading level is dictated by one's interest and ability.
5. The basis for a book conference can be a difference of opinion between the student and the teacher and may end with unresolved differences.
6. A summary of the book's plot (oral or written) is probably a waste of time for all but the slowest of students.
7. The teacher must be supportive in the conference and avoid making derogatory evaluations of books which have meant much to the student.
8. The teacher must leave each conference feeling the student has gained a clearer understanding of the book and his program.

Conclusion

Although many teachers and administrators agree with an individualized reading program in essence, they are reluctant to start the program on a complete semester basis because of administrative problems or simply through fear of being unable to cope with the awesome task of reading all the books adolescent readers might consume during a semester period. Aware of this, we recommend starting with two-week to four-week units of individualized reading with the regular English curriculum. The total number of books to be read by the teacher will be less oppressive and when the success of the short unit has been evaluated, another unit or units can be scheduled.

A related feature of this program concerns the use of the school library. We have found it valuable to ask each student to keep a list of the books he would like to have checked out of the school library if he could have found them there. We turn these lists over to our librarian to use as one basis for buying new books or for stocking additional copies of existing titles for the school library. This practice builds better student relations with the school library as well as provides us with books students really want to read.

It would be unwise to conclude without asking: Is individualized reading a valuable way for students to become acquainted with literature? Perhaps one way to answer this question is to recall the top forty books which NCTE Achievement Award winners for 1960, 1961, and 1962 believed most significant for them. Heading the list is Salinger's *The Catcher in the Rye*. We don't believe that this book was introduced as common reading in many English classes. Irwin Edman (*Saturday Review,* November 4, 1950) writes of the joys of unrequired reading for students and adults: when the pleasure of reading includes the pleasure of knowledge and thought. James R. Squire (*The Responses of Adolescents While Reading Four Short Stories,* NCTE Research Report No. 2, 1964) believes that teachers need to develop better techniques for assessing the quality of an *individual's* responses to literature (italics ours). Individualized reading has provided the students at University High School with the opportunity to discover the pleasure of learning through reading they enjoy. They have shown their enthusiasm through such heavy enrollment that the course must be offered every semester rather than alternate semesters as originally planned. Even then, it is impossible to include all students who would like to take this course. Individualized reading has become an important way of reading at University High!

Jerry L. Walker

In the program Jerry Walker suggests, the teacher can handle a heterogeneous group of thirty-five students pursuing separate goals. The teacher, however, must know what skills are to be taught. For a catalog of examples of word attack-decoding skills see Clyde Roberts' Word Attack, *(New York: Harcourt Brace and World, 1956). And, for a depth resume of comprehension skills, you may want to consult Ruth Strang et al.,* The Improvement of Reading *(New York: McGraw-Hill, Inc., 1965).*

Conducting an Individualized Reading Program in High School

"Curioser and curioser!" cried Alice (she was so much surprised that for the moment she quite forgot how to speak good English). "Now I'm opening out like the largest telescope that ever was! Good-bye, feet!" (for when she looked down at her feet, they seemed to be almost out of sight, they were getting so far off). "Oh my poor little feet, I wonder who will put on your shoes and stockings for you now, dears? I'm sure I shan't be able! I shall be a great deal too far off to trouble myself about you: you must manage the best way you can—but I must be kind to them," thought Alice, "or perhaps they won't walk the way I want them to go!"—Lewis Carroll

Alice's predicament is ours. As our school population opens out like the largest telescope that ever was, we cry, "Good-bye, students! With our large classes we certainly shan't have time to bother with you as individuals." And so, more often than not, we are too far off; and students do manage the best way they can. It really shouldn't be surprising to read the latest dropout statistics and discover that many of them are not walking the way we wanted them to go.

There is nothing economical in trying to teach students what they are not ready to learn or in making students who have already learned a fact or skill mark time until others learn the same thing. But that is what we

Reprinted with permission of Jerry L. Walker and the International Reading Association.

do, and we cannot afford that waste. If we are really concerned about maximum utilization of time, energy, and materials, we will have to stop crying about how busy we are and how we can't possibly teach such large classes and, instead, start finding ways to keep every student busy in his individual pursuit of knowledge.

English teachers must lead that search, for nowhere else are proximity and concern for the individual more important than in the English class where language is the focus of study. Growth in language facility closely parallels physical, psychological, intellectual, and social growth. Recent studies have found correlations between language learning and age, sex, I.Q., body chemistry, tissue damage, cognitive style, achievement motivation, and anxiety. The importance of special interests, abilities, and aptitudes and the relationship of experience to all these factors have long been recognized. The total number of variables that emerges when the newer findings are added to the older ones is so great that it precludes any possibility of treating all students alike. Single-factor homogeneous groupings, moreover, don't make the impossible possible. Any single factor we use as the criterion for group membership will prove inadequate as a predictor of performance unless it is viewed in relation to other factors that operate within the individual.

English teachers, however, are noted for their perseverance; they are determined to do the impossible, especially in their literature classes. Ready or not, everyone must read *Silas Marner* in the eleventh grade, or perhaps the twelfth, but read it he must unless, of course, he's in the bottom track (however it's defined). In that case, it doesn't make much difference what the student reads as long as he reads something.

It should be unnecessary to say that the reading and study of literature must be individualized; it cannot be otherwise. In common reading, only the selection is common; the effect is individual. The study of literature derives its value from its effect, which depends upon the personality, experiences, abilities and purposes of the reader as they enable him to interact with the literature he reads. The effects of literature can be predicted with some accuracy, but only through thorough knowledge of the reader and the literature; the teaching of literature is largely a job of producing effects.

The Individualized Program

The first step in conducting an individualized program is to gather as much information as possible about each student. Cumulative records, test scores, and inventories can supply some of the information, but much of it must be collected through observation and interview. It isn't enough to know the facts about a student's physical condition, academic history, socio-economic background, interests and aptitudes. More important is knowing how those factors affect the student's behavior, and only daily observation can reveal that.

The year should begin with individual interviews, which can easily be conducted while the other students are reading at their desks. Part of the interview should be spent getting acquainted with the student. Questions about his likes and dislikes, his work habits, his goals, and his view of himself in the world can elicit much necessary information. The rest of the interview should be spent listening to him read and questioning him about the material in order to gauge his ability to read, comprehend, and interpret on different levels. Initial interviews usually last perhaps ten minutes. At a rate of five interviews an hour, it is possible to interview a hundred and twenty-five students during a week.

The teacher's homework during that first week consists of using the information gathered from records and interviews to draw up individual courses of study. The plan for each student should include a list of the specific literary skills, knowledges, and appreciations he needs as determined by his past experiences, his present knowledge and abilities, and his future plans. One student might need the ability to follow the chain of events in a story, a skill already mastered by the other students in the class. He might also need to know and recognize the uses of figurative language. He might also need to appreciate reading as an enjoyable activity, and he should know the names and works of writers who have written about a subject in which he's interested. The initial list of things to be learned need not be exhaustive. It should be revised and added to during the year as a means of directing the student's time and energy as well as plotting his growth.

Included, also, in the individual's course of study should be the titles of selections to be read and the writing or study assignments to be done in connection with them. The reading and writing assignments included will depend upon the effect, or effects, which the teacher is trying to produce through the required readings. In planning for a ninth-grade boy who has a seventh-grade reading level and who doesn't like to read, the teacher might decide that his first reading assignment should be a couple of stories from *Teen-Age Tales,* hoping they will show the boy that he can complete a reading assignment and that some stories deal with problems like his. The student's next assignment might be to read Felsen's *Hot Rod,* again to produce the same effects. While the student is reading, and certainly after he has completed the reading, the teacher will want to discuss the stories with him and perhaps require some writings about them. For another student, the teacher might suggest the reading of *The Pearl, The Old Man and the Sea,* and *Lord of the Flies* to show the student that some stories can be read on different levels and that the use of symbols can add depth and interest.

Courses of study should also include directions on how the students should proceed with their work. The student who was assigned the reading of *Teen-Age Tales* and *Hot Rod* might be given no directions other than to read the stories and arrange for a conference with the teacher when he's finished. The student who read *The Pearl, The Old Man and the Sea,* and *Lord of the Flies* might have been directed to check several sources on the use of symbolism before reading those books and to write a paper on the nature of allegory after reading *The Pearl.*

One of the great advantages of having individual courses of study complete with directions in the hands of the students is that the teacher is freed from having to attend to the whole class during the entire period. While everyone is pursuing his own work, the teacher is free to circulate, to ask questions, to have conferences, and to help students locate materials. He is free to seek out those students with common problems and perhaps conduct some small-group instruction, and he is free to help the three or four students who have been reading similar materials prepare a class presentation. In short, the teacher is freed to have a much greater influence on each student by being available when he's needed.

Ideally, the teacher should be freed, also, from rigid restrictions in his choice of materials. Since the criterion for selecting material should be its potential effect on a particular student, having a wide assortment of books, magazines, and newspapers is obvious. Having an extensive classroom library is desirable, but not essential. Since the students know by looking at their courses of study what they should read, they can take the responsibility for getting the materials and bringing them to class.

The need to be acquainted with a great variety of literature on many different levels frightens many teachers and keeps them from trying an individualized approach to teaching. It is true that the more literature a teacher knows, the greater are his chances of matching the right student with the right selection, but it is also true that there are many resources the teacher can draw upon to supplement his knowledge. The librarian and other teachers can often be called upon to supply titles for specific students as well as quick run-downs on the significant features of the selections. Collections of annotations, arranged by subject and grade level, are available in nearly every library and they, too, can be used to extend the teacher's literary range.

A good individualized reading program is marked not so much by what a student reads as by how he reads. Consequently, even a teacher who is restricted to using a single anthology, through choice or force, can individualize the instruction effectively. When the selection of literature is restricted, individualization can be provided by the reading sequence, by the kind and amount of preparation for reading, by the pace, by the amount of follow-up work to be done, and by the kind of evaluation the teacher uses —all of which will depend upon the effect the teacher wants to produce on the individual. Through the use of conferences, study guides, preliminary questions, or all three, the teacher can effectively channel the effect of a given piece of literature on a student. Too narrow a selection of materials is a handicap, but not a death-knoll. The deadly aspect of such a program occurs only if the decision is made that since all students have read the same selection, all of them should have the same understanding of it and be affected in the same way by it.

Evaluation

Evaluation of growth must be a continual process in an individualized program. The teacher must check constantly on the effects of the work the student does so that he can revise or extend the course of study as needed. After checking a student's writing assignment, the teacher might discover the need to add more selections to the list of readings or to prescribe more careful preparation for the readings already listed. The major purpose of evaluation is to give direction to future actions, but teachers must also give grades. Letter grades can represent many things, but in an individualized program it is imperative that the grade reflect the work a student has done and the growth that has resulted from it. The grade should indicate how much the student has learned in relation to his potential, not how much he has learned in relation to what other students have learned. A student's grade should tell nothing about anyone but himself.

The keeping of records in an individualized program is vital to its success, not only for evaluating a student's growth, but also for providing continuity from one teacher to another. Included in the record should be the course of study the student has completed and samples of the different kinds of writing assignments he completed. It should also contain observations made by former teachers regarding the student's work and study habits and his personality characteristics.

The more complete the record, the less time it takes a new teacher to start the student on a new course of study. With every new teacher, the student can make a new start toward the realization of his uniqueness. An individualized program is an extension of the way one views the world and the individual's place in it.

Ruth E. Reeves

For many years, school curriculum builders have suggested that "every teacher is a teacher of reading." It sometimes appears that no one is very serious about it. In this essay from Houston, a junior high school individualized reading program demonstrates not only how to individualize, but how to move the reading program into content fields.

An Experiment in Improving Reading in the Junior High School

Elementary teachers are fairly well satisfied with their answer to the problem of teaching children to read—grouping in the classroom according to ability. Their answer does not, however, solve the problem for anyone but the elementary school child. In the first place, the answer sounds like a simple one, but to keep purposefully busy three groups of less-than-dedicated children—one group working perhaps on a second grade level, one on a fourth, and one on a sixth—requires the forethought of a stage manager, the sense of timing of a master chef, and "a banner with a strange device—Excelsior!" Not every elementary child, then, marches steadily forward for six years to his maximum potential in reading ability.

In the second place, as these children leave elementary school, they leave the comfortable atmosphere of expectation that they perform only according to their ability. Secondary teachers are in a sense specialists in their subjects, and they assume, consciously or unconsciously, that children have been taught to read in elementary school. Hence those who last year in the sixth grade were reading in second grade books are now, in the seventh grade, often presented with the same textbooks as are their more able classmates. The material is beyond their comprehension. Besides, this same material that is too hard for the retarded reader may be too simple to challenge the exceptionally capable student.

Can this reading situation be met in the junior high school? This was the question considered by a group meeting in the office of the principal of

---

Ruth E. Reeves, "An Experiment in Improving Reading in the Junior High School," *English Journal.* Copyright © 1958 by the National Council of Teachers of English. Reprinted by permission of the publisher and Ruth Reeves.

a Houston junior high school*—the principal, the assistant principal, the assistant superintendent in charge of curriculum and instruction, and two supervisors. A plan for teaching reading was sought that would provide not only stimulating material for students at all levels of ability but an incentive for their reading extensively.

First Year of the Experiment

It was decided to experiment during the following year with three low-eighth grade classes:

> 1. The principal would set up three low-eighth grade classes composed of below-average, average, and above-average readers.
>
> 2. These classes would be given a standardized reading test in the fall and another the following spring.
>
> 3. Three English teachers, three social studies teachers, and a science teacher who would be willing to assist in the working out of the plan would be selected for these three classes.
>
> 4. Instead of using one textbook in each of these classes the students would read extensively in books on their level of ability.

A few days later the seven teachers who had been selected met with the original group. It was spring and there were report cards to make out and school to close; meanwhile, however, plans could be made for fall. After school that same day the supervisor of English met with the three English teachers.

Since reading is one of the subjects considered to be especially the province of the English teacher, we felt particularly responsible. We decided to make our plans very specific, in order that we could all help each other. We decided, too, that the reading done in English classes should contribute in some way to the work being done in social studies and science. During several spring meetings, we decided to limit our activities for the first semester to the following three units:

> *First Six Weeks*—mythology and folklore. The fact that the first social studies unit in the low-eighth grade dealt with Old World backgrounds gave us some reason for this choice. Besides, the teachers had all felt a lack in their students of knowledge of mythology—and the teachers themselves liked mythology and wanted the opportunity to teach it.

---

*Sidney Lanier Junior High School: principal, Mr. G. C. Scarborough.

An Experiment in Improving Reading in the Junior High School

Second Six Weeks—backgrounds of Colonial times. Turning full-face to the social studies department, we would deal with fiction and biography based on Colonial times.

Third Six Weeks—biographies of Americans with an emphasis on scientists.

These units would be introduced by material in the basic and supplementary readers and with audio-visual aids. Individual reading, however, would be done in library books carefully chosen to suit the ability of each child.

For this individual reading, we needed some special bibliographies—some guides to the material on the shelves of the school library and to the degree of difficulty of each book dealing with each subject. Each of the three teachers agreed to prepare one bibliography during the summer. Since there certainly would not be enough material in the school library for all three classes to be reading on the same subject at the same time, the classes would rotate in their study of these units. During each six-weeks term, the teacher who had made the book lists would use the books on her subject first. Thus, necessary changes could be made. The book lists were an important part of the project and took some time to prepare. With the help of the librarian and with frequent reference to the *Children's Catalog,* the teachers arranged book titles in three sections: for the below-average reader, for the average, for the mature reader.

As soon as possible after the opening of school in the fall, standardized reading tests were given and scored. It was discovered that in this school reading levels varied from fourth grade to college graduate—that is above grade sixteen. The teacher who had compiled the list on mythology was ready to begin. Mythology, of course, has many echoes in modern life; there is the flying horse of gasoline fame, the car named for a fleetfooted god. Once started, eighth grade students were helpful in suggesting trade names based on names of gods and goddesses. Next, the teacher assured the class that myths were not "just silly stories," but the first science, answering such questions as "What is thunder?" and "Why do flowers grow?" Mythology, she told them, composed the first literature and the first religion. She told them the story of Adonis and the anemones, of Narcissus and Echo. So well did she do the job of interesting the class that when the time came to choose books, the greatest number of students chose mythology over folklore and fairy tales.

In the library students found books that appealed to them. In the library and later in the classroom they were given time to find out what kind of material was in their books. Then they formed groups on the basis of the types of reading they were doing. There was one group on American folklore, two on Greek and Roman mythology, one on fables. Three boys who were reading epics did not join a group but wished to report individually. Several students read three or four books on the subject; everyone read one complete book.

As time drew near for reporting to the class, the groups met to decide how the report was to be made. The teacher stipulated only that it was to be a serious presentation—a panel discussion, perhaps, or an imitation of a television program—and that it must stay within a time limit. Television programs took the day. The adaptations were wonderfully ingenious. In fact, so much was made by the adults who were invited to the program of the cleverness of the reporting techniques that the next reporting of this class was cumbersome with cleverness and very short on reportage. The reading had been done, but the presentation of the class had little evidence of the material read. The third unit was more seriously presented.

Methods of presentation in the three classes naturally reflected the formality or informality of the teachers; however, there was always strong interest, both on the part of the audience and the performers. Greatest feature of the programs was that each group contained children of different abilities; each child made a real contribution.

At the end of the semester, classes were asked to comment on the program. Most of the children had liked the project very much; a few objected to being told what subjects to read about. Their evaluations seemed completely honest:

> Since we have studied this project, I have learned to read more books, and to read books I do not like as well as others. I thought the idea of dividing us into groups according to the book's subject was an excellent one. The next time we do a unit like this, I think it would be an improvement if we were asked the type of book we would enjoy. Then the class could be divided into groups according to our choice of reading material.
>
> I thought it was a lot of fun and it taught us how to work together and use our brains. It made me like English more than I ever had before. It made me want to read more. . . .
>
> It didn't help me any. I'll read what I wish after I've read what I have to. I like books on the wars of the Indians all except the New England Indians and the peaceful Indians. I don't think these books can help me become too much of a better reader, although this might help greatly a poor reader.
>
> My opinion of this project is that it didn't complete its purpose because: (1) people are going to read what they please after the project is completed anyway and (2) they were mostly adventure and the readers paid more interest to the adventure than the facts contained therein. I believe it would have had more effect on the readers if we would have read

biographies, because we would have gotten much more factual material from them than the books that were read.

I believe this project was good. . . . During school hours we absorb all our interest in our school work and do not read many books. But during this project we had a chance to catch up on our reading without neglecting our other school work.

Results of Standardized Reading Tests
Class A

September
   7 below average (below eighth grade level)
   7 average (eighth or ninth grade level)
   20 excellent (tenth to twelfth grade level)

May
   None below average*
   2 average
   28 excellent, with a gain in most cases of at least two years. Four students were reading at the sixteenth grade level.

*Of the former below-average group, one left school, two were retained at midyear and were not part of the group for the second testing. One was absent, two were on eighth grade level, and one was on tenth grade level.

Class B

September
   13 below average
   9 average
   7 excellent

May
   8 below average*
   7 average
   16 excellent

*Of the former below-average group, one moved away, one was retained at midyear, seven were reading on the seventh grade level, two on the eighth, one on the tenth, and one on the twelfth.

Class C

September
   11 below average
   5 average
   13 excellent

May
   2 below average*
   6 average
   20 excellent (tenth to sixteenth)

*Of the former below-average group, four were retained, two were absent, one was reading on the seventh grade level, two on the eighth, one on the tenth, and one on the twelfth.

After reading these evaluations by the students, we decided that for the second semester we would ask each student to become an expert on some one subject of his own choice—family relationships, animal stories, science fiction, sea stories. Class reading time was to be spent, for the most part, in using basic readers, and the extensive reading would be done outside of class. During the latter part of the semester each student was to have time to report to the class on his specialty; he was to have something to show —a graph, a model, a set of pictures—and he was to have a bibliography of books he had read. After his report the class members were to have the opportunity of asking him questions.

I visited the classes to hear a few of these reports, and they were interesting. There were more submarines than sea stories, more wives-of-presidents than family relationships. Perhaps the eighth grade comes at a factual age. Although the school librarian reported that less reading was done during the second semester than during the first, the librarian in the branch of the public library near the school reported much more use of her books. Some of the student reports showed evidence of very wide reading. Questions following the reports were pertinent to the subject and were competently answered.

Meanwhile, in their social studies and science classes the same students were reading library material on their own reading level. When the reading tests were given at the end of the year, everyone was convinced that we were making progress.

We congratulated ourselves and the students. Looking at the graphed results of the standardized reading tests, we felt that we, along with the elementary school teachers, had found our answer to the problem of teaching children to read. Since the experiment had succeeded with three classes, the next year all the low-eighth grade classes in the school were to follow the same plan.

Second Year

What followed is what often happens in life. Of the three English teachers who had been involved in the experiment the first year, one married and moved away, one was given a different teaching assignment in which she was especially needed, and the third acquired some extra-curricular duties that were time- and energy-consuming. Thus two of the three English teachers had had no experience with the plan. The supervisor went on to another project. The book lists on the three original units were the only ones at hand. Naturally, there were not enough copies of those books to satisfy the increased demand.

In short, while during the first year three teachers, the English supervisor, the principal, the assistant principal, and the librarian were all intensely interested in the English phase of the project, now during the second year individual teachers were working alone. The results of the spring testing showed us that we were not now on the right track. It had been the control of the experiment, the organization by the group working together, the focus of interest on improvement in reading that had made for success.

Third Year

We are trying again this year. Again there are three teachers of low-eighth grade English; this time, however, each teacher is working with five classes instead of one. Each of the three teachers is selecting two units to work on each six weeks—one unit for three of her classes and the other for the remaining two classes.

First, she is teaching the material on each unit in the basic textbook with great care, doing intensive work on specific reading skills and vocabulary. Afterward, after all the material on the unit in the textbook has been covered, she holds a class discussion on the type of material. If the unit has concerned adventure, for example, such questions as these may be suggested: Is it necessary, in a story of adventure, that the hero be in physical danger? If he is in physical danger, do you like for him to rescue himself, or may he be rescued by someone else? What qualities of character or personality should the hero of an adventure story (true or fictional) possess? How does the author let you know, before the climax of the story, that the hero has these qualities? Must the reader like the hero? If so, how does the author make you like him? Do you like adventure in far-away places or near at home? Why? Such questions, suggested as often as possible by the members of the class, are written on the board and then copied into notebooks and used as guides to interest in subsequent reading.

The classes are then taken to the library to choose books on the subject of their unit. Lacking time to make graded lists for each unit, the teachers are allowing children to make their own selections, under the helpful supervision of the librarian and the teacher herself. For each book he reads, however, the student makes a bibliography card, annotating it and saying whether he has considered this an easy or a hard book. The reading ability of the child is taken into consideration, of course, as these opinions are interpreted. As teachers find time and efficient student help, they check the ratings given by the children against the *Children's Catalog* and their own evaluation. Cards describing the books are eventually on file in the library.

Reports to the class are for the most part given in panels. Instead of reporting on each book separately, members of the panel select topics to discuss as they pertain to individual books. For example: From reading your book, how much of the actual farm work would you judge was done by children in Colonial times? What was the attitude of the characters in your book toward England? Did the women have any fun or were their lives full of drudgery? What did you learn about the life of the times that you would not learn from reading a history book? Composition ideas grow from this type of discussion, sometimes imaginative stories, sometimes thoughtful paragraphs about character motivation.

Another feature of our revised program came out of a meeting of social studies and English teachers before the opening of school. One of the English teachers observed that children read only for the story and do not remember, when they have finished the story, the place or the time in history. It was suggested that we try to remedy this tendency toward superficial reading. At the beginning of the year, then, each low-eighth grade student received a booklet containing "A Time Line for Eighth Grade Students in English, Social Studies, and Science," a map of the United States, and a map of the world. He enters the title of each book he reads during the year on the time line and on one or both maps. A display of these completed booklets is planned for the spring.

It is hoped that by this means not only will the actual reading level of students improve but that children as they read will become more sensitive to many literary values. Now that we are again organizing our thinking and pooling our ideas, perhaps in the spring test results will show that students have improved in their reading techniques and that their reactions will prove their heightened interest in literature and many fields of study.

CHAPTER ELEVEN

Language-Experience Approaches for Student Initiated Materials

For many reasons, the language-experience approach seems to offer some exciting potentials for high school reading programs. Basically what is meant by "the language-experience approach" is that reading is taught through the medium of the students' real experiences and using their own language. Although attention is paid to language-experience approaches in elementary education, relatively little has been said of it in the literature of the secondary school.

One reason for its neglect, of course, is the comparative recent entry of the high school onto the scene of direct reading instruction. When reading was formally added to the high school curriculum, it was perhaps natural that this new input would resemble the "subject areas" that were then being taught. Reading instruction, then, was added as a course of study to be taught during some specified time and with a designated group of materials. The language-experience approach does not happily fit that mold, for this approach depends for vigor upon the shared experience of a group, flexible time, and variable content. And, the materials must grow out of the experience. One could never know ahead of time just what they might be.

Another inherent difficulty of this strategy is the degree of teacher preparation required. In order to be comfortable with the flexibility of student-generated experiences and materials, teachers often feel they must know a great deal about the skills involved in the reading process. The relatively brief time spent in teacher training is rarely long enough to afford beginning high school teachers more than a passing glance at the whole field of reading. Without the security of such knowledge, high school teachers have tended to seek materials that "covered" the skills, anthologies and readers of designated grade levels, and workbooks or supplements for drill.

The relevance and concomitant involvement from using the student's own language and experience should be a selling point for this approach with the high end as well as the low end of heterogeneous classes. It is possible that dealing with the student's own language may free teachers from some of the erroneous shibboleths about the nature of language and its use. Another advantage may be the working together of all the language arts—speaking, writing, listening, as well as reading—in this approach. Many authorities have held that the language arts cannot be fragmented into separate programs of composition or reading. As reading programs develop and as high school educators piece together a real theory of reading instruction pertinent to the adolescent, there can be little doubt that a refined language-experience approach will play a prominent part.

Lawrence W. Carrillo

There has never been sizeable disagreement over the value of the language-experience approach to the teaching of reading. Although this article tends toward elementary education, Dr. Carrillo discusses the structure of this approach in a way that readily lends itself to adaptation to the secondary school classroom.

The Language-Experience Approach to the Teaching of Reading

Introduction

One of the major difficulties with any *published* materials for the teaching of reading, whether printed in traditional orthography or in i.t.a., is the necessary assumption of common experiential background. That is, the important thing in the teaching of reading, from the first word, is the fact that the process is made meaningful to the children. If the words, sentences, concepts included are full of meaning for the children, if they have linguistic relevance, if they have been heard and spoken by the children prior to their printed presentation, learning to read will be relatively simple for most. If, on the other hand, the printed page represents a type of communication which is different, and if the situations found in the story are some which have never been experienced, learning to read is difficult.

A large number of studies, including my own dissertation (4), have seemed to show that children from homes which provide a broad experiential background, especially in language-experience, have little difficulty in learning to read. Success in reading is more certainly guaranteed if you have the right parents, and they are economically fortunate enough to provide you with both experiences and conversation about the experiences. But let us examine this!

Such studies may only have proven that the materials with which we have been teaching reading are designed to fit *the particular experiences* of children from a particular kind of home background. Our school culture

---

From *The Second International Reading Symposium* edited by John Downing and Amy L. Brown (London: Cassell and Co. Ltd., 1967). "The Language-Experience Approach to the Teaching of Reading" by Lawrence W. Carrillo.

may be attuned to upper-middle-class values, language and concepts; children who do not have this background fail because *so much* is new and different. Perhaps, for children from different environments, there was so little meaning in the educational task that it is rejected from the outset. Another fact which may add to the possibility of this interpretation has to do with intelligence testing, where there is also the assumption of commonality of experience. We now know that you can trust intelligence-test results only insofar as commonality of experience and conceptual background holds (if that far).

This problem is brought home with great force when you attempt to be an educator in a country different from your own. In Liberia, where I have spent this last year, neither British nor American materials 'fit' the children well enough to produce much meaning from the reading process. To see a teacher attempting to describe something included in a primary grade story which the children (and perhaps even the teacher) have never seen is a very frustrating experience. It is worse because, even though you may have experienced this thing yourself, your own ability to communicate the concept will be as limited as the overlap between the two cultures. You must know the Liberian culture rather well in order to draw parallels for explanatory purposes. All this is true even though the official language in Liberia is English. Obviously, the answer is materials for the teaching of reading which fit the culture in which they are used. But in a small country, where only a small percentage of the population is literate, and without a great deal of money, the publication of suitable educational materials presents a nearly insurmountable problem.

There is a *partial* answer, however, in the language-experience approach. Recently, this way of teaching reading has become more widely known, to lay readers as well as educators, through Sylvia Ashton-Warner's book *Teacher* (3). I find Peace Corps Volunteers using an adaptation of this approach deep in the bush, simply because this book and its inspirational account of a comparable situation (in New Zealand) has made such an impression on them.

Backgrounds and Sources—Professional

The first account in the United States of a way of teaching reading resembling the language-experience approach occurs over sixty-five years ago (6). Then, in the 1920's, along with the project method, activity teaching, and the introduction of manuscript writing in primary grades, many educators described methods which utilized the children's own language in the production of reading materials (7,10,18). Those who employed these methods emphasized the meaning and relevancy of the resultant materials, though all studies do not agree completely on the efficacy of the method.

All these studies were probably first combined and the method described and named the 'experience method' by Dr. Nila Banton Smith in 1934 (20). In most of the early studies, the experience method was used as a 'readiness' stage before employing the primer, in order to introduce reading informally as a thought-getting process. For a presentation of some of these early experiments and a complete bibliography, refer to Hildreth's recent article in *Elementary English* (12).

In the early 1940's, the method was given particular professional impetus through two separate books by Gans (9) and Lamoreaux and Lee (14). For a number of years most of the articles and pamphlets concerned with the experience approach had to do with its use with children of different cultural and language backgrounds (16,17,19). This emphasis continues, with the addition of articles showing the application of the method to older children from restricted backgrounds (8), and the revision of the method to what has come to be called the 'language-experience approach.' This latest name is an outgrowth of the findings of a five-year study with this approach and others in the San Diego (California) schools and by Dr. Allen specifically (1,2,13).

Two years ago, Dr. Allen collaborated with Dr. Lee to revise her book of twenty years earlier (15). This revision not only illustrates the method through real examples, but broadens the approach to include all the language arts, and shows how the approach may be individualized.

Very recently, still another book which emphasizes and illustrates the charts which grow from the use of the language-experience approach has been published (11). The practical nature and simplicity of this paper-bound book should have wide appeal.

One last publishing venture (5) must also be mentioned here, since it is an attempt to incorporate the language-experience approach into a series of carefully prepared readers, preserving the advantages of both. The language in the beginning books is the actual language of children, but the books have vocabulary control. The illustrations are actual photographs of children having the experience which produced the conversations on which the text is based. The situations are quite real for the particular group for which the readers are designed—the urban multi-racial group in the United States. Then, in later books, as the child's conceptual background broadens, the experiences are enriched and broadened. Since I am personally involved here, I will not describe these books further at this stage, but explain the language-experience approach and its attendant advantages and disadvantages.

The Language-Experience Approach

The language-experience approach may be basically outlined in only four steps, as follows:

1. *Experience.* The first essential is a first-hand group (or individual if the approach is applied in an individualized fashion) experience which contains sufficient inherent interest to produce a discussion. This may vary from daily events, including descriptions of the weather, to describing and evaluating experiences occurring on a study trip.

2. *Awareness.* The teacher leads the children in a discussion of the experience, recording (usually on the chalkboard) phrases and sentences used by class members. Manuscript writing is used in primary grades and either manuscript or cursive in higher grades.

3. *Composition.* The class, with teacher guidance, decides on the sentences and the order of these sentences needed to tell their story. The teacher may then write this story on the chalkboard in the order decided upon, and the class reads the story.

4. *Permanence.* Depending upon the nature of the story, the teacher may decide to give the material greater permanence by transferring it to an oaktag chart or large newsprint sheet. This step converts the class's effort to a large book form, and it may then be used again for review or reteaching at any later date. The several charts may be kept in order on a chart rack, hung in the room, or bound together in some way. These pages may be illustrated, preferably by children. It is possible to duplicate copies in a smaller size, so that each child has a 'book' of his own. This is particularly appropriate for more advanced pupils.

This basic method is applicable to both individuals and groups, and may be employed at any grade level. Most often it is used as a step in teaching beginning reading. The use of other media, such as the basal reader or i.t.a., is easily possible in conjunction with the language-experience approach. In short, this is an extremely flexible approach, adaptable to any conceptualization of the teaching of reading which you may prefer. It may be used anywhere, even if the sand is your 'chalkboard.' And since it starts with the children themselves, it is almost guaranteed to fit them better than use of published material alone.

Advantages and Disadvantages

As in any approach to a skill as complex and abstract as that of reading, there are both advantages and limitations to the language-experience method. Anyone who claims that any 'system' of teaching reading will

The Language-Experience Approach to the Teaching of Reading 263

be successful with all children and adults is doomed to disappointment. But let us see what the language-experience approach has to offer on the positive side.

1. The language, since it comes directly *from* the children, is the most meaningful possible language *to* the children. This applies not only to the vocabulary, but to the word order and degree of complexity within sentences. The teacher may use *his own* experience to exercise a few judicious choices in what finally appears in permanent chart form, but these changes must be applied very gradually.

2. The experiences, since they are recent and real to the children, provide intrinsic motivation, interest and vitality in the reading materials resulting from these experiences. Occasionally such materials may even be used with another class, depending upon the applicability of the material to the overlap in background experience between the two groups concerned.

3. Teaching of all the language arts is possible in a single, unified method. Oral communication, listening, handwriting, spelling, the mechanics of composition and grammar, creative writing and reading are taught together—without the artificial separation into subject-matter areas which tends to destroy them.

4. The basic concept of reading fostered by the method is both professionally sound and easily understood by children. The 'oneness' of all the communication skills becomes obvious; the association of the written form to the spoken form is made directly both in sound and sense; and the process of reading becomes something children have already known in another form and, therefore, easier because it is less puzzling.

Limitations found in the use of the language-experience approach are likely to be:

1. The vocabulary can range widely, providing insufficient repetition for any word to ensure retention, or providing such a variety of words that the learning of many of them is unlikely.

2. The oral discussion and organization of the story may be dominated by a few individuals. Very careful and skilful teaching is required to attain the objective of total group-participation. This one problem is likely to be the reason why the method is not employed more. Teacher security is a key factor.

3. Chart stories, because of their size (to be seen clearly by the entire group, they must be large), have a tendency to be quite short, and may therefore be easily memorized. This may cause a serious misconception of the reading act on the part of the child in the beginning stages. This is often quite difficult to overcome later.

4. Since the approach depends upon a daily teacher-led activity, the teacher must be extremely conscious of the developmental sequence of the

multiple skills with which he is working. Otherwise the learnings are more accidental than systematic, and the method is time-wasting.

5. The daily preparation of sufficient material takes a great deal of teacher time.

6. The method does not adapt easily to the practice of teaching several reading groups at their different levels in a single classroom.

Conclusion

The language-experience approach to the teaching of reading is enjoying a recent resurgence. An increasing concern over children with different environmental backgrounds and the effect of these different backgrounds on learning seems to be basic to this resurgence. The language-experience approach uses and incorporates environmental differences, rather than ignoring them, to produce materials which fit the group.

For many years in education, we have been saying "We must start where the child is." The language-experience approach is one way of doing just this.

But a caution is in order. No one method of teaching reading will, when used exclusively, do the complete job. A combination of methods will reach and teach more children than any single method.

Combining the language-experience approach with almost any other approach should produce more children who read with meaning, who understand what reading is, and who therefore enjoy their reading. Not only that, but it will make the very process of learning to read more enjoyable. Sufficient reason, in spite of difficulties, for at least occasional employment of the language-experience approach? I think so.

References

1. Allen, R. Van. "Concept Development of Young Children in Reading Instruction." *Twenty-fourth Yearbook.* Claremont, California: Claremont College Reading Conference, 1959, pp. 12-21.

2. Allen, R. Van, and Halvorsen, Gladys C. *The Language-Experience Approach to Reading Instruction.* Contributions in Reading No. 27. Boston: Ginn and Co., 1961.

3. Ashton-Warner, Sylvia. *Teacher.* New York: Simon & Shuster, 1961; London: Secker & Warburg, 1963.

4. Carrillo, Lawrence W. *The Relation of Certain Environmental and Developmental Factors to Reading Ability in Children.* Ed.D. dissertation, Syracuse University, 1957.

5. *The Chandler Language-Experience Readers.* San Francisco, California: Chandler Publishing Co., 1964.

6. Cooke, Flora J. "Reading in the Primary Grades." *The Course of Study.* Vol. 1. Chicago: Publication of the Chicago Institute, 1900, pp. 111-15.

7. Dickson, Julia E., and McLean, Mary E. "An Integrated Activity Program Try-Out in a First Grade of the Public Schools." *Educational Method* 9 (1929):31-42.

The Language-Experience Approach to the Teaching of Reading 265

8. Edwards, Thomas J. "The Language-Experience Attack on Cultural Deprivation." *The Reading Teacher* 18 (April 1965):546-51.
9. Gans, Roma. *Guiding Children's Reading Through Experiences.* New York: Bureau of Publications, Teachers College, Columbia University, 1941.
10. Gates, Arthur I.; Batchelder, M.; and Betzner, Jean. "A Modern Systematic versus an Opportunistic Method of Teaching." *Teachers College Record* 27 (1926):679-700.
11. Herrick, Virgil E., and Nerbovig, Marcella. *Using Experience Charts with Children.* Columbus, Ohio: Charles E. Merrill Books, 1964.
12. Hildreth, Gertrude H. "Experience-Related Reading for School Beginners." *Elementary English* (1964):280-97.
13. *Improving Reading Instruction. Description of Three Approaches to the Teaching of Reading.* Monograph No. 2. San Diego, California: San Diego County Department of Education, May, 1961.
14. Lamoreaux, Lillian A., and Lee, Dorris May. *Learning to Read Through Experience.* New York: Appleton-Century, 1943.
15. Lee, Dorris M. and Allen, R. Van. *Learning to Read Through Experience.* 2nd ed. New York: Appleton-Century-Crofts, 1963.
16. Meriam, J. L. "An Activity Curriculum in a School for Mexican Children." *Journal of Experimental Education* 1 (1933):304-8.
17. Nesbitt, Marion. *A Public School for Tomorrow.* A Description of the Matthew F. Maury School, Richmond, Virginia. New York: Harper & Row, 1953.
18. Report of the National Committee on Reading, Part I. "Appropriate Materials for Reading Instruction." *The Twenty-Fourth Yearbook of the National Society for the Study of Education.* Chicago: The University of Chicago Press, 1925, chapter 7.
19. Smith, Charles A. "The Experience Method in Beginning Reading." *Elementary School Journal* 38 (1937):96-106.
20. Smith, Nila B. *American Reading Instruction.* New York: Silver, Burdett and Co., 1934, pp. 229-44.

Evelyn Jan-Tausch

Evelyn Jan-Tausch insists upon a reexamination of reading instruction and its relation to total communication. Concerned about the fragmented bits and pieces of English language instruction, Dr. Jan-Tausch places much blame upon reading teachers who have been too eager to focus upon reading in isolation.

Reading as Language

One of the more disturbing aspects of the author's observation of reading instruction for the past twenty years has been its rapid metamorphosis into a subject area taught in separation from the rest of the curriculum for grades one through twelve. Two essential components of the reading process seem to be ignored—at a measurable cost—when reading instruction is departmentalized, compartmentalized, and grade-stratified. The first of these constituents is the understanding of reading as an integral part of the total language and thinking development of the individual; the second, realization that reading is a *skill* to be employed for the acquisition of knowledge and self-growth. It has no subject content sacred to its domain unless one is concerned with learning how to teach reading or doing research into the reading process. There seems to be no valid reason, therefore, for teaching reading apart from the rest of the curriculum; rather one might expect it to be taught as part of every subject that involves the use of language. It is difficult to think of exceptions to this last qualification.

Language for Communication

The purpose of language—and of teaching—is communication. While the linguist generally defines *language* in terms of articulated, structured, arbitrary *vocal* sounds, the fact remains that writing is an invention to extend the space/time range of language; and reading is a process of abstracting the communication conveyed by the written-down vocal symbols.

Reprinted with permission of Evelyn Jan-Tausch and the International Reading Association.

In oral communication the transmission takes place through the medium of sound waves; in reading, by means of light waves, but the essential function of language—to communicate—remains unaltered.

In the Communications issue of the *Kaiser Aluminum News* (1) the passage of ideas from one person to another is referred to as "human transactions," and the basic ingredients of the transaction—whatever the method of symbolization—are listed as:

> Something taken in
> Something transformed
> Something retained
> Something created
> Something transmitted

The quality of the message communicated through language symbols depends upon the cognitive level of the sender. The receiver, in turn, must rely upon his power of cognition to assimilate, transform (interpret), and retain the message conveyed. In the happy instance of the receiver possessing a creative facility over and beyond his purely intellectual endowment, the thought or action that he, in turn, transmits may add to the storehouse of human cultural treasures.

The language-reading communication at the first level of "something taken in" involves the receiver (pupil), the sender (author) and the teacher who clears the lines for transmission of the message by careful assessment of both the receiver's capacity and the frequency level at which the sender is communicating. Without skillful intermediation on the teacher's part, the reading or communication may fail to occur or the message received will be garbled and misleading. Evaluation of the perceptual strengths of the receiver aids the teacher in selecting the appropriate method of conveying the message.

Reading—Language Functioning

It must be stressed that the total reading act encompasses more than the take-in stage although, admittedly, the reading process must *begin* here. Reading is only *one* form of language and while it is certainly a most vital one, the teacher needs to understand that it is not the only way in which the human transaction takes place and information is transmitted. The point is made, albeit it may seem irrelevant here, because subject teachers often insist a pupil cannot *learn* because he cannot read. The terms are not synonymous nor do they necessarily have a cause-effect relationship. It is equally important for the teacher to realize that reading can and should be taught as part of the language-communication cluster in every subject area. In this way the teaching of reading rather than being an esoteric and "magical" affair reserved for the reading specialist becomes a matter of communication inseparable from each and every teaching situation.

The concept of reading as language requires not only acceptance on the part of the teacher verbally, but in actual practice. Personal experience leads this author to feel that many elementary teachers are apt *mentally* to feel uncomfortable if they do not meet with their reading groups each day for a reading period devoted to work in the basal reader. There is a real danger that this may come to be considered *all* that needs to be done in the course of the day for reading skill development. Whereas in the secondary schools the division between reading instruction and the other curriculum offerings is marked concretely by periods and bells, in the elementary school the separation is often just as definite *in the teacher's mind* and is reflected in his teaching.

Grouping has been used by teachers for some time to accomplish certain purposes in instruction; the technique of achieving a change in the teacher perception and functioning by a different kind of grouping of the elementary staff and teaching assignments than is customary in the self-contained graded school is a relatively new but growing development. Emphasis is usually placed when talking about the ungraded school and the continuous progress program on the effect that it has on the *pupil* and his learning. Equally important from the viewpoint of the elementary supervisor is the opportunity it affords to break through the limits imposed on the teaching of reading by the notion that it is a separate subject, and to develop teacher understanding that reading is language; it not only can but should be taught through the medium of the different subject material throughout the entire school day.

A New Approach

In September, 1968 one of the elementary schools (grades K-four) in Glen Ridge initiated a change-over to the ungraded continuous progress program. As a first step the previous year, the faculty and the supervisor had struggled to get down on paper a sequential listing of reading skills. One of the supervisor's basic tenets about reading instruction has been the conviction that only the word attack skills can be put into any reasonable kind of sequential development order. The comprehension skills remain the same throughout the grades; it is the level of difficulty of the material and of the concepts to be understood that must be sequentially planned. Such a developmental order already exists in the subject areas to some extent and things are happening *there* to make the material and the ideas presented not only appropriate to the cognitive growth of the youngster, but designed to develop his thinking abilities. In the transmission of subject material the reading skills can be taught in a meaningful and practical manner once the teacher has accepted the idea that reading is language and whatever develops the language or communication facility is, in effect, teaching the child to be a better reader.

Fortified then with a philosophic conviction and an admittedly incomplete listing of what was considered needed for the development of reading skills, the supervisor divided the teaching staff into two teams. To one group was assigned the teaching of Language Arts, reading, and Social Studies; the other carried responsibility for Math and Science. The school day was divided into five large time blocks with Language Arts and reading to be taught in the *one* largest time period.

The Language Arts program currently in use is one that lends itself very well to easing teachers into an understanding and active acceptance of teaching reading as an inseparable component of language. The program is the Nebraska *Curriculum for English* (2). It is an extension of suggestions made in the Woods Curriculum Workshop of 1961. The basic premise of this program is that children have a need to come in contact with literature, that even children who do not yet read should find attractive those communications of fine literature appropriate to their level of intellect, imagination, and rhythmic sense. Storytelling, modeled and unmodeled, is a foundation activity in this curriculum. The elementary program is divided into nine units, groups or "pseudo-genres": folk tales, fanciful stories, animal stories, adventure stories, myth, fable, and other lands and people, historical fiction, biography. This classification serves the purposes of the curriculum in that it allows for stress on certain story elements and thus a sequential development of the principles of the program. Literary works of substantial merit have been selected and those versions or editions of the stories that are most useful to the program or are of the highest degree of literary integrity. The literature is often read to the children. Work in oral language and composition is included in the units.

The makers of the curriculum do not want it confused with a reading program, and they state that the "development of methods for the teaching of reading is the proper concern of the reading expert." One can appreciate the natural concern of the curriculum planners not to infringe upon the discipline of another group of specialists, but their disclaimer only serves to emphasize the exclusion of reading from the rest of the language program and reduces it to the status of a course in code-breaking. The following are the goals and methods of this program:

1. Reading to children and their own story telling are included in this program because its authors believe "The child's basically oral approach to literature will change as he masters reading skills, *but he must know and feel that these reading skills are worth learning.* . . . Our concern is with showing such literature as will make reading worth the effort."

2. Oral exposure to literature, it is assumed, may quicken the child's ear to the "tunes" of the language, sharpen his sense of syntax, and continue to widen his oral vocabulary.

3. Oral discussion of the stories read builds a foundation for the interpretation of stories and the recognition of motifs.

4. Writing of original stories is suggested by the story read. These are the levels of "Something created—Something transmitted" and form a legitimate part of the total reading process. In the first few months of first grade, the teacher prints the story developed by members of the class on the board or on a large, lined experience chart paper. The story is then used for reading instruction—oral and silent—and is copied to go into a class booklet of original writings. The class booklets are useful for library material for primary "free reading periods." The first graders in this program are doing a great amount of original writing. Motivation for their writing stems from awareness of the outstanding stylistic characteristic of the stories which serves as a writing model (e.g. repetition of words and situations in folk tales) and the fertility of material which has demonstrated a lasting and basic appeal to the human mind.

5. The *Language Explorations* section of each unit, from grade one through grade six, deals with specific vocabulary word meanings; use of punctuation, underlining, illustrations, capital letters to illustrate *graphically* the oral intonation patterns; word changes by adding letters or taking letters off; syntactical experimentation by sentence expansion, changed word order, etc.; use of dialect; figures of speech; dictionary use, word derivations.

This listing of what is included in the Nebraska *Curriculum for English* is not meant to be all-inclusive of the skills covered, but to illustrate that any imposed separation of the teaching of reading from the rest of this language arts program would be an arbitrary and artificial one.

The time periods assigned to both math and science instruction are also large ones. Originally some of the teachers expressed doubts about too much time being allotted to these subject areas for first and second graders. They learned, however, that it is not just the methods of science or the skills of computation that they are to impart, but that the language of the subject is to be taught and that part of that language instruction is teaching reading through the use of math or science content. They are asked to develop reading not from the basal reader but by devising activities that will bring together the language and concepts specific to the subject. They are responsible for teaching the vocabulary used. This involves visual presentation of all new words or terms, sounding out to achieve oral mastery, learning of the appropriate meaning within the subject context, and frequent use of the word or term *by the pupil* in all subsequent oral or written work. Lists of these words are kept prominently on view in the classroom or in bulletin board displays. Manipulative devices are employed freely in math where the processed visual symbol system must be connected to other kinds of information—*action* in the case of mathematics—if comprehension is to happen. Experience charts are written to relate sequential steps in an experiment, mathematical quantities and measurements used to describe. Practical use and application enable the pupils to comprehend the difference between fact and fiction, author's purpose in communicating, the need for clarity and correct terminology.

Shared Responsibility

It seems relevant to point out that Stroud (3) has stated that the responsibility for teaching a pupil to comprehend does not rest primarily with the teacher of reading. Comprehension he feels is a generalized ability to the development of which all teachers and the educative process *in toto* contribute. The pupil draws from a stored fund of knowledge in all linguistic behavior whether it be reading, talking or writing. If one accepts this premise there is little doubt that the subject area teacher who refers a pupil to the reading teacher for improvement of comprehension has erroneously prescribed. The reading teacher who accepts the assignment and who painstakingly works on teaching the pupil to select main ideas and key words, to read paragraphs and to answer the questions that follow, may find that the pupil's reading comprehension, when measured by the subject area teacher in terms of functioning in his class, may show little or no improvement. The key to unlock the storehouse has been carefully oiled but the storehouse still remains empty. It is the clarification of terms and understanding of the processes or data concerned with the specific subject area that is needed for the improvement of reading *comprehension.*

The separation of reading instruction from the rest of the curriculum and failure to comprehend its nature as a language skill that must be closely allied to concept formation has produced sterility and staleness in far too many reading programs. Where the elementary grades remain self-contained and one teacher plans each day's total learning experience for the group, there is often a fusing of the reading and language arts that satisfies the pupil's unexpressed but very real need for a logical coherence and purpose for what he is learning. Beginning with the junior high program, however, the reading specialist emerges as a subject teacher in his own right with developmental reading classes separate and apart from those of the English teacher who at this point in the educational set-up generally is of the opinion that somebody else should teach the pupil *how* to read since he has not been prepared to do so. Visits to these secondary reading classes will often reveal that they are nothing more or less than duplications of what is already being done in the English class.

There are times when one wonders if reading experts have not succeeded too well in their struggle to achieve recognition for the need to teach reading. Putting the spotlight on a particular part of the curriculum to define its needs is admirable; to cut it off, however, may be to deprive it of sustenance and cripple its essential function.

References

1. Communications. *Kaiser Aluminum News* 23 (1965):3.
2. Nebraska Curriculum Development Center. *A curriculum for English.* Lincoln, Nebraska; University of Nebraska Press, 1966.
3. Stroud, J. B. *Psychology in the schools.* Iowa City: University of Iowa, 1964.

Josephine T. Benson

For the culturally different or children who use a different dialect from general American English, methods must be employed that place reading instruction in an understandable context. Because all of the language arts are integrated in the language-experience approach, it seems likely to yield dividends. Some techniques and the rationales for them are here described.

Teaching Reading to the Culturally Different Child

The culturally different child may be the product of many different environments. There are: (1) the transient child who moves often from one school to another within the city; (2) the child of migrant workers; (3) the child who moves from a rural community to the city where life is much more complicated; and (4) the bilingual child to whom English is a second language, little used and poorly spoken.

Teachers must recognize that just as there are wide differences among children in general, so also are there many differences among the culturally different. They differ in mental ability and reading, in motivation, and in interest and tastes as well as personality. Their cultural and educational backgrounds may be very different. Some children who have the ability to read well prefer not to because they may be excluded from their neighborhood gang. Other children are not necessarily culturally deprived. They may recently have come from another country whose language they speak and read easily, but are just beginning to learn English.

There is no easy solution to these problems. What is good for one is not necessarily good for all. We must accept each child as an individual with his strengths and weaknesses. Different techniques must be used for maximum learning. As we develop better understanding of the individual child, reading programs will improve giving each child a better opportunity to more nearly reach his potential.

The culturally different child usually comes from a home atmosphere in which there is very little furniture, few pictures and toys, if any. His

---

Josephine T. Benson, "Teaching Reading to the Culturally Different Child," *Progress and Promise in Reading Instruction.* Conference on Reading, University of Pittsburgh Report 22, 1966.

273

parents have very little education, work at unskilled jobs or "go on welfare." They have little ambition and no hopes for the future. Consequently, these children are not motivated and have no one to emulate. Their homes are void of any intellectual stimulation such as books, magazines or even a newspaper.

Motivation

For these children a good learning atmosphere is imperative. They need a classroom atmosphere which will attract and hold their interest through its many "on-going" activities.

Many books on different grade levels and on various subjects will help to spark an interest. Building libraries with a trained librarian are excellent, but, if we want children to be attracted to books, there must also be books in the classroom where the child can reach for one if, and when, he desires to do so. Attractive bulletin boards and pictures; a poetry corner; science and social studies displays; a sand table; a listening corner equipped with a sound recorder, a tape recorder and ear phones add interest. A special-interest table or corner for the display of rock collections, sea-shells, a piece of coal or stalagmite, etc. will stimulate oral discussion. Every classroom should have a magnifying glass and a small inexpensive telescope for exploring. A well-equipped classroom should include picture dictionaries for first grade and possibly second and regulation dictionaries as soon as the children are ready for them. Encyclopedias, maps, and a globe are helpful to children who have acquired the skill to use them. The classroom newspaper should be included in all classroom activities.

To further stimulate these children, many of whom tend to be apathetic and passive, some teachers make posters with slogans and appropriate illustrations such as "Put a Tiger in Your Reading" or "Put Your Reading in Orbit." It could be even more effective, providing they were able to have the older children decide upon a slogan for the group and an illustration and then have them elect one or two of the members to make the poster.

Oral Language

By the time the child comes to kindergarten his language patterns are set. He has already learned to speak and use language as he has heard it in his neighborhood and home. This may be the vernacular of the region in which he lives, a combination of English and the foreign language of the parents or the language of the street. He experiences difficulty in school because the language that he hears there, and is expected to use, is different from the language that he has learned at home. This is not only confusing but is also frustrating.

An investigation of the oral language patterns of culturally different children, conducted by Dominick Thomas from the Detroit Public Schools, showed that these children used shorter sentences with fewer words and less variety than children from higher social status groups. It also showed a deficiency in the amount, correctness; and maturity of their oral expression. Furthermore, he found that children living in low socio-economic urban areas used approximately only 50 percent of the words found in three leading basal first grade readers. These same children made no use of approximately 20 percent—50 percent of such word lists as the International Kindergarten Union, Dolch, Gates, Rinsland and Thorndike (15).

We know that a child's progress in learning to read depends to a great extent upon his previous experience with oral language. We also know that a child finds it easier to recognize words in print if they are already a part of his speaking vocabulary. The culturally different child has an extremely limited vocabulary. Parents of these children have little communication with their children. Their own vocabularies are very meager. These children speak in phrases rather than in sentences, make many grammatical errors, and often mispronounce words and enunciate poorly. Therefore, it is most imperative that oral language should be a major part of the readiness program both at kindergarten level and first grade.

Children can be given rich experiences by taking them to visit a farm, a circus, an airport, a fire and police station. Since many of these children never have an opportunity to go any farther than a few blocks from their homes, the teacher should not overlook many possibilities for extending experiences within walking distance of the school. Even the experiences they have encountered usually have very little meaning because there was no one to discuss these experiences with them. They are lacking in the conceptual foundations needed to build new concepts.

Language development should not be limited to the primary grades. Many of the older children could profit by first hand experiences commensurate with their abilities and interests. Many of them have never seen a movie or eaten in a restaurent. They should have opportunities to ride on buses, streetcars, trains and in taxicabs.

There should be much free and spontaneous conversing; sharing and relating experiences; talking on a toy telephone; playing they are on radio or television; manipulating puppets, especially finger puppets; and, dramatizing and choral reading.

Culturally disadvantaged children should be given opportunities to tell stories from pictures. At first they may only be able to enumerate objects seen in the picture. Later they should be able to interpret the picture. After they learn to tell a story from a single picture, they should then be able to tell stories from two or more pictures in sequence. Along with this experience in interpreting pictures a child should be given the experience of telling a story by means of pictures he has painted or drawn. Since the child, when drawing or painting a picture, often has much more in mind than appears in the finished product, he should be given the opportunity to tell his story from his picture.

Their speaking vocabularies increase as they learn the words to their songs, and through the stories and poems told or read to them by their teacher. Children in first and second grade love the Nursery Rhymes and ask to repeat them again and again. Dr. A. F. Watts, an Englishman, maintains that forty nursery rhymes introduce four hundred new words (17).

A kindergarten teacher may play this game with her reading readiness group of culturally disadvantaged children. She takes a small object from her desk. Holding it in her closed hand she asks the children, "What do I have in my hand?" The various children ask, "Do you have a ball in your hand?" etc. The teacher replies, "No, I do not have a ball in my hand," etc. The idea is to encourage and aid children to talk in sentences and the teacher refuses to answer anyone who does not.

Sensory Experiences

Because of limited verbal ability and inadequate experiential background, the culturally different child learns best through concrete and visual experiences. He needs much practice in the use of descriptive adjectives. These children have very few toys, if any, and are not familiar with many ordinary objects found in middle-class homes. As a result, the tactile skills are not fully developed. They should be given every opportunity to identify numerous objects by shape and texture, noting if they are smooth or rough; hard or soft; round or square. In the classroom, many opportunities are present for developing better tactile skills. Primary children are always interested in the teacher's clothes and in each other's. What kind of fur is on the collar of the teacher's coat? How does it feel? Is Billy's coat made of wool? Is it smooth like silk? A box containing samples of velvet and satin ribbon, velveteen, wool, cotton, and silk, which the children could feel, would be useful. Another box might contain a miscellaneous collection of objects which they could handle to feel the differences in textures such as: a sponge, a piece of coal, wood, cotton, stalagmite, a pebble. Ask children to describe how they feel; also have them make a game of it by having individual children close their eyes and identify an object handed to them.

The other senses of taste, smelling, seeing and hearing must also be developed. The sense of "seeing" is probably their best developed sense. They have a certain awareness of their environment. They see the river but, as mentioned previously, it has little, if any, meaning to them because they have never had an opportunity to ask questions and to voice their thoughts about the river. These children need to become more conscious of some of their surroundings.

Some afternoon ask the children to report the next morning on all the things they observed on the way to school. The assignment must be given in advance; otherwise the teacher will find they are aware of very little in their environment. They must be taught to be observant. On other occasions they should be directed to listen for different sounds, or to report on different odors such as bread baking, coffee, fruit, gasoline, spices, etc. Let them taste white and brown sugar; maybe vanilla, molasses, chocolate and ginger cookies. Several books about the five senses have been published by Crowell Company recently for reading to the children (12).

Listening

For many years teachers were so absorbed in teaching children written language that little attention was directed towards speaking and listening. It was taken for granted that children acquired these abilities before they came to school. With the advent of the radio and television, the emphasis has shifted to oral communication. Children who live in crowded homes in slum areas where the radio or television is rarely turned off have learned to tune out many of the noises surrounding them. As a result, their attention and memory spans are limited. They cannot distinguish slight differences in sound and therefore possess little auditory discrimination. Reading research tells us that the ability to note differences and similarities in words and the ability to hear separate sounds and be able to blend them into a known word are essential. Teachers should impress upon children the importance of careful listening. It will be just as important to them when they are adults as now. Both listening and reading are dependent upon the learner's ability to understand words quickly and meaningfully. Children should be taught specific skills for listening and how each is necessary for a particular purpose or kind of listening such as reading for information, for critical evaluation, and for appreciation. Good listening habits need to be developed at all grade levels.

These children need an abundance of auditory readiness to prepare them for phonics skills. Have them listen for rhyming words in nursery rhymes and other poems. Have them listen for the two words that rhyme out of three words given; such as: "man, pan, book." Vary the exercise by asking for the word that does not rhyme with the other two words. Have the children divide a paper in two columns and write the words you say beginning with "p" in the first column and the words beginning with "t" in the second column. The same exercise could be used with words beginning or ending with "m" and "n," "b" and "d."

Children like to listen to recorded music and interpret the sounds. Mendelssohn's *Spring Song*, Herbert's *March of the Toys*, *The Blue Danube Waltz*, by Strauss, and *The Carnival of the Animals*, by Saint Saens, among others are good for listening skills (9).

Reading

When the teacher feels that the children are ready for reading she then has the task of helping them to acquire a reading vocabulary while continuing to help them to enlarge their speaking and hearing vocabularies. Words which are already in their speaking and hearing vocabularies will be easier to learn when met in print.

Children can learn the names of nouns through pictures. Pictures can be cut from old reading readiness books or mail order catalogues and pasted on 3 x 5 cards with the name printed below the picture and on the back of the picture. The name should be cut off the card. The pictures can then be matched with the words. These can be self-checked by turning over each picture to see if the word on the back matches the word placed under the picture.

Picture dictionaries help children to recognize words. In addition, each child should have a picture dictionary which he has made up for his personal use by cutting pictures from magazines, catalogues.

Some teachers like to label various objects in the room to aid in word recognition and meaning.

Make a small shoestring chart (9" x 12") with blocks of various colors on one side and the names of the colors on the opposite side in a different order. Use a black shoelace or colored yarn to connect the color with its name. This can be used by individuals who need practice.

Since culturally different children have poor auditory discrimination, they need much practice in phonic analysis. Sound games such as Dolch's Consonant and Vowel Lotto are more popular than work-book exercises (7).

Many different word games should be used with these children. They like the element of suspense that games offer. Games not only create interest but also hold attention. They give a child a chance to win even if someone else knows more words and this builds self-confidence which these children need.

By the time the culturally different child has reached the fourth grade, he is more than likely to be approximately one and one-half years retarded in reading. He often has a language of his own through which he communicates with his friends. It is very different from the language of the classroom. For example, these children may say they had to "carry" a brother to school where we would use the word "take." They may talk about a "shoe bite" when they have a blister on a foot or they ask if they can "hush" out the light. They often use prepositions incorrectly when they comment that they went *by* a friend's house when they actually went *to* his house. To help children overcome this, have them play a game with prepositions in which they are asked to put an object on, in, under, around, beside, on top of, or behind a table, etc.

Many words have double meanings and children sometimes make a game out of them. Teachers should encourage this by calling attention to the fact that cartoonists draw heavily from these words for many of their cartoons. Encourage the children to watch for these cartoons and to bring them to school to share with their classmates. Interest in words may be heightened by asking children to watch for articles on the origin of words and on certain expressions which often appear in the newspaper. A recent article on the origin of "blue jeans" and another on the origin of "OK" should have interested them. Ask the children to draw a picture of the following: a home run, a ghost writer, a horse doctor, raising cats and dogs, etc.

Dictionary readiness should be introduced in the primary grades and dictionary skills in the third or fourth grade depending on when the children were ready. Many exercises are available in dictionaries, teachers' manuals and workbooks to give practice on these very important and useful skills. To encourage the use of the dictionary set aside a prominent corner of a blackboard for writing a provocative question such as: "If someone said you were agile, would you be insulted?" or "Is this true? If you are pugnacious, you are quarrelsome."

What kind of reading program can we plan for this culturally different child whose different speech patterns cause him to distort certain words such as "iron" which he pronounces "arn," whose recognition and understanding of words is so meager that he too often meets words in print which are not in his understanding or speaking vocabulary? Some teachers are using the Language-Experience Approach and finding it more effective than using standard reading books. While this approach is versatile and informal, it must be carefully and thoughtfully planned. It must be preceded by an adequate readiness program as described earlier in this paper. Provision must be made for teaching word-attack skills and the various comprehension skills. The topic of discussion should reflect the interests and experiences of the entire group. The lesson may be the aftermath of a field trip or a project or some vicarious experience such as a film or filmstrip. The Language-Experience Approach does not differentiate between reading and other language activities. Each child is encouraged to share his ideas with the other children. He quickly develops a writing vocabulary and soon can write his own stories independently. Books are a vitally important part of this type of program. The children read many books and use them as a source for their writing.

The teacher stimulates discussion and acts as a resource person in locating and supplying needed information; she also records and aids the children in organizing the material.

Through the Language-Experience Approach these children can identify with the reading material and are highly motivated to read it because it is their experiences, and, therefore, something they can understand. Their writings give them a feeling of accomplishment and add to their self-esteem. This approach provides an excellent opportunity for children to learn to take notes, to outline, to organize and to read critically.

While the Language-Experience Approach is more often thought of as a reading approach for the primary grades, there is no reason why it could not be just as effective in the intermediate grades.

Teachers who use the basal reader approach will find that experience charts can be a very helpful supplementary aid in teaching reading to all children.

A study by Dr. Brazziel gives additional proof of the close relationship between reading deficiency and the below-standard language usage of school children (3). The children in the intermediate grades are overwhelmed with the great number of new words introduced in the content subjects. These technical words are often very abstract. Sometimes it is better for the teacher to introduce fewer concepts in the content subjects and to explain and teach them more thoroughly. Using a topical unit approach may be more satisfactory because each child could be given reading material on his reading level. Sometimes trade books can be substituted for textbooks in Social Studies. These may help to clarify the concepts in the history text. Books like Laura Ingalls Wilder's *Little House in the Big Woods* give a clear and more interesting account of pioneer life than some history books. The content fields provide rich experiential background as well as good material for the development of thinking skills.

Culturally different children should have ample time for recreational reading so that they can make individual choices of what they want to read.

Since these children are usually lacking in motivation, there must be available many books on various subjects at all grade levels to stimulate and satisfy their interests. Taste for good literature must be developed gradually. Children who read nothing but the "comics" can not be expected to jump from that type of teading to a "Junior Great Books" selection. The change must be very gradual.

In middle-class communities, the number of children retarded in reading averages between ten and twenty percent while in low socio-economic areas it may range as high as eighty percent. These children have double problems. Their lack of self-esteem and experiences, low motivation and low acceptable verbal facility is further accentuated by their reading failure. A thorough testing program is needed to ascertain mental ability and to diagnose their difficulties. They must then be given reading material on their reading level. Motivation is a real problem. Although we now have a number of books which are known as "High Interest—Low Vocabulary Series," these books do not include multi-racial groups nor is the reading material something with which they can identify. A modified language-experience approach where the child dictates to the teacher his reactions to an experience or incident, etc., can be typed and used as reading material for him. *Ten Great Moments in Sports* (14), *The Deep Sea Adventures* (6) and *The Morgan Bay Mystery Stories* (10) will satisfy their taste for sports, mystery and surprise endings. *The American Adventure Series* (1) are popular with children who are reading retardates. Many children enjoy the ridiculousness of the Dr. Seuss books (8). *The Reading Skill Builders* (11) contains a variety of short selections. Reading games, vocabulary and phonics skills, mentioned previously, should also be included in this program.

In the past few years much concern has been shown in the large cities for the culturally different child. The Detroit Public Schools are presently developing the *City Schools Reading Series* (5) for grades one through three. The project was started in 1959 under the direction of Dr. Gertrude Whipple. The program follows the basal reader methodology and includes teachers' manuals, workbooks and word cards, etc. Five pre-primers have been published instead of the usual three, but the books are shorter so that they may be completed more rapidly and thus give a feeling of accomplishment earlier. The books show children of multi-racial groups in urban settings to give the children an opportunity to identify themselves with characters that are familiar. The environment shown in these books is not that of the tenement or housing development type, but is one to which culturally different children might reasonably aspire. The illustrations used in the books are large and colorful with one center of interest and no unnecessary details. The stories are humorous or have a surprise ending to sustain interest. The vocabulary was carefully chosen to meet the needs of these children and much repetition of words has been provided. An evaluation of the first three pre-primers showed the City Schools Series to be significantly more effective in stimulating interest in reading and word recognition than the regular basal series.

The *Bank Street Readers* (2) prepared by the Bank Street College of Education in New York City is also an "urban-centered" series of eight books for grades one through three. A reading readiness program is followed by two pre-primers. Since sixty percent of Americans live in cities, these readers are designed for children of all economic, social and cultural background and not just for the culturally different. The publishers of the Bank Street Readers claim they have broken with tradition by including such forms of literature as vignettes, poems, stories, dialogues and essays for greater interest. The vocabulary used is taken from the children's speech rather than from established word lists.

Another new reading series is the *Skyline Series* (13). Recommended by the publisher as a co-basal series in grades two, three and four or with remedial pupils through the junior high level, these books are also about urban life. There is only one teacher's guide to the three books, but specific suggestions are given for each lesson. The authors and artists of this series are from mixed racial and cultural backgrounds and the stories are reflections of their own experiences. The brief sentences and the natural phrasing are typical of the culturally deprived city child. These stories could also be used with children who were not culturally deprived to give them a better understanding of how other children live. This program was developed for the St. Louis Public Schools.

The *Chandler Language-Experience Readers* (4) are being developed to use with culturally deprived children in the San Francisco Public Schools. Knowing that many more boys than girls have reading problems, they have made a special effort to develop experiences which will foster their interests. Like similar series, they have built their stories on familiar experiences of urban, culturally deprived multi-racial groups and have developed the vocabulary from the children's speech. All pictures used in the books are actual photographs of culturally different children participating in familiar experiences. The program is to extend gradually through grade six. It includes six paperback pre-primers and, at the present time, extends only through second grade. An added feature is the five (4 minute), 8 mm. color films which are integrated with the series.

The *Urban Education Studies Album* (16) consist of eight basic albums each of which has twelve 18 x 18 inch photographs to be used to develop basic languages skills and responsible citizenship. Special City Albums, each containing twenty-four photographs of New York, Denver, Detroit, Washington, D.C., Los Angeles and San Francisco have been designed for use not only in those cities, but also by any one interested in the growth of large cities. Prepared with the aid of Ford Foundation funds, these albums have been used in the New Haven, Connecticut, schools with much success. A detailed teacher's guide accompanies each album.

These are only a few of the many programs that are being developed throughout our country to motivate and to interest the culturally different child in learning to read.

References

1. *The American Adventure Series.* Chicago, Illinois: Wheeler Publishing Co., 1948.
2. *Bank Street Readers.* New York: The Macmillan Co., 1965.
3. Brazziel, William F. Report given at the American Educational Research Associations Meetings. Atlantic City, New Jersey, February, 1962.
4. *Chandler Language-Experience Readers.* San Francisco, California: Chandler Publishing Co., 1964.
5. *Cities Schools Reading Program.* Writers' Committee of the Great Cities School Improvement Program of the Detroit Public Schools. Gertrude Whipple, Chairman. Chicago, Illinois: Follett Publishing Co., 1964.
6. *The Deep Sea Adventure Series.* San Francisco, California: Harr, Wagner Publishing Co., 1959 and 1962.
7. Dolch, Edward W. *Dolch Games.* Champaign, Illinois: Garrard Publishing Co., 1948.
8. *Dr. Seuss.* New York: Beginners Books, Inc., Random House, Distributors, 1958.
9. Logan, Lillian. *Teaching the Young Child.* Boston, Massachusetts: Houghton Mifflin Co., 1960, p. 216.
10. *The Morgan Bay Mystery Series.* San Francisco, California: Harr, Wagner Publishing Co., 1962.
11. *Reading Skill Builders.* Pleasantville, New York: Reader's Digest Services, Inc., Educational Division, 1958.
12. Showers, Paul. *Find Out By Touching.* New York: Thomas Y. Crowell Publishing Co., 1961.
13. *The Skyline Series.* New York: Webster Division, McGraw-Hill Book Co., 1965.
14. *Ten Great Moments in Sports.* University Park, Pennsylvania: Penn's Valley Publishers, Inc., 1961.
15. Thomas, Dominick. "Oral Language of Culturally Disadvantaged Kindergarten Children." *Reading and Inquiry,* edited by J. A. Figurel. I. R. A. Conference Proceedings. Vol. 10. Newark, Delaware: International Reading Association, Inc., 1965, pp. 448-50.
16. *Urban Education Studies Albums,* edited by Betty Warner Dietz. New York: The John Day Co., 1965.
17. Watts, A. F. *The Language and Mental Development of Children.* London: George C. Harrap and Co., Ltd., 1964, p. 40, p. 31.

CHAPTER TWELVE

Library Resources for Extending Reading Instruction

An anomaly in public high school reading instruction has been the almost deliberate ignorance of public library services for young adults. Some of this may be due to the reluctance on the part of some librarians to serve adolescents, for libraries, too, have been involved in the conflicts in values that have startled schools over the past decade. Emerging from this is a new look at the role of the library in public service.

Today, the young adult librarian offers a greatly expanded range of services to youth. The activities offered by the library are as diverse as film festivals and poetry readings. Some libraries harbor an underground press while others have Saturday art classes or little theatre activities. Opponents to this role of the library object to what they claim are nonbook or even antibook aspects about these new services. Where these new programs are successful, teenagers see the library as a friendly and inviting place to be. All in all, for whatever reasons, the youth who are enticed are indeed brought to libraries and in contact with reading adults.

As the library seems to be changing the kinds of activities it provides, the nature of its book-oriented services are changing, too. Paperbacks, as one example, with their expendable nature and all that that implies, take greater and greater portions of the new library budget. The book mobile and "media machines" take books and services to the community, away from the old marble-stepped Carnegie buildings. The storefront black history collection, movies in the park, the clowns and the children's story teller in the shopping arcade—these are all new faces of the library without walls. As teachers of reading, we need to tie in to these activities, coordinate our efforts with these compatriots in the right to read.

Anne E. McGuinness

Here are hints for the librarian as well as the library-oriented teacher for bringing students to books in a lively way. In these suggestions, this librarian has included some of her personal warmth and the nostalgia of generations of readers she has helped. The good school library will campaign for new readers.

Reading Guidance in the Junior High School

With proper coordination we should be able to streamline our library reading from kindergarten through the senior high school. The elementary library starts the reading habit. Here the child is introduced to the book, to the idea of quiet reading, to the idea of replacing the book on the shelf. In the junior high school we try to carry on. Our job is to enrich the reading experiences of children already acquainted with a library and books.

Reading guidance is the alpha and omega of library work with young people. All library work is important; none should be neglected, all phases are necessary. Yet, I feel that while a conscientious librarian may be able to organize, equip, and efficiently conduct a library in a junior high school, unless she has that certain spark which enables her to put her finger on the pulse of the adolescent child's needs, she is not reaching the spirit of the child, and so is missing one of the real thrills of library work.

We all know that it's a strange, elusive thing, this ability to draw people to you, so that they want to share their problems. As Barrie's Maggie says about charm in *What Every Woman Knows,* "it's a sort of bloom. If you have it, you don't need to have anything else."

Senior high school librarians may not agree with me when I say that junior high school librarians have the greater advantage in reading guidance. We work with the fresh unbroken ground, which must be plowed and cultivated; then we plant the seed. The children come to us with reading tastes unformed, and challenge us with their reading attitudes of indifference, overconfidence, or with tragically impoverished backgrounds, or hap-

---

Reprinted by permission from the April 1954 issue of the *Wilson Library Bulletin.* Copyright © 1954 by The H. W. Wilson Company.

pily with a natural love for reading. What a field day for reading guidance! Because they are programmed, we meet all of them. What a challenge!

We might roughly divide our readers into four large groups: First: the slow, indifferent, over-age, reluctant, or nonreader, who has seldom, if ever, read a book clear through to the end. We've made giant strides in the material for this group, also, I must add, in the use of the energy, patience, and fortitude of the librarian. The lovely new adaptations of Huck Finn, Lorna Doone, Monte Cristo are all too difficult for these readers. They need picture books, the larger, the shinier the cover, the better. Just what is best for this group it is difficult to say. They must not be neglected. They make some progress it is true, but must they continue to try the strength and patience of the librarian? It sometimes takes eight or nine months to train them to take a book from the shelf and sit down quietly. Perhaps a six-month's assignment of library once a week, might be the solution.

Disinterested Reader

Secondly: the average reader of impoverished background who makes haphazard book choices, who is not particularly interested in reading, but who can be shown. This group cries for guidance. Here is our biggest challenge. It calls for all the library tricks for attracting attention to the books. Book talks, radio broadcasts, exhibit cases, hobbies shared and aired, games, contests—for this group we pull out all of the stops. One author to whom we are very grateful is Dorothy Smith, who wrote *Muddy Paws* and *The Secret of the Lighthouse.* She seems to have arrived at a happy combination of homespun story with a dash of sophistication. Her stories are very probable and are enjoyed by boys as well as girls. Other authors with this same appeal are Raftery, who wrote *Copperhead Hollow* and *Snow Cloud;* Carter, who wrote *Ghost Holly Mystery, Hinkle.* What would we do without Hinkle's horse and dog stories? Publicity plays such an important part in ensnaring this group. We keep a list of the most popular books borrowed each year. When *Seventeenth Summer* won first place, we put posters on all bulletin boards on each floor throughout the building which read; "Do you know Angie Morrow?" "Have you met Angie Morrow?" When she was discussed for a week, we added to the poster, "Read *Seventeenth Summer* by Daly if you'd like to know more about Angie." We did the same for *Thunderboats Ho!,* the most popular boy's book. Our whole school is conscious of our library.

Thirdly: the high I.Q. advanced reading grade child, who in some cases has a disorderly mind, with an inability to differentiate between the mediocre and the fine in literature. He reads, yes, but mostly science fiction, many of them "the standard brand books to be read only as something to pass the time and kill the pain: aspirin in chewing gum," as Gilbert Highet puts it. Here is one of the most difficult groups to reach; they are sure; they know all of the answers; it takes real finesse to reach them; yet, once they are reached they are happy for the help. Often one meets, despite all efforts, a hard shell of resistance. Many retain their false superiority which one never quite penetrates. One must learn to leave this group alone—to browse alone, to choose alone, to read and to keep one's findings to one's self. We've found that plastikleer covers on our books did wonders for this group. We've set aside a section of our library for these books which may all be borrowed for two weeks. A judicious handling, or placing, or remarking, about these books began to rouse suspicion, then sharing. Today, every time this group reports to the library the majority of them borrow one of these plastikleer covered books. We are beginning to put a little seasoning into their reading tastes.

Good Readers

Fourthly: the good readers—the children who want to read, who are avid for suggestions, who call reading their favorite hobby. One must just keep feeding the books—they are hungry to read them. One can often grow happy just watching these children come alive when they discuss with gratitude the books which you suggested. This is an appealing group, which brings out the best in the librarian's background. All the kinds of reading which she has loved—the hours spent on adult as well as juvenile literature, here find their reward—bits of poetry, parts of plays. In sharing and reliving them with this type of reader, the librarian experiences a warm glow which makes the work completely satisfying. But you must know the books; nothing can substitute for this firsthand knowledge. Once the children realize that you know these, their confidence is hard to shake. This builds up a feeling of camaraderie which spreads, until the library is looked upon as the place to come to for help and for fun.

Humor

This brings me to humor. We don't really use it enough in our work, do we? And is there anything which can relieve tension, ease the burden of overwork, clear the atmosphere and lift the spirits like the vivifying catharsis of laughter? It might only be a cartoon, a riddle, a small joke which you share, but the whole room is lighted up as with the light of many candles.

People of Note; and *Ted Cott's Musical Quiz Book, Fools and Funny Fellows, Joe Macarac, Pecos Bill, Paul Bunyan,* have jumped into the gap many times, and for me they've never failed. A very difficult discipline group can be brought round eventually with a good joke now and again, even if you have to explain it more than once.

It is a privilege to help to guide the reading of the very young. It keeps the librarian young in borrowing some of their enthusiasm as well as their courage. One realizes that in guiding the reading of the young, one is helping them to form a pattern for living. With no conceit you know that you have helped to steer many toward the path of years of enjoyment. To be sure, reading is only a part of living. One must also have the active living —the sports, the outdoor fun, travel, to keep a good balance in living—but in reading guidance we are in a position to open doors for them, for which they will one day be grateful.

One hears about these results in the strangest ways. During the last war, the letters from the boys in the service were revealing. The oddest things take hold in their minds—things which you never think about, or take for granted. We have a little statue atop our catalog case, of a small child reading a book. A pilot from Africa wrote to ask if the ivy still climbs around the book. From Alaska, there came a letter mentioning a picture of the interior of a cathedral which he remembered, because it always made him feel calm, quiet, serene. Each boy asked not to change these things— he wanted to find them just where they are, when he returned. From the Pacific area, came a letter describing a "bull session" among the officers when Brownings's *Forsaken Merman* was being discussed. The writer could recall the room, the warmth of the sun shining on his back, could hear the voice of the librarian reading the words which started him on a long journey in search of singing words. Twin girls invited the librarian to their wedding. In the note they took the opportunity to say "thank you" for helping them to emerge from scraggly, unkempt, overworked, drudges into individuals who are wanted. They even mentioned the books, *What Is She Like?, Personality Plus, Lessons in Loveliness,* which had been steps upon which they had leaned in their ascent to happiness. We give little pieces of ourselves to the children we meet. When we are worn out, and feel that we can't drag another step, this knowledge spurs us on.

Surprise

One of the things which has brought the greatest amount of success in library work is the use of the element of surprise.

With a glum, unresponsive group of good readers, we started the period by making a statement. "It has been said, that there is a direct ratio between observation and intelligence. There is something new in this room. Look around, see who is first to find it." One located a new painting. No one knew the name of the painting nor the artist who painted it. "Where would he look for this information? I'll give you five minutes. See who finds it first." There was real enthusiasm shared in this treasure hunt. After it was located in one of our art books, the chatter continued. They had not realized that we had such a beautiful art collection. Many of these books were borrowed right then and there.

At Christmas time, a quote was attached to the bulletin board, "CHRISTMAS IS A KIND, FORGIVING, LOVING TIME." We asked, "Where did the quote originate? Who said it? Where would you look to find the source? I'll give you five minutes to find it." Surprising were the results, not the least being a game of quotes from their own readings, with which to stump their neighbors.

A whole avenue of discussion was opened up by the boy who found prejudice in *Prester John* by Buchan. Almost as lively as the discussion which followed the statement that today Huck Finn would be called a juvenile delinquent. We should seize upon these interruptions in the reading of the group—you learn more about your readers, they learn more about your books.

We had fun with one idea—adopting an orphan. We explained that many fine books are lost in the shuffle and so remain unused. We called them orphans, took them off the shelves, and put them up for adoption. We put posters on bulletin boards around school such as: "I'm happy because Mary Brown, 7-6, has adopted me," or "I'm smiling because Tom Jones, 8-6, has given me a place in the sun." *Up the Mazarin for Diamonds, Courage Over the Andes, Tree of Liberty* are just a few of these discoveries.

A boy in the class was being ridiculed because he was wearing pants which were cut down from his father's. The librarian said, "I know a boy who had no shoes, could not go to school. After the truant officer got after him he came to school in his sister's shoes. The first day, he had a fight in the school yard with the first boy who laughed at him. That boy today is president of Eastern Airlines"—Eddie Rickenbacker's story goes over with a bang. All books in personal history came alive.

A boy objects to helping with the dishes—sissy stuff. Ike and his brothers and their football tactics used in doing Sunday night dishes, puts a new light on the job and sells Eisenhower's book, *Born to Command.* Again personal history comes alive.

It's so easy to win the confidence of these young readers, if you believe in them, believe in yourself and your ability to share the joy, the wonder, of living, and if you believe in books and their power.

Sound enthusiastic when you recommend a book—it's catching. Emphasize the "fun" in reading—in your book talks, in your posters. Positive thinking, "God's in His heaven, all's right with the world," have a far-reaching effect. Books let light into life; some children's lives are so much more dreary than we know. We have so much to offer these children.

They say that the best test of man's knowledge of books is to see what can be done without them on a desert isle. Try five or ten minutes' concentration on a book—think of the title, the plot, the characters. Try it on bright readers. One day—no books, just think of the finest book you've ever read. You are sometimes surprised with what they learn from reading. This practice helps them to plan for living in the future, also it gives the spiritual forces a chance in their lives by keeping company with the great. What joy if one can learn as Elizabeth Browning said, to "gloriously forget ourselves and plunge forward, headlong into a book."

There is an art of good reading as well as an art of good writing. Try asking a group of good readers to find in their reading examples of words that sing—laughing words—disturbing words—lifting words. This is when we discover that they read Richter's *Trilogy; Wind, Sand and Stars;* the *Verne Omnibus; Lantern in Her Hand; Green Mansions.* This helps them to see so much more than the printed words on the pages of a book.

Bibliotherapy is spoken of frequently today. Is it really new? Haven't we been using it since time began? No matter—it is good, sound, mental hygiene. We've had success with some. I'll mention only a few.

A child who feels that a parent does not love her has been greatly helped by *Anchor for Her Heart* by Newcombe; *Young Barbarians* by Helen R. Sattley.

A boy who knows that he is too young to take part in the war can lose some of his resentment about remaining in school when his older brother goes to camp, by reading *Thunderboats Ho!, A.W.O.L., Hull Down for Action, Sea Snake.*

A child who is afraid, a moral coward, and is sensitive, is greatly helped by *Call it Courage, Heroes and Hazards, Last of the Mohicans.*

A child who easily gives up when things become discouraging has been helped by *King of the Wind, Let the Hurricane Roar.*

A girl who is a tomboy is helped by *Cowgirl Kate, Tam Morgan.*

We have many broken homes. Our pupils (girls) who are disturbed have been greatly helped by the wholesome family life of *Seventeenth Summer, Anchor for Her Heart, Lantern in Her Hand, White Bird Flying, Meet the Malones.*

Lastly, a boy who is too fat, gauche, unathletic, is helped by *Bertie Comes Through, City Boy.*

The happiness in our work lies chiefly, in the appreciation of our good fortune, in working in a chosen medium. Our years of this "youthful encounter" have not dimmed our joy, nor our pride, nor our spirit. The "hyacinths" which we have bought to feed our souls, have proved a wise investment.

The challenge of our work is absorbing and rejuvenating. Always there will be new books written, and always a new generation to read them. Our work is progressive and no matter what comes next, it is certain to be interesting.

Margaret C. Hannigan *Librarians and libraries have traditionally served the information-seeking and recreation-seeking publics. Under the guise of these services, librarians, as counter-agents, have often slipped some serious purpose to their clients. Some notion of the diversity of library service is here noted, too.*

The Reader with Mental and Emotional Problems

How a chance encounter with a single book changed the course of a life is told by Frank Canizio in his autobiography, *Man Against Fate* (2). When he was a young convict, uneducated and rebellious, another prisoner about to be paroled tossed a worn copy of Emerson's *Essays* into his cell. One day because he was bored he started reading—rather, picking out the words for he had trouble understanding. But some meaning reached him. He felt that Emerson was talking directly to him in the essay, "Self-Reliance," especially in the lines: "Nothing can bring you peace but yourself. Nothing can bring you peace but the triumph of principles." Something stirred in him. He thought about them, memorized them, and kept on reading. He began to value knowledge and learning; he enrolled in correspondence courses; later he studied law. He says that a steady stream of books from the library entered and left his cell. After 23 years, during which he continued to read, study, and grow, he defended himself in a retrial of his case and was freed. Just as important is that he was prepared for the freedom of his remaining years.

Chance may be the only way that some people will ever discover the benefits and enjoyment of reading. The purpose of this article is to consider how librarians can remove the chance element for many people with mental and emotional problems, in particular, the ways in which librarians in hospitals and institutions can make their libraries serve as a "bridge to community life" for their readers and pave the way so that agencies, especially libraries, will be waiting, ready to help, at the other end of the bridge.

Margaret C. Hannigan, "The Reader and Mental and Emotional Problems," *ALA Bulletin,* October 1964. Reprinted from *ALA Bulletin* by permission of the American Library Association.

The function of the library as a bridge to community life or, to use a more common analogy, as an open door to the world's wisdom and knowledge is important and challenging in an institution. It ties in well with the intrinsic character of the library as a non-institutionalized, "outside-world" place even when it is located within the high walls of a prison—a place with a real library air about it and with real library materials. The very act of visiting the library, selecting reading material, talking about books to the librarian and to others, and borrowing chosen books—yes, and refusing those not wanted—allows the patient or inmate to see himself acting, for a short time, as a normal, free individual. This outside-world air gives the library a tremendous advantage in accomplishing its aim of serving as a bridge not only for readers but for potential readers in the institution community. It should never be forgotten; it should permeate everything about the library. Even rules and regulations should be as unobtrusive as possible so as to emphasize more important values.

Once the aim of making the library a bridge to the outside world is established, the library staff will find that regular library services bend themselves readily to achieve this purpose. Reader guidance, probably the most effective method we have of helping an individual, should be our most highly cultivated skill. Those who have been too busy with routines to give advisory service will have to revamp their ideas of a librarian's responsibilities. Fortunately, common sense and intuition aid the beginner and experience quickly gives confidence. But reader guidance is a skill which depends upon constant practice, continuous reading, insight into human nature, and a deep understanding and love of people. It is effective day in and day out, but when the librarian suggests just the right book to a person at just the moment he needs it, both are enriched by the experience.

No doubt every librarian has special cases he will never forget and a small collection of dependable titles that have worked with many readers. Louise Baker's autobiography, *Out on a Limb* (1), is one such book. My best success with it was with a young mother, an amputee, who found the courage and inspiration she needed in Miss Baker's story. She read many other books, but it was to this one she turned again and again during her rehabilitation in the hospital. The nursing staff traced the dramatic change in her attitude and morale to the very day she started reading it.

Often the librarian recommends a list of titles chosen to help the reader meet an immediate need, develop an attitude or point of view, or perhaps gain understanding and insight into his own situation. As discharge or parole time approaches, the person's need for support to help him face the setting where his troubles started becomes critical. Sometimes his "crutch" or his excuse for failure or for avoiding responsibility has been taken away from him, cured by surgery or treatment or controlled by drugs (this happens with an epileptic, for instance, who may have no more seizures but the hurt to whose personality is still there). How desperately he needs a source of strength, example, inspiration, and courage. Of all the aids he receives to help him make a good adjustment, books can be the most reliable and effective, if we help him find the right ones.

Hilda K. Limper, a specialist working with exceptional children at the Cincinnati Public Library, wrote me about a six-year-old girl whose psychiatric treatment was aided and hastened by books and her relationship with the librarian. Debby was extremely withdrawn, poorly adjusted socially, and seldom spoke. At first she was thought to be retarded, although as her treatment progressed she proved to be above average mentally.

The librarian established rapport with her when she first met her through the brightly illustrated counting rhyme book, *Over in the Meadow* (9). A pleasant relationship developed and continued throughout Debby's treatment; she was able to talk to the librarian, read with her, and enjoy many books.

When the time for her discharge approached, she seemed apprehensive about returning to her home and parents permanently. Books helped prepare her for this adjustment, one of which was *Lisette,* by Adelaide Holl (7). It is the story of a beautiful white poodle, lost and miserable among strangers in a big city, who found a friend in a fine German shepherd. Shedding her haughty manner, Lisette responded to the dog's affection and found love and laughter in her life with him.

Often the most effective way of reaching the individual is through group work. In the priority of library programs, reading and discussion groups rank high because of their adaptability to different types of people and situations and their beneficial results. Librarians are dedicated to making people aware of the pleasures and values of reading and to bringing people and books together. The medical team usually lists socialization as the top goal in work with those having mental and emotional problems, and the group members themselves have a variety of reasons for joining and participating. Reading and discussion groups can accomplish these aims and many more.

Group Work

So much has been written about group leadership, types of groups appropriate for library sponsorship, and techniques and materials that there is no need to repeat here. However, the opportunity group work provides for furthering our aim of making the library a bridge to the community is worth considering. The group offers the ideal setting for describing community library services and for building up each one's concept of himself as a library patron. It may start him thinking of the desirability of returning to the community. It may also give him the confidence he needs to join the public library and to take part in its programs. Librarians or others from the outside might be invited to speak to the members or to become leaders of discussion groups in the institution. In Cleveland groups of patients visit the public library and are put on the mailing list of the *Library Announcer*. The visits often result in the patients' becoming patrons of the nearest branch and attending library adult education programs. If patients can make the trip over the bridge to the community while still in the hospital, they surely will find their return home less frightening.

Two examples will illustrate ways in which groups within an institution can be effective in helping the members look toward the outside world with some confidence and anticipation. The first is described in an article, "Liberal Education behind Prison Walls," in the June 1959 *Adult Leadership* (8). It tells of Great Books discussion groups at El Reno Federal Prison in Oklahoma led by Raymond Johnson of the Great Books Foundation; Walter Gray, director of the Community Workshop of the Oklahoma City Library; and other volunteers. The main aspects of the program were: education, therapy (through group discussion), and rehabilitation (through a better awareness of ideas). The account of the discussions, which showed a growing maturity and ability to talk about ideas objectively, is heartwarming. As to how the experience will affect the men's future, Mr. Johnson says, "Our graduates swear they'll involve themselves in Great Books on the outside. Perhaps some of them will." The author's feeling is that, thanks to the leadership of a librarian from the public library, some, at least, will also turn to the great free resources of the library when they get out.

The second example involves William T. Henderson and the author who recently conducted a reading group project with thirty narcotics addicts in a New York State correctional institution. The project was reported in the July 1963 *Bookmark* (6). In an effort to make reading so important in the lives of these men that they could depend on it to help them through periods of discouragement, stress, and temptation, time was taken to acquaint them with public library services. Booklets which locate New York branch libraries and describe library services and programs were distributed. The name of a readers adviser at the central library, Robert Sheehan, was given to them and they were urged to go to him for guidance. Mr. Sheehan reports that three men who came to his office for guidance were from this group. The institution is following up on the project through parole officers to see how many are reading and using the library, but the report is not yet available.

Besides exerting direct influence on inmates and patients to make use of libraries, the librarian can help set up practices in the institution which will assure the inclusion of the library in counseling sessions designed to prepare the person for leaving the institution. He can talk at staff meetings and to individual staff members and see that those who conduct final interviews before discharge have an up-to-date supply of leaflets from libraries in the area served by the institution. It would be interesting and helpful if he could also keep in touch with social workers or others who see those on trial visit, in foster homes, or on parole.

In New York issuing library cards to inmates going on parole may be tried. Some in the library system are interested and willing to cooperate. The mechanics of handling such a project would be simple in areas where the universal borrowing privilege is honored.

Implications for Library Services

I have left until last the effects and the implications for library service of modern trends in treatment and rehabilitation of those with mental and emotional problems. Some trends are evident in the shortened hospitalization period not only of patients with physical ailments but of the mentally ill as well; in the establishment of small community facilities for the retarded and others with handicaps, institutions which permit them to spend weekends and vacations at home; in the open-door policy in many mental hospitals which allows patients the freedom of the hospital grounds and often of the local community; in day hospital treatment for mental patients; in the transitional type of treatment center exemplified by halfway houses for mental patients and, in some places, for paroled prisoners; and in self-help organizations like Alcoholics Anonymous. For prisoners the prospect of staying out of prison is improved by the addition in many correctional institutions of group counseling, psychotherapy, and vocational training and the revamping of educational courses.

The implication for libraries of having many people who formerly would have been hidden from sight—locked up in a hospital or prison—added to the great number with mental and emotional problems already in the community is tremendous. I believe that librarians have a serious responsibility to take the initiative in bringing library service into the lives of these people and in educating library staffs and the general public in areas such as mental health, epilepsy, and cerebral palsy.

The onus at this stage is largely on the public librarians although the librarian in the hospital or institution is in the best position to serve as a liaison between his agency and the public library. The initiative, in any case, for developing and offering services usually rests on the librarians' shoulders because, for some reason, those planning rehabilitation programs often seem to take the library for granted if they think of it at all. But, in my experience, these same people are more than glad to make room for library services once they are offered.

A natural starting place would be with an organization already in operation, for instance, the day hospital or day-care center. Many communities now have these centers where mental patients come for treatment while living at home. The focus of the treatment is away from the traditional hospital and toward the community, and the program often includes current events, play reading, and a literature group, led by a social worker, psychologist, or occupational therapist. In Albany, New York, the psychiatrist in charge of the day-care center connected with the Veterans Administration Hospital asked the public library to conduct a program for his patients. As a result Bruce Thomas, community services librarian, now has a weekly reading-discussion group which is well attended and is accomplishing the aims the psychiatrist had in mind.

The best known self-help groups besides Alcoholics Anonymous, in the author's opinion, are Recovery (The Association of Nervous and Former Mental Patients)* and Synanon Foundation† dedicated to the complete rehabilitation of narcotics addicts. The benefits of cooperation of the library with their programs seem self-evident, but, since the philosophy and methods of each are different, it would be wise for the library to work out a plan of service with each local group.

In Recovery, the treatment is based exclusively on writings of Dr. Abraham Low, the founder. Phil Crane, executive secretary, says that the association is interested in having Dr. Low's book, *Mental Health through Will Training* (10), in libraries. He mentions, too, that many Recovery groups across the country meet in public libraries.

The Cleveland Public Library has had experience with Recovery for some time. Clara Lucioli, head of their Hospitals and Institutions Department, writes that it began when the local office of the Veterans Administration asked for copies of Dr. Low's book on long loan so their field workers might understand his theories.

After a group was formed, members came to the library to borrow copies. One member, a former long-term patient who had responded well to this method of treatment, suggested that the library keep a set of the Low recordings in the reading room along with a reserve copy of the book and the monthly Recovery publication for the use of members who would feel free to drop in when they were downtown. He believed that many expatients

---

*For information, write to Recovery, Inc., 116 S. Michigan Ave., Chicago.

†For information, write to Synanon Foundation, Inc., 1351 Ocean Front, Santa Monica, Calif.

would enjoy a quiet place for relaxation where their interest would be understood and unquestioned and that those who had missed a meeting would appreciate a chance to catch up on the material in the library. The materials have been available for more than two years. They are used mainly by members who meet at a nearby church or who work downtown and come in on their lunch hour. Occasionally the Califone recorder with eight outlets and a portable victrola have been needed to take care of people who were at different points in the records.

Synanon Foundation has six houses in the United States. Gertrude Cavanough, associate director, recommends that libraries stock Dr. Daniel Casriel's book, *So Fair a House* (3), for information and insight as to the working of Synanon. She says that the Santa Monica house has two classes that librarians would be especially interested in knowing about, one on contemporary moral issues led by a UCLA professor and one in remedial reading.

Apparently no direct use is made of public libraries in the Synanon program although an important part of their work consists of seminars and other group discussions. Often the theme of a meeting is based on a concept from science or the humanities. Charles Dederich, the founder, has said, "... doses of an innerdirected philosophy such as that outlined in Ralph Waldo Emerson's essay entitled 'Self-Reliance' are administered to the recovering addicts." He added that the intellectual, emotional, and spiritual food fed to the recovering addicts is rather carefully selected.

Surely the public library has much to offer this group as a source of material to enrich its programs and as a community agency which members can use freely and without question.

In picturing the great need for libraries and their services by those with mental and emotional problems, I have tried to indicate what a large portion of a community falls into this group at a given time and to highlight the common goals and close relationships which need to exist between librarians in hospitals and institutions and those in public libraries if these people are to be helped by us. Above all I have wanted to prove that librarians can meet the real needs of these troubled people through regular library practices: reader advisory service, group work, orientation of staff and public to the problems, and cooperation with community groups.

As librarians we have no choice but to respond by using our resources and talents to improve the mental health of our communities and our nation.

References

1. Baker, Louise. *Out on a Limb.* New York: Lothrop, 1962.
2. Canizio, Frank. *A Man Against Fate.* New York: Fell, 1958, o.p.; Permabook, 1959, o.p.

3. Casriel, Daniel. *So Fair A House: the Story of Synanon.* Englewood Cliffs, New Jersey: Prentice-Hall, 1963.

4. Dederich, Charles. "Synanon Foundation." Reprint of a paper read before the Southern California Parole Officers in October 1958. Available from Snyanon Foundation, 1351 Ocean Front, Santa Monica, California.

5. Frame, Janet. *Faces in the Water.* New York: Braziller, 1961.

6. Hannigan, Margaret C., and Henderson, William T. "Narcotic Addicts Take Up Reading." Bookmark (July 1963).

7. Holl, Adelaide. *Lisette.* New York: Lothrop, 1962.

8. Johnson, Raymond. "Liberal Education Behind Prison Walls." *Adult Leadership* (June 1959).

9. Langstaff, John. *Over in the Meadow.* New York: Harcourt, 1957.

10. Low, Abraham A. *Mental Health Through Will Training.* 11th ed. Boston: Christopher.

11. ———. Recordings of his addresses to patients. Records available from Recovery, Inc., 116 S. Michigan Ave., Chicago.

Sarah Ryder

Reading teachers must use the school librarian as a resource to reading fare. In the school described here, the librarian is more than a resource for books and bibliography; she also shares in the planning and teaching.

The Librarian Goes to the Classroom

Nobody, not the teacher, nor the reading specialist, nor even the librarian with her eye on circulation figures, is interested in *reading* as an end in itself. Each of us is interested in educating the child, by the transmission of ideas and by getting him to think critically about himself and his environment.

And so when one of our English teachers approached me and asked me to deliver a book talk on some timely topic, I readily assented. Since Negro History Week and Brotherhood Week were in the offing, we both agreed that "Discrimination" would be a good subject.

Summaries of books are deadly. On the other hand, stimulating, provocative questions arouse interest, invite participation and attention, and result in awareness and recognition.

Armed with a half dozen books or so, I addressed the class. "Let's all relax," I said, "and pretend we are not in school but in someone's living room." The response was instantaneous: many smiled, a few slumped in their seats. There was general relief that this was not going to be a "lesson." "We are in someone's living room," I continued, "and we are expecting another guest. The guest is an Englishman. What do you think he will look like?"

Hands began waving in the air. I cautioned them to have a firm picture in their minds before they started speaking. In all classes that I did this, freshmen as well as seniors and at all academic levels, the answers had the same stereotype-images. The Englishman had a monocle, a cane, a mous-

---

Sarah Ryder, "The Librarian Goes to the Classroom," *English Journal.* Copyright © 1965 by the National Council of Teachers of English. Reprinted by permission of the publisher and Sarah Ryder.

tache. He was Restrained, Polite, Intelligent. I wrote all the characteristics on the blackboard, trying to elicit as many personality traits from them as I could.

"Oh, I'm sorry I made a mistake, I do not expect an Englishman at all; I am really expecting an Italian. What kind of man do you expect now?"

After a few seconds for them to get "a picture," their replies came through: Short, Fat, Emotional, Dark, Dirty, Rude.

"Oh, I'm sorry, I've made another mistake, I'm really expecting a Russian." They laughed, and then the words came tumbling out again: Bold, Fat, Light Hair, Impolite, Aggressive, Loud.

Next I said, "You know," (this time they were expectant and anticipating) "I'm really expecting a Chinese." The answers: Tall, Dark Hair, Polite, Intelligent, Family-minded, Studious.

How did they know what the Chinese were like? How many had met a Chinese socially? I told them about the early Chinese stereotype in 1930, the Fu Manchu-Myrna Loy-opium den-white slaver-Chinee. I asked how many had met a Russian, or an Englishman, or an Italian. Some few raised their hands, but I asked all the others who had had such ready answers.

What are Americans like? "Oh, we are all different." How come? Why are all the Italians alike, all Englishmen alike, and we all different? The answer was obvious and they came through: "Because we know each other better."

They said their images had come from reading, television, movies, etc. I pointed out that their stereotype of an Englishman was very much like Anthony Eden and that of a Russian was very like Khrushchev. I invited them to go to the library and look at a Russian magazine called *Soviet Life* and observe the people in the pictures. I reminded them that Northern Italians were blonde. I pointed out that our image of the Chinese had changed because of Pearl Buck's *The Good Earth,* that it was in danger of changing again because of China's involvement with communism. I also pointed out our different images of the Japanese during the war and now.

Then I switched back to the early 1900's and Bret Harte, and a poem he had written called "Plain Language from Truthful James." We read it together paragraph by paragraph, I making sure they understood the irony. (Briefly Truthful James, an American, and his friend, Bill Nye, attempt to cheat Ah Sin, a Chinese, at cards. Ah Sin is no fool and turns the tables on them.)

A brief summary then ensued about discrimination due to nationality. I asked what other types of discrimination there were. The items were listed on the board:

Religion.
What else?

Race.
You mean color?
Yes.

I mentioned Langston Hughes; no one had heard of him. I read his short essay called "That Word Black." Next I read "I, Too," also by Langston Hughes and finally, "And Yet Do I Marvel" by Countee Cullen.
What other types of discrimination are there? No one said anything. I suggested *sex.* No one had thought of that. After all women did have the vote, didn't they? What about discrimination in employment? What about a woman as President of the United States? Loud guffaws! I told them about the struggle women have had and mentioned Ibsen's *The Doll's House* and Barrie's *The Twelve Pound Look.*

What other kinds of discrimination? By this time they were at it again and mentioned *Rich* and *Poor* and *Status.*

I told them about Kipling's *Tommy* and discrimination against classes of people, or against people from another part of the country, the kind of prejudice our soldiers have encountered. I read two verses from this.

Next we discussed our feelings about physical deformities. If a dwarf came into the room, would they assume he was stupid? Were they prejudiced against somebody that stutters? I mentioned Philip in *Of Human Bondage* and his great cross.

We then talked briefly about the need to think a little before prejudging anyone, whether on the basis of color of skin, or nationality, or whatever. I finished by inviting them to the library to look at some of the books from which I had read. Some had their cards, and I stamped the books for circulation. I left with fewer books, more friends, and with the hope that I had implanted some significant doubts in their young and unquestioning minds.

Louis E. Barrilleaux

In this unusual classroom, the library is defended as a more natural solution to problems than the single-volume textbook. The results, although not surprising, pose some penetrating questions about the results we want from students who must outgrow textbooks.

Textbook and Library Usage in Junior High Science

Teaching in American schools is characterized by extensive use of the textbook. Yet at the focal point of the educational process—a student facing a problem—does it matter whether the student has a textbook with *a* ready answer? Isn't it more important that he learn to locate and use a variety of sources with differing views or explanations? Which route to a solution fosters the greater development of critical thinking, creativity, and rational powers (3)? Which route fosters the greater development of ability to find and create knowledge? Which contributes more to the development of the ability to weigh evidence and to make choices in complex situations where knowledge is less than complete and where ability to foresee the outcome is imperfect? If it is assumed that terminal behavior is predetermined in the student's experiences, how do these differing processes contribute to desired behavior in science education?

Enormous sums of money are invested in textbooks each year. The cost of those purchased for elementary and high schools during selected years is reported in Table I. Considering these facts on expenditures, it is puzzling that so little research relating to textbooks has been reported.

For comparative purposes, sums for school libraries are also reported in Table I. The American Library Association reports that in schools having 250 or more students, an annual expenditure between four and six dollars per student is recommended for regular library books. Additional funds are required for encyclopedias, dictionaries, magazines, newspapers, pamphlets, supplies, and equipment (1).

Reprinted with permission of Louis E. Barrilleaux and the International Reading Association.

TABLE I
Elementary and High School Textbook and Library Expenditures for Selected Years

	Textbooks[a]	Library
1955-56		$20,417,000[b]
1957	$134,135,000	
1957-58		$31,525,000[c]
1959-60		$44,568,000[d]
1960	$177,295,000	
1961	$195,460,000	
1962	$298,500,000	
1962-63		$63,208,000[e]
1963	$236,490,000	

[a] American Textbook Publishers Institute. "Total Number, Value, & Price Per Unit of Textbooks Sold" (a report prepared for the Institute by Stanley B. Hunt and Associates, New York, April, 1964).
[b] United States Office of Education. *Biennial Survey of Education: 1954-56. Statistics of State School Systems 1955-56* (Washington: Government Printing Office, 1959). p. 88.
[c] United States Office of Education. *Biennial Survey of Education: 1956-58. Statistics of State School Systems: 1957-58* (Washington: Government Printing Office, 1961). p. 57.
[d] United States Office of Education. *Biennial Survey of Education: 1958-60. Statistics of State School Systems: 1950-60* (Washington: Government Printing Office, 1963). p. 63.
[e] United States Office of Education. *Digest of Educational Statistics* (Washington: Government Printing Office, 1964). p. 157.

In the 1959–1960 school year, approximately 42,000.000 pupils were enrolled in the elementary and secondary schools of the United States (5). Actual school library expenditures for the 1959–1960 school year were $44,568,000. This figure would have been $200,000,000 if recommended library expenditures had been made.

This investigation was an attempt to present some evidence in regard to the most effective use of printed materials in junior high school science instruction. A longitudinal study compared the effects of different basic reading and reference materials upon library utilization of eighth-grade science students at the end of the ninth grade.

This report is limited to the evaluation of library utilization. The complete investigation, which is reported elsewhere, includes growth in science achievement, critical thinking, science attitudes, and writing in science as categories of educational outcomes which were evaluated (2).

Methods

In 1962–1963 as eighth-graders and in 1963–1964 as ninth-graders, 42 students at the Malcolm Price Laboratory School, State College of Iowa, were studied in a two-year longitudinal experiment. From the available sample, two instructional groups were "matched" with reference to mental ability and preference for science in the employment of a "treatments X levels" design (4) in which there was a high and an average level of predicted science achievement. There were 21 students in each section, and each had nine students at the high ability level and 12 at the average ability level. The assignment of students to the instructional groups and the assignment of the instructional hour were by chance.

The experimental group met 55 minutes daily. The obtained mean Otis I.Q. for this group was 111.2, and the mean science interest rank was 5.5.* The control group also met 55 minutes daily. The obtained mean Otis I.Q. was 110.5, and the mean science interest rank was 5.1.

The variation in experimental and control treatments did not result from a fundamental difference in method, but instead, from the use of different basic reading and reference materials. Although instruction was centered about units of study prepared by the teacher, the experimental group followed a planned sequence of topics which was essentially the same as those included in the textbook issued to the control group. A textbook and/or other study materials were not issued to the experimental group. The use of a variety of references and sources in the school library was encouraged.

Although instruction was centered about units of activities prepared by the teacher, the control group followed the content of the course as outlined in the textbook. Each student was issued a textbook and encouraged to use library materials as well.

Having had experience with both treatments, the investigator served as teacher for the experimental and control groups and attempted to teach each with equal enthusiasm and interest.

A major category of educational outcomes for which differences in the effect of the treatments were analyzed was library utilization. Where it was appropriate, obtained differences were tested statistically by the method of analysis of variance and the F-test. Interaction was also studied as the investigator determined if the effectiveness of the treatments depended upon the ability levels at which they were used. The .05 level was the adopted level of statistical significance.

Evaluating library utilization. During the second year (ninth grade) of the two-year longitudinal study, samples of the library behavior of experimental and control subjects were observed. Through the cooperation and assistance of school librarians and college-student assistants, the library behavior of the ninth-grade students was observed and recorded one day per week for an entire school day during 25 complete weeks of classes. On each day

---

*A rank of one denoted the highest of nine possible ranks of the scientific percentile rank on the Kuder Preference Record—Vocational Form B.

(randomly selected) an observer was posted in the school library for the specific purpose of recording the desired information. A card was prepared on which the data was recorded. The information gathered for each student included type of library activities, type of library materials used, and extent of library usage.

Results

Free reading. Table II reports the frequency of observed free reading by treatments and ability levels. All means, by ability levels as well as the overall means, favored the experimental group. There were no marked differences in means between ability levels within the experimental or control groups of students. On the average, students of the experimental group engaged in free reading 5.5 times during the 25 days of observation, while the students of the control group engaged in this activity an average of 3.6 times during the same period.

Locating and using library materials. The frequency of observation by treatments and ability levels for students engaged in locating or using library materials is also reported in Table II. This analysis shows that all

TABLE II

Mean Scores for Evaluative Procedures on Library Utilization of Treatments and Ability Levels

	Experimental (Library-nontext)			Control (Textbook)		
	High $N=9$	Average $N=12$	Total $N=21$	High $N=9$	Average $N=12$	Total $N=21$
Frequency of Free Reading	5.8	5.2	5.5	3.6	3.6	3.6
Frequency of Locating and Using Materials (Total)	13.1	11.4	12.1	8.2	5.8	6.8
Science			6.5			2.2
Non-science			5.6			4.6
Number of Checkouts (Total)	7.6	6.3	6.8	3.1	2.2	2.5
Science class			4.4			0.9
Non-science class			2.0			1.4
Number of Visits	22.1	21.3	21.6	14.7	17.3	16.2
Total Hours in Library Activities	12.3	11.7	11.9	8.6	9.8	9.3
Science class	4.6	3.2	3.8	2.2	1.5	1.8
Non-science class	5.0	5.5	5.3	4.4	5.2	4.9

means, by ability levels as well as the overall means, favored the experimental group; and within each treatment group, the means were in favor of the high ability level students. Students of the experimental group, on the average, were observed locating and using materials for science classes about three times more than the students in the control group. Students in the experimental group were also observed locating and using more non-science materials than the control group.

Library materials checked out. Table II shows the means for library items checked out by ability levels in the observation of experimental and control groups. The table shows that all means for students in the experimental group were at least double the corresponding means for students in the control group. While the overall mean for total observed check-outs by students in the experimental group was 6.8, students in the control group checked out a mean of 2.5 references. Table II also reports that students in the experimental group were observed checking out library items for a mean of 4.4 check-outs for purposes related to science classes, while students in the control group checked out library items for the same reason for a mean of 0.9 check-outs. Students in the experimental group also had a higher mean for the number of observed check-outs related to non-science classes.

Frequency of library visits. Table II reveals that both the high and the average ability levels of the experimental group exceeded the comparable levels of the control group in the mean number of observed library visits. A test of interaction of treatments with levels reported in Table III yielded a significant F of 4.420. This indicated that the comparative effectiveness of the treatments was not the same for high and average levels.

According to Table II, the mean number of observed library visits for the total experimental group was 21.6 The corresponding mean for the control group was 16.2. As shown in Table III, the F-test of treatments resulted in a significant F of 9.116. When high and average ability levels were combined, the difference in effectiveness of the treatments was statistically significant and in favor of the experimental group.

The mean of 22.1 for the high ability students of the experimental group exceeded the mean of 14.7 for the corresponding control group in the mean number of observed library visits. Table III shows the results of an F-test of treatments for the high ability levels only. The obtained F of 9.882 was statistically superior for students at the high ability level. The F-test of treatments for the average ability level, as reported in Table III, shows that the difference was not significant.

Time spent in library activities. Table II shows an analysis of the total number of observed hours devoted by students to total library activities.

TABLE III
Analysis of Variance for Means in Time Spent and Number of Visits to Library

Sources	df	Hours in Library Activity Mean Square	F	df	Number of Visits to Library Mean Square	F	.05F
Treatments X Levels	1	8.9325	0.924	1	111.4062	4.420*	4.10
Levels	1	0.6444		1	8.3304		
Treatments	1	74.2938	7.689*	1	229.7694	9.116*	4.10
Within Groups	38	9.6626		38	25.2053		
Total	41			41			
Treatments (High only)				1	249.0912	9.882*	4.10
Treatments (Average only)				1	92.1984	3.658	4.10

*Significant at .05 level.

Means at each of the ability levels and the overall mean of the experimental group were greater than the corresponding means of the control group. While there was no significant interaction of treatments with levels, Table III shows that the effectiveness of the experimental treatment for the high and average ability levels combined was statistically superior to the control treatment for the high and average ability levels combined. The statistical superiority of the experimental treatment did not depend on the level at which it was used.

Table II indicates that the mean number of hours at each of the ability levels and the overall mean of the total experimental group were greater than the corresponding means of the control group for time spent in library activities related to science classes. While there was no significant interaction of treatments with levels, Table IV shows that the effectiveness of the experimental treatment for the high and average ability levels combined was statistically superior to the control treatment for the high and average ability levels combined. The statistical superiority of the experimental treatment for time spent in library activities related to science classes did not depend on the level at which it was used.

Table II shows that the analysis of data on observed number of hours devoted to library activities related to non-science classes revealed that all means, by ability levels as well as the overall means, favored the experimental group. There was no statistically significant interaction of treatments with levels, and the overall effectiveness of the treatments was in favor of the experimental treatment but not to a statistically significant degree.

TABLE IV
Analysis of Variance for Means in Time Spent in Library Activities by Science and Nonscience Classes

Sources	Hours Spent in Science Related Activities			Hours Spent in Non-science Related Activities			.05F
	df	Mean Square	F	df	Mean Square	F	
Treatments X Levels	1	1.1254	1.052	1	0.3591	0.082	4.10
Levels	1	11.1251		1	3.5808		
Treatments	1	42.4200	39.634*	1	1.7640	0.403	4.10
Within Groups	38	1.0703		38	4.3794		
Total	41			41			

*Significant at .05 level.

Interpretations

When student utilization of the library was observed during the second year of the treatments, the experimental (library-nontext) group was statistically superior in overall effectiveness to the control (textbook) group in terms of number of library visits, time devoted to total library activities, and time devoted to library activities related to science classes. While the use of library materials without a text in science was statistically superior in overall effectiveness to the use of an issued basic textbook for the frequency of total library visits, students of high ability profited more from the experimental (library-nontext) approach. The means for time devoted to library activities related to non-science activities for the group of students using school library materials in science without a textbook were greater than the corresponding means for students who were issued a basic textbook. The differences, however, were nonsignificant at the .05 level.

While not tested statistically, the use of library materials with no textbook in science was, on the average, more effective than the use of an issued basic textbook when measured by the extent of free reading, the extent of locating and using library materials in science and non-science areas, and total library materials checked out in science and non-science areas.

The transfer value of library-nontextbook instruction in science, in terms of general library behavior, is suggested in view of the systematic findings that the students in this type of class participated more in free reading, located and used more library materials for non-science classes, devoted more time to library activities related to non-science classes, and checked out more library materials in non-science classes than students in the class with an issued textbook in science.

Implications for Practice

This study presents some evidence in regard to the influence of an issued textbook on library utilization. It demonstrates what *can* be done and what outcomes are likely to occur under certain established conditions.

Where it can be assumed that schools possess extensive library facilities and provide extensive opportunities during class periods and out of class for students to use the facilities toward the accomplishment of an accepted class responsiblity, the findings in this study have important implications. It gives evidence that it is possible to modify the program of junior high school science instruction to a more flexible one where students as individuals may select from a range of printed materials and perform as well or better in attaining desired outcomes of science instruction. The findings do not imply the abandonment of printed materials in junior high school science instruction. It is rather the more effective use of printed materials that must be sought.

A course of instruction should possess a structural and sequential nature, but within the framework, this study suggests permitting a high degree of independence and individual responsibility in the location, selection, and use of printed materials for the more effective attainment of accepted goals in junior high school science.

References

1. American Library Association. *Standards for School Library Programs.* Chicago: American Library Association, 1960, pp. 24-25.
2. Barrilleaux, Louis E. "An Experimental Investigation of the Effects of Multiple Library Sources as Compared to the Use of a Basic Textbook on Student Achievement and Learning Activity in Junior High School Science." Ph.D. dissertation, University of Iowa, August, 1965.
3. Educational Policies Commission. *The Central Purpose of American Education.* Washington: National Education Association, 1961, p. 4.
4. Lindquist, E. F. *Design and Analysis of Experiments in Psychology and Education.* New York: Houghton Mifflin Co., 1953, pp. 13-17, 121-155.
5. United States Office of Education. *Biennial Survey of Education: 1958–60. Statistics of State School Systems: 1959–60.* Washington: Government Printing Office, 1963, p. 1.

K